"Is there any verse in the Gospel of Mark tha[t] so central to the message of the evangelist th[at] six carefully coordinated chapters John J. R. L[... ... ...] ... lay out the interpretative options for this verse, they show how it contributes to the larger message of Mark's Gospel, and they probe what its message can mean for the life of faith. This is a book to be read and re-read for its deep and sensitive insights."

PAUL FOSTER, University of Edinburgh

"Is it possible to summarize a whole book of the Bible by studying one key verse in that book? Yes, and John Lee and Daniel Brueske show how it can be done effectively. For them, Mark 10:45 is the key for unlocking Mark's Gospel. They not only work through the interpretation of this verse phrase-by-phrase but also situate it within the occasion, purpose, overall structure, and message of Mark's Gospel. If you want to understand Mark's Gospel, study Mark 10:45. If you want to understand Mark 10:45, this book is a great place to start."

JOEL F. WILLIAMS, Biblical Seminary of the Philippines

"One might ask, 'A whole book dedicated to interpreting one verse?' But of course, an entire book should be devoted to Mark 10:45, which can be classified as 'The Whole Gospel in a Single Verse.' Lee and Brueske masterfully justify why this is so. They show how Mark 10:45 is the key to reading and unlocking the purpose of Mark's Gospel. It is also key for understanding who Jesus is and what he has done, and it is the mainspring for why disciples must follow Christ's example of radical self-giving service. This well-written book will be a prized resource for reading, teaching, and preaching Mark's Gospel."

DAVID E. GARLAND, Baylor University

"I love this introduction to Mark. It is thorough and thoughtful and through the lens of Mark 10:45. Lee and Brueske carefully walk through introductory material and then do the necessary work to establish Mark 10:45 as a key text for Mark's work as a whole."

PATRICK SCHREINER, Midwestern Baptist Theological Seminary

"Jesus came to seek and to save the lost. In this clear and accessible book, John Lee and Daniel Brueske demonstrate how this simple but extraordinary claim lies at the heart of the Gospel of Mark and the center of the gospel message. By considering the place of this verse in the book, Lee and Brueske provide a wonderful introduction to Mark and his purposes for writing. I would happily recommend this book to anyone who is serious about understanding Mark more clearly and living in the light of its message."

CHRIS BRUNO, Training Leaders International

"This book which considers the substitutionary nature of Jesus's death is a welcome addition to the literature on the Gospel of Mark. Lee and Brueske mine the riches of God's Word by considering the inner-biblical connections and significance of the so-called 'ransom statement' of Mark 10:45. The authors help readers appreciate the importance of Jesus's death in Mark, and the integrated structure of the Gospel."

BRANDON D. CROWE, Westminster Theological Seminary

"Lee and Brueske guide us in a careful and intensive examination of Mark 10:45, situating the verse in its historical, literary, and theological context. They also interact with recent scholarship on this verse as they explore the famous ransom saying of Mark 10:45. The meaning, significance, and importance of this central verse is unpacked for readers in this illuminating study."

THOMAS R. SCHREINER, The Southern Baptist Theological Seminary

A Ransom for Many

Mark 10:45 as a Key to the Gospel

A Ransom for Many

Mark 10:45 as a Key to the Gospel

John J. R. Lee and Daniel Brueske

LEXHAM
ACADEMIC

Print ISBN 9781683595618
Digital ISBN 9781683595625
Library of Congress Control Number 2022941654

Lexham Editorial: Derek Brown, Andrew Sheffield, Katrina Smith, Mandi Newell, Jessi Strong
Cover Design: Lydia Dahl, Brittany Schrock
Typesetting: Abigail Stocker

CONTENTS

CONTENTS

PREFACE

*"Even the Son of Man did not come to be served
but to serve and to give his life as a ransom for many."*
— Mark 10:45

This book presents our case that Mark 10:45 is key to understanding the Second Gospel. In this single short verse, we find both a summary of Mark's message and a hint towards his purpose. We believe that Mark composed his Gospel with the desire of motivating his audience to remain faithful to Jesus in the face of the hardship, suffering, and shame that any follower of Jesus was likely to encounter at various times in the first century. From this desire, Mark narrates a story that concentrates on Jesus's identity and his mission, highlighting Jesus's dedicated servanthood and his unwavering loyalty to God even to the point of death on a Roman cross. Mark 10:45 specifies the height of that ultimate servanthood and loyalty. Mark's narration of who Jesus is and what he has done is the means by which Mark accomplishes the purpose of encouraging his audience to follow in the footsteps of Jesus the Nazarene, persevering through hardship and contempt, shame and loss, persecution and death, and enduring all things for him who came not to be served but to serve and to give his life as a ransom for many. In Mark's mysterious story, faithfulness to God and devotion to Jesus truly become one as we follow his ultimate example of loyalty and servanthood.

ABBREVIATIONS

Ann.	Tacitus, *Annales*
BBR	*Bulletin for Biblical Research*
BDAG	*A Greek-English Lexicon of the New Testament and Other Early Christian Literature, 3rd edition*
Cons.	Augustine, *De consensu evangelistarum*
Dial.	Justin Martyr, *Dialogue with Trypho*
ESV	English Standard Version
JBL	*Journal of Biblical Literature*
JSNT	*Journal for the Study of the New Testament*
JSNTSS	Journal for the Study of the New Testament Supplement Series
Haer.	Irenaeus, *Adversus haereses*
Hist. eccl.	Eusebius, *Historia ecclesiastica*
LEB	Lexham English Bible
LNTS	Library of New Testament Studies
Marc.	Tertullian, *Adversus Marcionem*
NETS	New English Translation of the Septuagint
NIV	New International Version
NIV11	New International Version, 2011 edition
NIV84	New International Version, 1984 edition
NTS	*New Testament Studies*
TNIV	Today's New International Version
WUNT	Wissenschaftliche Untersuchungen zum Neuen Testament

I

THE WHOLE GOSPEL OF MARK
IN A SINGLE VERSE

O N THE EVENING OF THURSDAY, February 28, 1889, Charles Haddon Spurgeon ascended the steps of the Metropolitan Tabernacle pulpit in London, England, to preach a sermon that would come to be titled, "The Whole Gospel in a Single Verse." Spurgeon's text was 1 Timothy 1:15. In this verse, Spurgeon sees "the great truths of the gospel … pressed together by a hydraulic ram," and he goes so far as to claim, "[T]his text contains the gospel in brief, and yet I may say that it contains the gospel in full."[1] We believe something similar could be said about the place of Mark 10:45 within the narrative of the Second Gospel. Mark 10:45 is not just one verse among many; it is a *key* verse for understanding Mark. It summarizes Mark's thematic emphases in brief, and yet we may say that it contains the core of Mark's message in full. As a result, Mark 10:45 carries implications for how we read and interpret Mark's Gospel as a whole.

Many interpreters have recognized the importance of Mark 10:45. But as with every consensus, there are some who disagree. Julius Wellhausen, for example, in his monumental commentary downplayed the weightiness of Mark 10:45 and, relatedly, the atoning significance of

---

1. Charles Haddon Spurgeon, *The Metropolitan Tabernacle Pulpit Sermons*, Vol. 39 (London: Passmore & Alabaster, 1893), 134.

Jesus's death within Mark's Gospel.[2] Nevertheless, most biblical scholars do agree that Mark 10:45 is important. Even popular Bible teachers
like Irving Jensen, Warren Wiersbe, Max Lucado, and Chuck Swindoll
have presented 10:45 as a key verse. For many, the significance of Mark
10:45 within the Second Gospel is self-evident.

But there is a problem. Even though many scholars recognize the
importance of Mark 10:45, not much discussion exists as to *why* or *in
what sense* this verse is so crucial. There are brief remarks here and
there, but most offer no more than a few lines, mentioning the matter
almost in passing and then quickly moving on to other issues. The significance of Mark 10:45 is, thus, usually assumed rather than explained.
In this study, we aim to move from simply presuming and asserting the
significance of Mark 10:45 to demonstrating it and, ultimately, to considering how proper attention to this verse should guide our reading
and interpretation of the rest of Mark's narrative. Such a task must
include a careful examination of the verse and its context. Moreover,
a careful reading of Mark 10:45, integrated as it is within the Second
Gospel, requires some understanding of the setting and intention
behind the book's composition. No writing exists in a vacuum, and
Mark's Gospel is no exception.

Therefore, in what follows, we will explore both the occasion (chapter 2) and the purpose (chapter 3) that gave rise to the Second Gospel.
There is little consensus regarding the specific *occasion* for Mark's
Gospel, but we believe some details about the audience are more plausible than others. Given the uncertainty of Mark's occasion, our argument for his purpose will be built primarily on the narrative itself.
Nevertheless, reading Mark's Gospel with some regard for its historical setting helps us imagine how Mark's message would likely have
been received by his earliest audience. We will argue that a composition in the middle to late 60s CE, though not certain, is more plausible
than alternative suggestions. We will also contend that Mark's earliest

---

2. Julius Wellhausen, *Das Evangelium Marci*, 2nd ed. (Berlin: Reimer, 1909),
84–85.

audience was likely facing either the prospect or the reality of suffering for their faith in Jesus of Nazareth.

In exploring the author's *purpose* for writing (chapter 3), we will survey the entire narrative of the Second Gospel for indications of the author's concerns and goals. Unlike Luke (1:4) and John (20:30–31), Mark contains no explicit statement regarding his compositional intention. Therefore, careful consideration of the total narrative is prudent, especially given the *strategic placement* of Mark 10:45 within the structure of Mark's Gospel (a point we will advance in chapter 5). We will give particular attention to the Evangelist's competence as an author, which is implied by various details found throughout the narrative at both the macro and micro levels. If Mark were rather careless in his composition, then determining his purpose would be a presumptuous goal. However, Mark's thoughtful and deliberate handling of his material justifies our pursuit of his purpose and, ultimately, the pursuit of our target verse's meaning and significance based upon both its content and its location within the narrative. Readers will not be surprised to find that Mark's narrative focuses on the person and work of Jesus from its opening to its close. Who Jesus is (his identity) and what he has done (his mission) comprise the content of this gospel. However, Mark's narration of this Jesus story is not meant simply to offer historical data or theological beliefs about Jesus. Mark is *persuading* his audience to remain faithful to Jesus even in the face of suffering and trials.

Following the discussion of Mark's purpose, we will proceed to the interpretation of Mark 10:45 itself (chapter 4). We will offer observations about the narrative context of Mark 10:45 and then move on to a phrase-by-phrase analysis of the verse. Through our investigation, we will note that Jesus directs the attention of his disciples toward the supreme model of honor and splendor, that of the "one like a son of man" from Daniel 7:13–14.[3] And we will see that even this glorious

---

3. Unless otherwise indicated, quotations from the English Bible are from the Lexham English Bible (LEB). Where LEB uses italics to indicate interpretive

Son of Man is not too exalted to serve others and to suffer shame and abuse in order to "give his life as a ransom for many."

Chapter 5 will then highlight this verse's critical function within Mark's narrative and its contribution to our interpretation and appreciation of the Second Gospel. We will explore the strategic placement of Mark 10:45 at the conclusion of the carefully crafted threefold cycle of passion and resurrection predictions (8:27–10:45). This arrangement situates our verse at the climax within the Journey section (8:22–10:52) and also enables it to set the tone for the subsequent Jerusalem section (Mark 11:1–16:8), especially the narration of the Messiah's passion (Mark 14–15). In addition to the strategic location of 10:45 within Mark's narrative sequence, we will also discuss the value of this verse as it relates to the purpose of Jesus's mission and the meaning of his death. We will then consider several implications of this verse's crucial role within Mark's narrative, giving particular attention to the prominence of Jesus's atoning death and the inseparable link between his passion and the necessity of servanthood among those who follow him. We will also consider other ramifications, such as the significance of Mark's literary characteristics for its proper interpretation.

Finally, we will close with a reflection on how today's readers can and should apply the message of Mark 10:45 here and now. But before thinking about our "here and now," we must first deal with the "here and now" of the author and his intended audience. The Evangelist wrote his Gospel in the context of a specific time and place, so any serious discussion of this Gospel must consider its occasion and purpose. This is where our study begins.

---

glosses without an equivalent word in the original texts, we have removed those italics for the sake of clarity.

THE OCCASION OF MARK'S GOSPEL

I N THE HISTORY OF BIBLICAL INTERPRETATION, Mark's Gospel has held a rather humble station among the Synoptic accounts.[1] Early on, a presumption persisted that Mark's Gospel served primarily historical (rather than theological) purposes[2] and, more significantly, that it was occasioned as an *epitome* of Matthew's Gospel.[3] Since Matthew includes most of Mark's[4] material, and any uniquely Markan

---

1. See Sean P. Kealy, *A History of the Interpretation of Mark's Gospel*, 2 vols. (Lewiston: Edward Mellen, 2007), and the brief discussion in the introductory chapter of William Telford, ed., *The Interpretation of Mark*, 2nd ed. (Edinburgh: T&T Clark, 1995), esp. 1–9.

2. By "historical" purpose, we mean that the author's primary intention was to provide a historical record of the life of Jesus—without assuming that ancient historiographers wrote the same way we do today. Historical purposes are often set against theological purposes, but the two are not necessarily mutually exclusive. For a short survey of interpreters holding to a historical purpose, see Adam Winn, *The Purpose of Mark's Gospel: An Early Christian Response to Roman Imperial Propaganda*, WUNT 2.245 (Tübingen: Mohr Siebeck, 2008), esp. 4–9.

3. Augustine, *Cons.* 1.2.4. *Epitome* (from Greek ἐπιτομή, meaning "abbreviation" or "summary") is a popular style in classical literature that summarizes longer documents or works.

4. For the sake of convenience, the term "Mark" is used variously throughout this book to refer both to the work known as the Gospel of Mark and to the author of that work.

material missing from both Matthew and Luke is scarce,[5] many of the unique literary and theological contributions of the Second Gospel were underappreciated, if not altogether ignored. This low regard for Mark among the New Testament Gospels does not mean that its canonicity was disputed.[6] Mark's early association with the authority of the apostle Peter marked its unique significance.[7] But it was not until scholarly opinion regarding Mark's occasion and purpose shifted in the nineteenth century that this Gospel came to be appreciated for its own sake.

The first development to elevate Mark's status was the growing consensus that Mark was actually the first Gospel published rather than

---

5. The largest sections of Mark that do not appear in Matthew are 1:23, 25–28, 35–38; 3:20–21; 4:26–29; 5:4–5; 7:33–36; 8:22–26; 9:21–24; 9:38–40; 12:40–44; 14:51–52. Of these passages, the only ones that do not appear in Luke either are 3:20–21; 4:26–29; 5:4–5; 7:33–36; 8:22–26; 9:21–24; 14:51–52. There are several other instances of unique Markan material, but none of these is more than a verse long.

6. In the fourth century, Eusebius (*Hist. eccl.* III.39.15) presents the tradition from Papias (ca. 100 AD) that Mark was the "interpreter" of Peter. While some may take the comments from this tradition that Mark "wrote down accurately, though not indeed in order" as indicating some criticism of Mark's Gospel contemporary to Papias, there is nevertheless no indication that Mark was not regarded as authoritative (quote taken from Arthur McGiffert's translation in "The Church History of Eusebius," in *Eusebius: Church History, Life of Constantine the Great, and Oration in Praise of Constantine*, ed. Philip Schaff and Henry Wace, A Select Library of the Nicene and Post-Nicene Fathers of the Christian Church, Second Series, vol. 1 [New York: Christian Literature Company, 1890], 172).

7. Other ancient sources connecting Mark's Gospel to Peter include Justin Martyr, *Dial.* 106.3; Clement of Alexandria, "Fragments of Clemens Alexandrinus," *Fathers of the Second Century: Hermas, Tatian, Athenagora, Theophilus, and Clement of Alexandria (Entire)*, ed. Alexander Roberts, James Donaldson, and A. Cleveland Coxe, trans. William Wilson, *Ante-Nicene Fathers*, vol. 2 (Buffalo: Christian Literature Company, 1885). 1 Clement is also cited by Eusebius in *Hist. eccl.* II.15.1–2; Irenaeus, *Haer.* III.1.1; Tertullian, *Marc.* IV.5. It is interesting that a rising appreciation for the unique contributions of Mark's Gospel has somehow coincided with growing suspicion toward its connection with Peter.

just an *epitome* of Matthew's Gospel. In the early nineteenth century, New Testament scholars advanced various solutions to the Synoptic Problem, some proposing that both Matthew and Luke used Mark's Gospel as a source.[8] This new approach to the relationship among the Synoptics understood Mark as providing more historical value than the other Gospels, since its composition was chronologically closer to the events described. As a result, Mark enjoyed the spotlight of significance, especially in historical Jesus studies.[9]

A second development that increased the prominence of Mark's Gospel among New Testament scholars was a new understanding of the purpose behind its composition. Reading Mark as the first written Gospel required a drastic reassessment of the circumstances that occasioned its composition; Mark could no longer be considered a summary of another Gospel. Still, there was no immediate reason to dispense with the long-standing assumption that Mark's primary purpose was to provide a historical record of Jesus's words and deeds. William Wrede, however, challenged this assumption at the turn of the twentieth century. In his 1901 book, *The Messianic Secret*, Wrede argued that Mark's Gospel was written—and that the so-called "secrecy motif" was employed—to explain why Jesus was not believed, in Wrede's view, to be the Messiah until after his death.[10] For Wrede, Mark's driving motivation was not historical but theological; Mark wrote this gospel to *explain* his community's beliefs about Jesus. This view that Mark's intention was theological rather than historical resulted in the diminishment of Mark's historical reliability among critical New Testament

---

8. Examples include Christian G. Wilke, *Der Urevangelist oder exegetisch kritische Untersuchung über das Verwandtschafts-verhältniss der drei ersten Evangelien* (Dresden: Fleischer, 1838); Heinrich J. Holtzmann, *Die Synoptischen Evangelien* (Leipzig: Engelmann, 1863).

9. See the brief discussion of Mark's nineteenth-century ascendance in popularity in Robert H. Stein, *Mark* (Grand Rapids: Baker Academic, 2008), 15–17.

10. William Wrede, *The Messianic Secret* (Cambridge: Clarke, 1971); originally published in German as *Das Messiasgeheimnis in den Evangelien* (Göttingen: Vandenhoeck & Ruprecht, 1901).

scholars. Still, interest in Mark continued to mount as scholars shifted their attention from the historicity of this Gospel to its theological significance and especially to the question of what Mark was hoping to accomplish with his "gospel of Jesus Christ" (1:1).[11]

In light of this shift of attention toward the Evangelist's motivation for writing, it is proper to begin our examination of the meaning and significance of Mark 10:45 by considering the occasion and purpose that moved Mark to compose his Gospel. After all, knowing *why* Mark was writing will inevitably aid us in interpreting *what* Mark has written. In this chapter, we will proceed by considering the plausible historical and geographical settings in which Mark was writing, with particular attention to those elements within Mark's Gospel that indicate an expectation (or actuality) of suffering for the sake of Jesus.

It will be helpful first to distinguish clearly between Mark's *occasion* and his *purpose*. The *occasion* of Mark's Gospel refers to the circumstances surrounding its composition. The primary circumstances we will consider in this chapter are (1) the date of its composition and (2) the location and situation of its audience (and the related historical circumstances). The *purpose* of Mark's Gospel is a more specific concern within the consideration of its occasion and refers to the *motivations* and *intentions* of the author when he composed his Gospel. We care about the occasion, ultimately, because we care about the purpose. Mark's purpose does not arise in a vacuum; it is a product of the occasion that generated it. Any knowledge we can gain about the situation into which Mark was speaking will contribute to our understanding of what he hoped his work would accomplish. Therefore, our understanding of Mark's purpose for writing, which we will discuss in

---

11. See Telford, *The Interpretation of Mark*, 3–4. See Janice Capel Anderson and Stephen D. Moore, eds., *Mark and Method: New Approaches in Biblical Studies*, 2nd ed. (Minneapolis: Fortress, 2008) for an introduction to various methodological approaches to Mark's Gospel. See also Jin Young Choi, "Mark," in *The State of New Testament Studies*, ed. Scot McKnight and Nijay Gupta (Grand Rapids: Baker Academic, 2019), 297–314. See Winn, *The Purpose of Mark's Gospel*, for a summary of major proposals regarding the occasion and purpose

the next chapter, should be informed to some degree by the occasion of his composition. To be clear, our case for Mark's purpose does not depend directly on the specific occasion that we believe is most likely. But even a provisional understanding of the circumstances Mark was addressing can still guide our pursuit of Mark's purpose and enhance our understanding of the meaning and significance of Mark 10:45. Therefore, we will content ourselves with arguments for the general plausibility of one set of circumstances over others.[12] We argue below that the most likely occasion for the Second Gospel is that Mark was writing to Jesus-followers in Rome during or after the Neronian persecution of Christians that began in 64 CE.[13]

---

12. Two other caveats are pertinent in reconstructing the original occasion, circumstances, and audience of Mark's Gospel. First, while certain inferences may be necessary to reconstruct the circumstances, the further removed these inferences are from the actual data of the text, the less reliable they will be for interpreting the text. Consequently, a second caveat in this pursuit is to prioritize the interpretive strength of those facts that are most directly indicated by the text and to relativize those facts that are more speculative. At face value, this principle is obvious, but it is not always easy to practice because we all tend to root for our own reconstructions.

13. We use the term "Neronian" to indicate that the persecution took place in and around the city of Rome during Nero's reign and that it was an occasion of civil hostility toward followers of Jesus. It is not necessary that Nero directly ordered this persecution, especially as a result of the fire of July 64. The tradition of this civil persecution of Roman Christians is rooted in the testimony of Tacitus in *Ann.* 15.44, but it is also connected with the presumed execution of Paul after his appeal to the emperor (Acts 25:10–12). Brent Shaw questions the historicity of Tacitus's reference to Nero blaming Christians for the fire of 64 CE in "The Myth of the Neronian Persecution," *Journal of Roman Studies* 105 (2015): 73–100. For responses to Shaw's argument, see Christopher Jones, "The Historicity of the Neronian Persecution: A Response to Brent Shaw," *NTS* 63 (2017): 146–52; and Pierluigi Leone Gatti, "Much Ado about Nothing: An Answer to B. D. Shaw's The Myth of the Neronian Persecution," *Augustinianum* 59 (2019): 201–15.

WHEN DID MARK WRITE
HIS "GOSPEL OF JESUS CHRIST"?

New Testament scholars have advanced dates for Mark's Gospel anywhere from the 40s through the 70s CE. Most contemporary Markan scholars propose a date between 65 and 75 CE. We will begin by making a case for the middle to late 60s CE as the most reasonable date for Mark's composition. We will then respond to some potential objections to this date as we interact with alternative proposals.

THE PLAUSIBILITY OF A COMPOSITION
IN THE MIDDLE TO LATE 60S

One source worth consideration when dating Mark's Gospel is the testimony of the early church. The tradition of Peter's association with the Gospel of Mark has served as the primary evidence for its date throughout most of church history. By way of example, Irenaeus of Lyons writes, "After [Peter's and Paul's] departure, Mark, the disciple and interpreter of Peter, did also hand down (παραδέδωκεν) to us in writing what had been preached by Peter."[14] The most explicit testimony to a date of composition after Peter's death appears in a document referred to as the Old Latin (Anti-Marcionite) Prologue to Mark's Gospel. The Prologue contains the following line in its shorter recension: "After the death (*post excessionem*, lit. "after departure") of Peter himself he wrote down (*descripsit*) this same gospel in the regions of Italy."[15] However, there is disagreement about whether these early

---

14. Irenaeus, *Haer.* 3.1.1. The translation is from "Irenaeus against Heresies," in *The Apostolic Fathers with Justin Martyr and Irenaeus*, trans. W. H. Rambaut, ed. Alexander Roberts, James Donaldson, and A. Cleveland Coxe, *Ante-Nicene Fathers*, vol. 1 (Buffalo, NY: Christian Literature Company, 1885), 414. See also the evidence for an association between Mark and Peter in footnotes 6 and 7 of this chapter.

15. This English translation is taken from Martin Hengel, *Studies in the Gospel of Mark* (Philadelphia: Fortress, 1985), 3.

writings place Mark's composition before or after the death of Peter.[16] Adam Winn contends that *post excessionem* in this source is a euphemism for Peter's death rather than referring to Peter's departure from a particular location.[17] Reading the Prologue as referring to Peter's death would rule out a date of composition in the 40s or 50s. However, such a reading would also directly contradict the testimony recorded by Eusebius in book II, chapter 15 of *Ecclesiastical History*:

> Nor did they cease until they had prevailed with the man, and had thus become the occasion of the written Gospel which bears the name of Mark. And they say that Peter, when he had learned, through a revelation of the Spirit, of that which had been done, was pleased with the zeal of the men, and that the work obtained the sanction of his authority for the purpose of being used in the churches. Clement in the eighth book of his Hypotyposes gives this account, and with him agrees the bishop of Hierapolis named Papias.[18]

Unless "the work" that "obtained the sanction of [Peter's] authority" was the *plan* to compose the Gospel of Mark rather than the *completion* of it, this excerpt indicates that Peter was still alive after Mark's Gospel

---

16. For example, it is not clear whether Irenaeus describes the *composition* or the *transmission* (παραδέδωκεν) of Mark's Gospel after the deaths of Peter and Paul. Similarly, the Old Latin Prologue may refer to Peter's departure from one location to another rather than to his death. However, Winn, in *The Purpose of Mark's Gospel*, 44–48, convincingly contends that the testimonies of both Irenaeus and the Old Latin Prologue can plausibly describe a composition of Mark's Gospel after the death of Peter but acknowledges that the testimony discussed below from Clement of Alexandria through Eusebius (*Hist. eccl.* II.15.1–2; VI.14.5–7) clearly describes a composition during the life of Peter.

17. Winn, *The Purpose of Mark's Gospel*, 47. Relatedly, scholars have argued against a 40s date on the implausibility of Peter's presence in Rome during that decade. This argument assumes a Roman provenance for Mark's Gospel, but it is commonly used to push the date of composition into the 50s or 60s. See the section below on proposal for a date of composition in the 50s.

18. Eusebius of Caesarea, "The Church History of Eusebius," 116.

was written. Furthermore, E. Earle Ellis has argued that the testimonies of Irenaeus (*Haer.* 3.1.1-3) and the Old Latin Prologue describe the "transmission" (*descripsit* in the Prologue) of Mark's Gospel in Italy rather than the composition of it.[19] This reading would undoubtedly undermine the strength of the Old Latin Prologue as evidence for the composition of Mark's Gospel after the death of Peter. Ellis concludes that neither Irenaeus nor the Old Latin Prologue offers information about the timing of the actual *composition* of Mark's Gospel.[20]

In light of such contradictory testimony within the ancient external witnesses to Mark's Gospel, many scholars shift the focus to the internal evidence in the text of Mark's Gospel to establish a date. One common argument from the text for a composition in the middle to late 60s is the striking sense of rejection, mistreatment, and persecution that followers of Jesus should expect to face. This theme of rejection and mistreatment is most prominent in the threefold "passion prediction" cycles of Mark 8:27–10:45, but it is also present at a number of other points (4:14-19; 6:11, 17-29; 8:15; 12:1-11, 38-40; 13:9-23; 14:51-52, 66-72).

The theme of persecution may reflect rising tensions between the church and civil authorities. It is true that much of the opposition to Jesus and the disciples in Mark's narrative comes from unbelieving Jews and the leaders in Jerusalem. But the call of Jesus in Mark 8:34 that anyone who follows after him must take up his *cross* refers to a specifically Roman threat, given that crucifixion was the Roman (not Jewish) way of execution in the first century CE (cf. 13:9). The Jewish conflict experienced by Jesus and his disciples in Mark's Gospel illustrates the hostility believers will experience or are already experiencing from various authorities as a result of their loyalty to Jesus. If Mark understands the ultimate source of opposition to Jesus as spiritual (see 3:20-27; also, 1:21-28; 5:1-20; 9:14-29), then it is not surprising that

---

19. Edward Earle Ellis, "The Date and Provenance of Mark's Gospel," in *The Four Gospels, 1992,* ed. Franz van Segbroeck (Leuven: Peeters, 1992), 803, 814.

20. Ellis, "The Date and Provenance of Mark's Gospel," 805.

the agents of that opposition may be represented by religious leaders at one point and by Roman authorities at another. Conflict between first-century followers of Jesus and the Roman authorities varied at different times depending on the location, but the Neronian persecution of Christians in Rome in the mid-60s offers a very plausible backdrop to the warnings about suffering and persecution (e.g., 8:34; 10:29-30; 13:9-13) found in Mark's Gospel. Before this time, there does not seem to be an instance of significant Roman persecution of Christians.

One reason for dating Mark in the middle to late 60s and *not earlier* is that Paul never seems to refer to Mark's Gospel—or any other written gospel for that matter. It is natural to expect that Paul would have made some reference to a written account of the life of Jesus had he been aware of it. There are several references throughout the Pauline epistles to the life of Jesus (in Romans alone, see, e.g., 1:3-4; 3:25; 4:25; 5:18-19; 6:3-4).[21] But none of these requires a written source; each can easily be explained as the result of oral tradition circulating among early followers of Jesus.[22] There seems to be no clear indication that Paul was aware of Mark's Gospel (or any other written gospel).[23] This silence in the Pauline corpus is especially notable since the traditional

---

21. See also the section, "Paul and the Historical Jesus," in Gordon Fee, *Pauline Christology: An Exegetical-Theological Study* (Peabody, MA: Hendrickson, 2007), 524-26, for other examples of Paul's knowledge of or reference to the life of Jesus; cf. David Wenham, *Paul: Follower of Jesus or Founder of Christianity?* (Grand Rapids: Eerdmans, 1995).

22. There are even instances in which Paul appears to agree with teachings that are found in Mark, for example, Romans 14:14, which seems to correspond to Mark 7:1-23. But this does not necessitate that Mark was Paul's source.

23. On the contrary, arguments can be made for a Pauline influence on Mark's Gospel, e.g., the worldwide mission of the gospel (Mark 13:10; 14:9). For discussions of possible Pauline influences on Mark, see Martin Werner, "Der Einfluss paulinischer Theologie im Markusevangelium," *Zeitschrift für die neutestamentliche Wissenschaft und die Kunde der älteren Kirche Beihefte* 1 (Berlin: de Gruyter, 1923); Joel Marcus, "Mark—Interpreter of Paul," *NTS* 46, no. 4 (2000), 473-87; Eve-Marie Becker, Troels Engberg-Pedersen, and Mogens Müeller, eds., "Mark and Paul: Comparative Essays, Part 2," *Beihefte zur Zeitschrift für*

author of Mark's Gospel seems to be mentioned favorably (Col 4:10; Phlm 24; 2 Tim 4:11). When this silence is considered not simply on its own but alongside the expectation of persecution from Roman authorities described above, a composition *after* the Christian suffering under Nero in the middle 60s becomes even more plausible.

There are also reasons for dating Mark *no later* than the middle to late 60s, that is, after the siege of Jerusalem in 70 CE. The most significant difficulties with a later date are the details in Jesus's prediction of the temple's destruction in Mark 13—interestingly, Mark 13 is at times cited *in support* of a post-70 date, and we will deal with those arguments for a later date below. We believe that Mark 13 supports a date of composition before the fall of the Jerusalem temple because Mark's details of the events surrounding the temple's destruction are relatively general compared to parallel details in Luke's Gospel. For example, Mark 13:14 (also Matt 24:15) references the "abomination of desolation," whereas Luke describes this specifically as "Jerusalem surrounded by armies" (Luke 21:20). Furthermore, Luke 19:43–44 contains a very specific warning (unparalleled in Matthew and Mark):

[Y]our enemies will put up an embankment against you, and will surround you and press you hard from all directions. And they will raze you to the ground, you and your children within you, and will not leave a stone upon a stone within you, because you did not recognize the time of your visitation.

Another detail that makes good sense of a composition before the fall of Jerusalem is the line in Mark 13:18, "But pray that it will not happen in winter." If Mark is writing after the temple's destruction and the siege actually occurred between spring and fall, then it is peculiar that Mark includes the detail about praying it would not happen in winter. One of the purposes of prophecy *ex eventu* (after the event) in the ancient world was to establish the prophet's credibility by highlighting

die neutestamentliche Wissenschaft und die Kunde der älteren Kirche 199 (Berlin: De Gruyter, 2014).

the accuracy of his prophecy.[24] Mark 13:18, however, might defeat the purpose of impressing readers with Jesus's prophetic accuracy.[25] To be clear, this is not an argument against the validity or truthfulness of 13:18. The only point we are making here is that such a detail could undermine the appeal to prophecy *ex eventu* as an explanation for why Mark includes this passage in his narrative.

Given the evidence above, we contend that a middle to late 60s date, *after* the Neronian persecution of Christians began but *before* the destruction of the Jerusalem temple, is most likely for the composition of Mark's Gospel.[26] Other dates are also commonly proposed, but we find the arguments for these dates less persuasive. Below we will consider and evaluate the two primary alternatives to a middle to late 60s date.

---

24. John J. Collins discusses *ex eventu* prophecy as a major similarity between ancient genres of apocalyptic and quotes A. K. Grayson on the purpose of *ex eventu* prophecy as establishing credibility. John J. Collins, *The Apocalyptic Imagination: An Introduction to Jewish Apocalyptic Literature*, 3rd ed. (Grand Rapids: Eerdmans, 2016), 33. Grayson is specifically describing Akkadian prophecy, but credibility as a purpose for *ex eventu* prophecy in general seems plausible.

25. Verse 18 would certainly not falsify the prophecy of Mark 13. It is not as if Jesus declares that the siege *will* or *must* happen in winter. Rather, the point of v. 18, especially before the events take place, would be to highlight the hardship that people will face during the time of which Jesus is speaking.

26. Other notable scholars to advance a similar date for Mark's Gospel include Charles E. B. Cranfield, *The Gospel According to St. Mark* (Cambridge: Cambridge University Press, 1959); James R. Edwards, *The Gospel According to Mark* (Grand Rapids: Eerdmans, 2002); Austin Farrer, *A Study in St. Mark* (New York: Oxford University Press, 1952); Hengel, *Studies in the Gospel of Mark*; Willi Marxsen, *Mark the Evangelist: Studies on the Redaction History of the Gospel*, trans. James Boyce, et al. (Nashville: Abingdon, 1969; originally published in German as *Der Evangelist Markus: Studien zur Redaktionsgeschichte des Evangeliums* [Göttingen: Vandenhoeck & Ruprecht, 1956]); Vincent Taylor, *The Gospel According to St. Mark* (London: Macmillan, 1952). For a list of several other scholars and when they date Mark's Gospel, see Markus Vinzent, *Marcion and the Dating of the Synoptic Gospels* (Leuven: Peeters, 2014), 161–63.

EVALUATING THE ALTERNATIVES

There are a couple of major alternatives to a composition in the middle to late 60s. Some push the date later, usually to the early 70s, insisting that Mark's Gospel as we have it was completed after the destruction of the Jerusalem temple. Others place Mark's date before the deaths of Paul and Peter, often into the 50s, though there has been renewed interest in a date as early as the 40s.[27]

AFTER THE SIEGE OF JERUSALEM (POST-70)

The argument for a date after the siege of Jerusalem in 70 CE rests primarily on the presumption that Mark's description of the total destruction of the Jerusalem temple (Mark 13:2) makes more sense *after* the temple has already fallen. The basic argument usually proceeds as follows.

> Premise 1: The specificity of 13:2, namely, that "not one stone will be left here on another stone that will not be thrown down!" indicates that a complete razing of the temple is in mind.

> Premise 2: Though an attack on Jerusalem may have been anticipated as early as the late 60s, it is highly implausible that anyone expected the complete razing of the temple.[28]

---

27. A 40s date is certainly a minority view. See James G. Crossley, *The Date of Mark's Gospel: Insight from the Law in Earliest Christianity* (New York: T&T Clark, 2004), for a relatively recent argument for dating Mark to the 40s.

28. See, e.g., Joel Marcus, "The Jewish War and the *Sitz im Leben* of Mark," *JBL* 111, no. 3 (1992): 441–62, who suggests that the "precision" of Mark 13:1–2 "indicates that it has been written after the event" (460). However, Marcus seems less certain in *Mark 1–8: A New Translation with Commentary*, Anchor Yale Bible 27 (New Haven: Yale University Press, 2008), 38–39.

Conclusion: It is, therefore, more reasonable to think
that Mark composed this "prophecy" after the fact as
a device meant to impress a post-70 audience with
Jesus's prophetic accuracy.

The first premise is uncontroversial. There is no reason to doubt that
Mark is describing a complete razing of the temple. The weakness of
the argument lies in the second premise. We need to ask whether it is
really implausible that *anyone*, even the Jesus whom Mark describes,
would have expected the Jerusalem temple to be completely razed
before it actually happened.

This question cannot be settled solely based on naturalistic presuppositions. Obviously, most people with a supernatural world-
view will find objections to genuine prophecy unpersuasive. But we
believe that the above argument for a post-temple composition is
weak even from a naturalistic perspective. There are a few reasons
why the complete destruction of the Jerusalem temple was not utterly
unthinkable before the siege of Jerusalem. The first and most obvious
point is that 70 CE was not the first time that Jerusalem had lost its
temple. It is likely that, even in the Roman period, there was among
Judeans a community memory of the destruction of Solomon's temple
during the Babylonian conquest similar to the reflections we see in
later portions of the Hebrew Bible (e.g., 2 Kgs 25:8–11; Ezra 5:11–12;
Lam 2:1–7). The destruction of the Jerusalem temple was not a novel
concept. When the prediction of the temple's destruction is understood in the context of God's judgment on the religious leadership in
Jerusalem and linked to prior destruction of the Solomonic temple,
this prediction appears far less risky for Mark to include beforehand
than many suppose.

Another point to consider regarding the plausibility of predicting the temple's destruction is the Roman practice of *evocatio deorum*.
John Kloppenborg describes *evocatio deorum* as "the 'calling out' of
the tutelary deity or deities of a city prior to its destruction, the
'devoting' of its inhabitants to death or, more usually, slavery, and

the razing of its buildings and temples."[29] Kloppenborg argues that
anyone familiar with this widespread aspect of Roman siege warfare
or the demise of cities like Carthage or Corinth could have easily sur-
mised that such destruction would be an inevitable result of war with
Rome.[30] If Kloppenborg is correct and Mark 13:2 describes an inevitable consequence of war with Rome, then the prediction of the razing
of Jerusalem's temple may only be as specific as a prediction that the
God of Israel would remove his protection from the earthly temple,
with the result that Rome would take the city and raze the temple.
Kloppenborg himself prefers a date *after* the fall of the temple for Mark
13 on the specific grounds that he views *evocatio deorum* as a "*literary
motif* ... [that is] usually retrospective"[31] and that "the destruction of
a temple entailed the belief that the deity had departed."[32] However,
we are not arguing that Mark is employing *evocatio* as a literary motif.
We are simply noting that the practice of razing temples was a known
Roman military tactic in the first century.

Moreover, Mark does indicate an expectation that the God of Israel
would abandon the Jerusalem temple, thereby leaving it vulnerable to
destruction.[33] One example is Mark's sandwiching the so-called cleans-
ing of the temple within Jesus's cursing of the fig tree and the tree's
destruction (11:12–25). The intertwining of these two events suggests a
symbolic connection between the missing fruit of the fig tree and the
unfaithfulness of the religious authorities represented by the temple.[34]
In fact, this specific intercalation is itself located alongside a larger

---

29. John Kloppenborg, "*Evocatio Deorum* and the Date of Mark," *JBL* 124,
no. 3 (2005): 434.

30. Kloppenborg, "Date of Mark," 447.

31. Kloppenborg, "Date of Mark," 434.

32. Kloppenborg, "Date of Mark," 441.

33. See the discussion of some of these indications in the section,
"Atonement and the Temple," in chapter 5 below.

34. See, e.g., Dane Ortlund's argument for reading Mark 11:23 as a picture
of judgment upon the temple in his article, "What Does It Mean to Cast a
Mountain into the Sea? Another Look at Mark 11:23," *BBR* 28, no. 2 (2018): 218–39.

section of controversies with the religious leaders (11:27–12:44) adjacent to the prediction of the temple's destruction (13:2). This arrangement likely indicates that Mark is linking Jesus's discourse on the temple's destruction to the religious leaders' unfaithfulness. Another example indicating an expectation that God would abandon the temple is Mark's description of the temple curtain tearing from top to bottom in 15:38. The destruction of this barrier would have significant implications for the legitimacy of the temple itself. In this way, an actual prediction of the temple's destruction simply reflects Mark's understanding of God's shifting relationship to the temple. Claims that such a bold prediction would be too risky to include before the fact underestimate the likelihood that Mark and his readers would connect God's abandonment of the temple with its destruction before it actually took place.[35]

So then, is it really appropriate to argue that the complete destruction of the Jerusalem temple would have been unthinkable before it actually occurred? Kloppenborg considers this question and ultimately acknowledges:

Is the substance of Mark 13:1–2 imaginable as a saying that circulated prior to August 70 C.E.? Given knowledge of the Roman ritual of *evocatio* and given conditions in which conflict with Rome seemed likely or inevitable, it is indeed conceivable that someone could conclude that the deity would depart and the utter demolition of the temple would result.[36]

Kloppenborg helps us reframe the issue from whether it is likely that a writer would predict an event as extreme as the destruction of the Jerusalem temple to whether a writer might predict God's abandonment of the Jerusalem temple, leaving it *vulnerable* to destruction. The latter question poses no difficulty for a date of composition in the middle to late 60s.

---

35. See the discussion in the section, "Atonement and the Temple," in chapter 5.

36. Kloppenborg, "Date of Mark," 447 (italics original).

BEFORE THE DEATHS OF PETER
AND PAUL (PRIOR TO MID-60S)

Another alternative often suggested is a date *before* the middle to late
60s. This proposal commonly results from certain presuppositions
about the book of Acts and the relationship between Mark, Luke, and
Acts. First, and most speculatively, some scholars presume Acts to be
composed before or shortly after Paul's death in the mid-60s, usually
because Acts does not mention Paul's martyrdom. Second, and most
reasonably, Acts is presumed to be written after, even if immediately
after, the Gospel of Luke. And finally, Luke is assumed to be written
after Mark's Gospel, with Mark serving as a source for Luke. If Acts
is written in the mid-60s, then there is probably not enough time for
Mark's composition, circulation, and implementation as a source for
Luke's Gospel unless we push the date of Mark earlier, with many
scholars suggesting a date in the 50s or even the 40s.[37]

According to this line of logic, if Acts was published before or very
shortly after Paul's death in the mid-60s, then we are left with two
choices: either give up a middle to late 60s date for Mark's Gospel or
give up Markan priority among the Synoptics. But we should first ask
whether the early 60s is a more certain date for Acts than the middle
to late 60s is for Mark. The most common arguments for dating Acts
before or around Paul's death are primarily arguments from silence.
Acts does not mention Paul's death, Paul's letters, the Neronian persecution in Rome, or the destruction of the Jerusalem temple. Therefore,

---

37. A few notable proponents of a composition in the 50s, for varying rea-
sons, include Adolf Harnack, *The Date of Acts and the Synoptic Gospels* (New
York: Putnam's Sons, 1911); Ellis, "The Date and Provenance of Mark's Gospel";
and Robert Gundry, *Mark: A Commentary on His Apology for the Cross* (Grand
Rapids: Eerdmans, 1993). Notable proponents of a 40s date include C. C. Torrey,
The Four Gospels: A New Translation, 2nd ed. (New York: Harper, 1947); J. A. T.
Robinson, *Redating the New Testament* (London: SCM, 1976); Maurice Casey,
Aramaic Sources of Mark's Gospel (Cambridge: Cambridge University Press, 1998),
259–60; and more recently, Crossley, *The Date of Mark's Gospel*. For a more com-
prehensive list of various scholarly positions on the date of Mark, see again
Vinzent, *Marcion and the Dating of the Synoptic Gospels*, 161–63.

many assume that those events had not yet happened. However, arguments from silence, on their own, do not provide a sufficient basis to insist on a date for Acts before the death of Paul.[38]

While the ancient testimony may be contradictory at points, the date of composition for Mark that best explains both the external and internal evidence is the middle to late 60s. We believe that much of Mark's Gospel, especially the references to persecution at the hands of the Roman authorities (e.g., 8:34; 13:9), makes more sense in the context of Nero's persecution of Christians in Rome. Even though this persecution was not widespread, the ancient testimony connecting Mark's Gospel to Rome (discussed below) improves the likelihood of this proposal. Although our understanding of the purpose of Mark's Gospel does not directly depend on one date of composition over another, we do believe that the Neronian persecution and the years immediately thereafter comprise the most reasonable timeframe for Mark's writing.

TO WHERE DID MARK WRITE HIS "GOSPEL OF JESUS CHRIST"?

The previous references to Nero persecuting Roman Christians reveal our inclination toward a Roman audience for Mark's Gospel. But can a Roman audience be established on other grounds? Though scholarly opinion is somewhat more settled on Mark's audience than on the date, there is still disagreement over whether Mark wrote his Gospel for believers in Rome or somewhere in the East. Some of the same traditions that connect Mark with Peter (Old Latin Prologue to Mark; Clement of Alexandria) also link this gospel with Rome, but more recent proposals also include Galilee and Syria.

---

38. To be fair, we have advanced our own argument from silence above concerning the relationship between Mark's Gospel and Paul's epistles, but that argument is only supplementary to our case. The primary evidence for our dating Mark in the middle to late 60s is not its relationship with Paul's epistles but the theme of Roman (or civil) persecution of believers, among other factors (see our discussion above). We do not suggest that Paul's silence about Mark's Gospel is primary evidence for a post-Pauline composition of Mark.

ROME

Several scholars point to the Latinisms used throughout Mark's Gospel (esp. κοδράντης [Latin, *quadrans*] in 12:42 and πραιτώριον [Latin, *praetorium*] in 15:16) as evidence of a provenance in Rome or somewhere in the west of the empire.[39] But many of these Latin expressions were not out of place in eastern provinces, especially in locations with a military presence.[40] Thus, Mark's use of Latinisms should be considered supplementary to an argument for a Roman audience, not as independent evidence. There are stronger lines of evidence that point to an audience in Rome, and one of the most compelling is Mark's inclusion not of *Latinisms* but *Aramaisms*, more specifically, his inclusion of translations for these Aramaisms. Mark contains several Aramaic words and expressions translated into Greek (3:17; 5:41; 7:11, 34; 15:22, 34). These translations are quite natural if Mark is writing to an audience unfamiliar with Aramaic, but they would be rather peculiar if Mark were writing to believers in Galilee or Syria, where Aramaic would be common. Mark's explanation of Jewish purity regulations in 7:3-4 also makes more sense with a Roman audience than with a group of believers in Syria or Galilee, who would be familiar with such customs.

GALILEE OR SYRIA

Suggestions of a Galilean or Syrian provenance generally discard the ancient testimony as contradictory and unreliable and prefer to depend exclusively on the internal evidence within Mark's Gospel. For example, Willi Marxsen argues that Mark's emphasis on Jesus's ministry in and

---

39. For example, Hengel discusses these words in *Studies in the Gospel of Mark*, 29, and refers to Friedrich Blass, Albert Debrunner, and Robert Walter Funk, eds., *A Greek Grammar of the New Testament and Other Early Christian Literature* (Chicago: University of Chicago Press, 1961), 4-6 (§5) for a discussion of Latinisms in the Greek New Testament.

40. Gerd Theissen, *The Gospels in Context: Social and Political History in the Synoptic Tradition*, trans. Linda Maloney (Minneapolis: Fortress, 1991), 245-49; Marcus, "The Jewish War and the *Sitz im Leben* of Mark," 441-62; Marcus, *Mark 1-8*, 32.

around Galilee (nearly half of Mark's Gospel) and the note about Jesus returning to Galilee after his resurrection (16:7) indicate that Mark is writing for a Galilean audience awaiting Jesus's imminent return.[41] Joel Marcus has more recently argued for an audience in Syria based on some of the details in Mark 13 and the prominence of the conflict with Jewish authorities throughout Mark's Gospel.[42] These proposals deserve consideration, but as noted above, the inclusion of Aramaic expressions with Greek translations and the explanation of Jewish purity regulations do still present substantial difficulties for a Galilean audience. Given the geographic and linguistic proximity between Syria and Galilee, the same problems apply to a Syrian audience. In contrast, none of these details are evidence *against* a Roman audience. Mark indeed gives considerable attention to Galilee within his narrative, especially in the first half of his Gospel. But we must not confuse the setting of Jesus's public ministry with that of Mark's audience. Mark's attention to Galilee is a result of his subject matter rather than a hint as to the location of his audience.

NO SPECIFIC AUDIENCE?

Dwight Peterson argues that the pursuit of a so-called Markan community should be abandoned altogether, specifically because such speculations are inherently circular. Peterson complains that assertions about the Markan community seek to interpret Mark's Gospel in light of these reconstructed communities but these communities can only be reconstructed by *first* interpreting the text.[43] Peterson's concern is legitimate. It is true that the circularity of the process does not allow for an independent interpretive standard. Communities are

---

41. Marxsen, *Mark the Evangelist*. See Hendrika Roskam, *The Purpose of the Gospel of Mark in Its Historical and Social Context* (Leiden: Brill, 2004), for a more recent Galilean proposal.

42. Marcus, *Mark 1–8*, esp. 33–37. See also Theissen, *The Gospels in Context*.

43. Dwight Peterson, *The Origins of Mark: The Markan Community in Current Debate* (Boston: Brill, 2000).

hypothesized based on the a priori interpretation of the text (internal evidence), and these interpretation-shaped communities and circumstances then guide the (re-)reading of the text. But such is the nature of inductive investigations and, specifically, of hermeneutics. All interpretation involves an educated synthesis of the data and a reevaluation of that synthesis as new data are added. We have no other (or at least no better available) means by which to interpret the Gospel text. Solid external evidence about the recipient community would, of course, help alleviate this problem. But the scant external evidence we have of the occasions and circumstances that produced each Gospel is from neither the authors nor the audiences. It is also not contemporaneous with the composition, nor is it generally accepted by a broad spectrum of New Testament scholarship. Therefore, the internal evidence of the text, circular as it may be, is our strongest (drifting) anchor for interpretation. Furthermore, we are not arguing that it is impossible to interpret the text correctly without recovering the original circumstances of composition. We just believe that reading the text in light of even a provisional understanding of these circumstances is *more helpful* than ignoring the occasion altogether. A tentative and flexible picture of the circumstances and occasion is better than no picture at all. Of course, should we find sufficient reason to disregard a previously held understanding of what led Mark to write his Gospel, it would be foolish not to revise our reading. But interpreting the text with a specific setting in mind constructively stimulates our imagination to fathom how Mark's Gospel would have been read and heard by its original audience and how it would have impacted their own journey as they followed Jesus along the path of shame and suffering.

Similar to Peterson, Richard Bauckham argues against reading the Gospels with a specific audience or community in mind. In *The Gospels for All Christians*, Bauckham offers a chapter titled, "For Whom Were the Gospels Written?" in which he criticizes the long-standing tradition within New Testament scholarship of treating the Gospels as occasional documents similar to the epistles of Paul.[44] Bauckham contends that the Gospels were not occasional documents in this sense, written for one specific audience wherever they might have been, and that each author instead intended his work to be read by a vast audience in diverse locations.

This idea that Mark wrote for a universal audience has, however, been criticized.[45] There is reason to believe that Mark's text presumes a specific audience familiar with the details he includes. For example, in 15:21, Mark mentions Simon of Cyrene as the father of Alexander and Rufus, two individuals seemingly unknown elsewhere in early Christian literature. The inclusion of such a detail presupposes that the audience knew these names.[46] Specific details like this imply that universal readership is probably not Mark's primary expectation. Nevertheless, writing for one particular audience does not preclude an anticipation of broader circulation. If Mark did write to a specific audience, as the reference to Rufus and Alexander indicates, an audience in or around Rome explains his translation of Aramaic expressions, his explanation of Jewish purity regulations, and the references to Roman persecution better than the Galilean or Syrian alternatives.

---

44. Richard Bauckham, ed., *The Gospels for All Christians: Rethinking the Gospel Audiences* (Grand Rapids: Eerdmans, 1998), 9–48. Bauckham later published a summary of this chapter in his article "For Whom Were Gospels Written?" *HTS Theological Studies* 55, no. 4 (1999), 865–82. Refer also to Edward W. Klink III, ed., *The Audience of the Gospels: The Origin and Function of the Gospels in Early Christianity*, LNTS 353 (London: T&T Clark, 2010).

45. See, e.g., David Sim, "The Gospels for All Christians? A Response to Richard Bauckham," *JSNT* 84, no. 1 (2001): 3–27; Marcus, *Mark 1–8*, 25–28. For a response to several criticisms that have been leveled at Bauckham's hypothesis, see Michael Bird, "Bauckham's *The Gospels for All Christians* Revisited," *European Journal of Theology* 15, no. 1 (2006), 5–13.

46. Marcus, *Mark 1–8*, 27, also includes Mark 4:10–12; 8:14–21; and the ending at 16:8 as additional examples of "cryptic passages" that probably made more sense in the context of the shared knowledge between the author and the intended audience. Roskam, *The Purpose of the Gospel of Mark*, 15, also mentions 15:40.

WHAT DOES THE TEXT INDICATE
ABOUT ITS OCCASION?

As we examine the text of Mark's Gospel for clues to what may have been going on in the life setting of the author and his audience, we find a prominent emphasis on the shame and suffering that comes with following Jesus. In the first half of his Gospel (1:1–8:21), Mark describes various situations in which Jesus exemplifies the shame that those who associate with him should expect to receive. In this section, many readers focus on the awed reactions to Jesus's authority and power rather than on shame, but Mark narrates several significant instances in which shame is implied toward Jesus. For example, the scribes and Jewish leaders accuse Jesus of blasphemy (2:7; cf. 14:64). They ask why he eats with "tax collectors" and "sinners" (2:16), labels associated with shame, and why his disciples do not practice acts of piety like fasting or observe traditions like handwashing (2:18; 7:5). They also claim that Jesus is breaking God's law by violating the sanctity of the Sabbath (2:24). His family claims that he is out of his mind (3:20), and the scribes claim he is in league with Satan (3:22). Jesus is laughed at by those he serves (5:40) and rejected by those in his hometown (6:1–6). In each example, Jesus is associated with dishonor or shame for violating the norms and expectations of his contemporaries. The second half of the Gospel (8:22–16:8; esp. 8:31–10:45; 12:1–12; 13:3–23; 14:26–31), then, is primarily where Mark describes the *suffering* that Jesus and his followers are destined to face.[47] Peter's confession that

---

47. This does not mean that examples of suffering appear only in the second half and examples of shame appear only in the first half. For example, shame is very much a part of Jesus's crucifixion (15:16–20, 26–32). Martin Hengel describes several ways that crucifixion was meant to bring shame upon the victim, including being hung naked in public areas and denied a proper burial; Martin Hengel, *Crucifixion* (Philadelphia: Fortress, 1977), 39–40, 87. Likewise, suffering on the part of those who follow Jesus is implied as early as the parable of the sower (esp. 4:17–18). Hengel also suggests that the story of the man with an unclean spirit called "Legion" is an indication of Roman persecution; Hengel, *Studies in the Gospel of Mark*, 8. Our point here is that issues of honor and shame are most frequent in the first half of Mark's Gospel, and only after

Jesus is the Messiah prompts Jesus to begin teaching the Twelve about his own suffering and death (8:27-31). But when Peter rebukes Jesus for announcing this suffering and death, Jesus emphatically counters that his disciples, too, must be willing to endure suffering and shame if they indeed want to follow him (8:34-38).

While Mark's narrative presents the topics of suffering and shame as teachings directed toward the twelve disciples, these teachings also apply to future disciples, not least, Mark's audience—after all, Mark did not write his Gospel for the Twelve. At least two passages portray suffering and shame for Jesus's sake as an experience that applies to more than just his twelve disciples. The first of these is seen shortly after Jesus first announces his passion and resurrection (8:31). In Mark 8:34-38, in particular, Jesus describes what disciples must be willing to do: deny themselves, take up their crosses and follow him (v. 34), and give up their own lives for his sake (v. 35). Perhaps most emphatically, they must also be willing to bear shame for his sake:

> For whoever is ashamed of me and my words in this adulterous and sinful generation, the Son of Man will also be ashamed of him when he comes in the glory of his Father with the holy angels. (8:38)

Mark underscores the universality of this teaching by noting that Jesus "summon[ed] the crowd together with his disciples" (v. 34). He is speaking not just to the Twelve but to "anyone" who would follow after him. The Twelve are not the only ones who will bear shame for their association with Jesus. Anyone who would follow him must be willing to endure scorn and rejection from the world.

Another passage implying that followers of Jesus will face suffering and shame for his sake occurs within Jesus's teaching on the Mount of Olives in Mark 13. After the preceding controversies in the temple complex (11:27-12:44), Jesus announces that a time will come when

---

Jesus begins to teach his disciples that he must suffer and die does the theme of suffering become prominent.

the Jerusalem temple is destroyed (13:1-2). When Jesus's disciples ask him about the timing of these things, he replies with one of the most extended discourses in Mark's Gospel, describing what those who follow him, not just the Twelve, should expect to face *after* his death and resurrection (13:3-23). The Twelve are not the only ones who would be handed over to councils and beaten in synagogues (v. 9), brought to trial, and delivered over (v. 11). And they certainly are not the only ones who will be "hated by all because of my name" (v. 13). Mark is not recording these words for the disciples to whom Jesus is speaking but for his own audience and, in a broader sense, for any who would follow after Jesus, as the concluding verse of the thirteenth chapter clarifies: "what I say to you, I say to *everyone*" (13:37; emphasis added). Although this verse concerns eschatological vigilance, its universal language implies that Mark has in view not just a few disciples (13:3) but a much wider range of Jesus-followers, not least the original audience of his Gospel.

These passages corroborate the likelihood that Mark wants his audience to be ready for suffering and shame for Jesus's sake. This expectation is prominent in Mark's Gospel, and such prominence probably relates to the occasion and purpose for which Mark is writing, implying that his original audience was either experiencing or anticipating such suffering and shame.[48]

---

48. One could argue that if the mere presence of these two passages indicates Mark is especially concerned with suffering, then we must assume that the other Synoptic Gospels (Matt 16:24-28; 24:1-51; Luke 9:22-27; 21:5-36) are equally preoccupied with this theme and that it is not a unique emphasis of Mark's Gospel. But this objection misses two key differences between Mark and the other Synoptics. First, we agree with the majority of NT interpreters that Mark is a source for the other Synoptics. As a result, Matthew and Luke are both more likely to *inherit* concerns that are more direct and explicit in Mark. Second, while both Matthew and Luke *contain* discussions of suffering for the sake of Jesus, neither Gospel has as proportional of an emphasis as Mark. This particular interest in suffering within Mark's Gospel will be highlighted in the following chapters as we survey the text and discuss its themes and structures.

CONCLUSIONS REGARDING
THE OCCASION OF MARK'S GOSPEL

Whatever uncertainty may still exist about the occasion of Mark's Gospel, one thing we can say with relative confidence is that Mark's audience was either expecting or already facing suffering because of their allegiance to Jesus. Although no clear-cut evidence renders any date from the 50s through the 70s impossible, the evidence favors a composition in the middle to late 60s. Concerning the location of Mark's original audience, on the other hand, Rome makes the most sense of both the external and internal evidence. For a Syrian or Galilean proposal, the linguistic peculiarities (i.e., repeated translation of Aramaic expressions) coupled with the explanation of Jewish purity customs pose a significant challenge. Furthermore, some of the details in Mark's Gospel (e.g., 15:21) imply a specific rather than universal audience, though the expectation of an eventual wider circulation is possible.

When we consider the location along with a date in the middle to late 60s, it seems likely that Mark wrote to an audience in Rome experiencing or anticipating persecution for their loyalty to Jesus. The cases for an audience facing suffering, a Roman audience, and a middle to late 60s date complement one another. Each increases the respective plausibility of the others. Neronian persecution of Christians in Rome during the mid-60s provides a suitable and persuasive backdrop against which we may read Mark's Gospel, especially passages like 8:34–38 and 13:9–13. Even if readers disagree with the location of Mark's audience or the date we have suggested here, most will find it reasonable that Mark's audience is likely anticipating or experiencing persecution for their commitment to Jesus (cf. 2 Tim 3:12).

Since we believe that an audience made up of Jesus-followers in Rome in the middle to late 60s is more plausible than the alternatives, we will provisionally utilize that specific historical situation as we consider Mark's narrative, bringing it to bear on the text where appropriate, and tentatively so. We do not intend to interpret Mark's Gospel exclusively through the lens of these provisional conclusions so that they color our interpretation of every passage. Rather, we aim to reflect upon the circumstances that gave rise to this Gospel in order to better evaluate various interpretive options and to try, as best we can, to put ourselves in the shoes of Mark's original audience. Reference to a provisional understanding of the historical occasion of the Gospel is inevitable, even beneficial, as we seek the author's purpose. However, our reading of Mark's Gospel—and especially our proposal that Mark 10:45 is key for understanding it—does not depend exclusively on a specific audience or date of composition. The arguments we will offer regarding Mark's purpose (chapter 3) and the meaning and significance of Mark 10:45 (chapter 4) stand on their own apart from the specific reconstruction that we have put forward above. The primary reason for considering the occasion of writing is to gather whatever additional light may be available as we discern Mark's purpose for writing. With these clarifications in place, we now turn our attention to that question of purpose, that is, what Mark hopes to accomplish as he writes to his original audience.

III

THE PURPOSE OF MARK'S GOSPEL

UNFORTUNATELY, MARK NEVER PLAINLY STATES what he hopes to accomplish through his writing. He offers nothing like the statement in John 20:31, "but these things are recorded in order that you may believe that Jesus is the Christ, the Son of God, and that by believing you may have life in his name," or the prefatory remarks in Luke 1:4, "so that you may know the certainty concerning the things about which you were taught." Therefore, any attempt to establish Mark's purpose requires a careful examination of what has, in fact, been written. The following sections will examine how the content of Mark's Gospel sheds light on his purpose for writing. We will then discuss the literary features of Mark's Gospel that demonstrate competency and intentionality on the part of the author. Finally, we will survey the major sections within Mark's Gospel to consider how the whole of Mark's narrative relates to and supports the purpose for which he wrote this Gospel. We will argue that Mark has written a story that focuses substantially on who Jesus is and what he has done *in order to motivate his audience who are facing rejection and persecution to remain loyal to Jesus.* Mark does this by carefully and deliberately constructing his narrative to illustrate precisely how this Jesus, the Son of Man, served and gave his life as a ransom for others, thereby modeling true servanthood and faithfulness to God in the face of even the most extreme shame and suffering.

If most New Testament scholars are correct in their assessment that Mark is the earliest written Gospel, then Mark is something of a

31

trailblazer in the gospel genre. Of course, Mark did not coin the word "gospel" (εὐαγγέλιον). As a term referring to a good report, there is evidence for the use of εὐαγγέλιον as far back as Homer.[1] The word also appears in a plural form (εὐαγγελία "good tidings," NETS) at various points in the LXX of 2 Samuel. The most prominent Old Testament use of this root may be Isaiah 61:1, where the aorist middle infinitive εὐαγγελίσασθαι occurs: "The spirit of the Lord is upon me, because he has anointed me; he has sent me *to bring good news* to the poor" (NETS, emphasis added).[2] However, the verbal root also occurs several times throughout 1-4 Kingdoms (1-2 Samuel and 1-2 Kings in English Bibles).[3] In the first century, when Mark was writing, the noun εὐαγγέλιον was used as a term for military victory or the inauguration of a new ruler (esp. in the plural form).[4] So, with regard to Mark's composition, the novelty is not in the term εὐαγγέλιον itself but in its designation of a literary genre, namely, a narrative story about the sayings and works of the one through whom God was fulfilling his promises.

WHAT DID MARK HOPE TO ACCOMPLISH?

If we hope to discover the purpose for which Mark wrote his Gospel, we must first ask why he considered this genre most suitable to his goal. Many New Testament scholars recognize that the gospel genre is closely related to the Greek literary genre of *bios*.[5] Generally speaking,

---

1. See Homer, *Odyssey* 14.152.

2. Other occurrences of this verb in Isaiah include 40:9; 52:7; and 60:6. If Isaiah is Mark's primary source for the concept of "gospel" (εὐαγγέλιον), it is peculiar that he would not include the quotation of Isaiah 61:1 in his description of Jesus's rejection at Nazareth as Luke does (Luke 4:16–30).

3. 1 Kingdoms (1 Samuel) 31:9; 2 Kingdoms (2 Samuel) 1:20; 4:10; 18:19, 20, 26, 31; 3 Kingdoms (1 Kings) 1:42. The noun also occurs in 2 Kingdoms (2 Samuel) 4:10; 18:20, 22, 25; 4 Kingdoms (2 Kings) 7:9. See also 1 Chronicles 10:9; Psalm 67:12; 95:2; Joel 3:5; Nahum 2:1; Jeremiah 20:15 for other uses of this root in the Greek Old Testament.

4. See, e.g., Josephus, *Jewish Wars* 4.618.

5. For more information on the genre of the New Testament Gospels, see Craig Keener and Edward Wright, eds., *Biographies and Jesus: What Does It Mean*

ancient Greek *bioi* were narrative accounts of the deeds and sayings of historical figures, and this description would undoubtedly apply to Mark's Gospel. But we want to ask whether Mark's intent was simply to provide such a record of Jesus's life or whether, perhaps, this record of the life of Jesus was for Mark a means to an end. What did Mark hope to accomplish *through* this Gospel? Some have suggested that Mark's purpose is to teach—or even to correct existing teaching—about Jesus.[6] Indeed, Mark's Gospel has the effect of teaching, but other genres are more amenable to didactic, hortatory, and polemical material. Mark did not write a letter to an erring congregation, nor has he written a homily to people who need consolation—though Mark's audience may well have included such people. Instead, Mark chose to write a *narrative*; he chose to tell a story about Jesus and his followers. It is in this sense that a "gospel" is an ideal means for delivering his message. By writing a narrative about the person and work of Jesus Christ, Mark is able to capture the imagination of his audience and *motivate them to remain loyal to Jesus* despite the expectation of shame and suffering that they may have to endure for his sake. And so, Mark begins his narrative by answering the question of who Jesus is. But his answer to this question is not merely propositional; it is also descriptive and

---

for the Gospels to Be Biographies? (Lexington: Emeth, 2016); Richard Burridge, *What Are the Gospels? A Comparison with Graeco-Roman Biography* (Waco: Baylor University Press, 2018); Craig Keener, *Christobiography: Memory, History, and the Reliability of the Gospels* (Grand Rapids: Eerdmans, 2019). For a discussion of the genre of Mark specifically, see David Aune, "Genre Theory and the Genre-Function of Mark and Matthew," in *Matthew and Mark: Comparative Readings*, ed. Eve-Marie Becker and Anders Runesson, 2 vols., WUNT 2.271 (Tübingen: Mohr Siebeck, 2011); Helen Bond, *The First Biography of Jesus: Genre and Meaning in Mark's Gospel* (Grand Rapids: Eerdmans, 2020).

6. For example, Theodore Weeden, "The Heresy that Necessitated Mark's Gospel," *Zeitschrift für die neutestamentliche Wissenschaft und die Kunde der älteren Kirche* 59 (1968): 145–58, sees Mark correcting a θεῖος-ἀνήρ Christology. See also Werner Kelber, *The Kingdom in Mark: A New Time and a New Place* (Philadelphia: Fortress, 1974).

illustrative.[7] Mark does not just assert who Jesus is. He *narrates* who Jesus is *through* Jesus's words and actions.

THE TOPIC OF MARK'S STORY:
THE IDENTITY AND MINISTRY OF JESUS

The topic of Jesus's identity is pervasive throughout Mark's Gospel.[8] The very first words identify Jesus as Messiah (Χριστός) and Son of God (υἱὸς τοῦ θεοῦ, 1:1).[9] The climax of the story, Jesus's death (which is foreshadowed as early as 3:6 in the conspiracy of the religious leaders and perhaps even as early as 2:7 with the charge of blasphemy), is followed by an affirmation of his heavenly identity: "Truly this man was God's Son!" (15:39). The turning point of the narrative centers on the confession of Peter, "You are the Christ!" (8:29), after which Jesus begins to teach his disciples about the rejection and suffering that he, the Son of Man, must face. But, again, Mark is a *storyteller*, and direct discourse is not his only technique for communicating Jesus's identity.

---

7. Propositional expressions of Jesus's identity can be found in both the various christological titles applied to Jesus by the author and the direct statements of different characters in the story (e.g., 1:11; 3:11; 8:29; 9:7; 14:61-62; 15:39) and even in prescript of the Gospel: "The beginning of the gospel of Jesus, Messiah, Son of God" (1:1, our translation). We will discuss below several passages in which Mark's answer to the question of Jesus's identity is presented illustratively via descriptions of Jesus's words and actions, but a few obvious examples of such passages would be 2:1-12; 4:35-41; and 11:1-11, among others.

8. For example, see 1:27-28; 2:6-7, 12; 4:41; 6:2-3, 14-16, 48-50; 8:27-29; 10:17-18; 11:27-28; 12:35-37; 14:61-62; 15:1-5, 39. Several of these verses relate to the authority of Jesus, which we propose below is a consequence of his identity. In this way, the identity and authority of Jesus are two sides of the same coin.

9. The phrase "Son of God" in 1:1 is disputed by some textual scholars, as is evident even in the footnotes of many English translations, because some early witnesses to Mark's Gospel lack this phrase. This textual issue will be discussed in more detail in the analysis of Mark 1:1-13 below.

Mark also reveals to (or *reminds*) his readers who Jesus is through his vivid narration of Jesus's actions.[10] The identity of Jesus—often expressed through words or actions—permeates nearly every passage, and we will discuss several examples below as we survey Mark's Gospel. Whatever Mark's purpose in writing was, it seems clear that he chose to write a story to provide his own answer—through the words and actions of Jesus—to the question, "Who then is this?" (4:41). This again is why a "gospel" of Jesus Christ provides an excellent vehicle for his purpose. For Mark, Jesus's words and actions demonstrate his authority. And Jesus's *authority* is both a consequence and an expression of his *identity*. This authority is not a merely delegated authority (cf. esp. 2:7), as with a prophet or priest or even a king or angel. His authority to heal the sick, forgive sins, cast out unclean spirits, calm the rebellious waters of the sea, and override prevailing religious traditions is rooted in his own divine identity.

THE PURPOSE OF MARK'S STORY:
STAY ON THE PATH!

As stated above, we believe Mark's purpose for his Gospel is to remind his audience precisely who this Jesus is *in order to motivate* them to remain faithful to Jesus, even in the face of shame and suffering. This purpose fits well with the background of Nero's persecution of Roman Christians in the middle 60s. But our discussion of Mark's purpose cannot rest solely on hypothetical reconstructions of the situation in which his Gospel arose. The *best* evidence for Mark's purpose will come from the text itself. The purpose we have proposed accounts for both the genre and the content that Mark has selected for his Gospel. By choosing to write a "gospel of Jesus Christ" (1:1), Mark is able to capture the imagination of his audience through his narration of Jesus's words and actions and through his descriptions of various reactions from the disciples and others. He reminds his audience who Jesus is

---

10. For example, see 1:21-28; 2:1-12, 23-28; 3:1-6; 4:35-41; 5:21-43; 6:30-44, 45-52; 11:1-10, 12-33.

by inviting them to follow alongside Jesus and his disciples during his ministry. Regarding the content of Mark's Gospel, we have already discussed the prominent focus on the shame and suffering of Jesus in the narrative.[11] We will highlight this theme more thoroughly in our survey of Mark's content below. The theme of shame and suffering is not restricted to the passion narrative alone or even to the second half of Mark's Gospel, in which Jesus has announced the necessity of his death (8:31; cf. 10:45). Rather, this theme is introduced as early as the initial accusation of blasphemy in 2:7, and it surfaces repeatedly throughout the Galilean section (e.g., 2:7, 16; 3:20-22; 5:40; 6:1-6). But just as important as the *fact* of Jesus's shame and suffering in Mark's story is Jesus's *reaction* to it, namely, his resolute acceptance and steady faithfulness. Mark is not simply telling the story of Jesus's life and ministry. He is telling the story, specifically, of Jesus's steady faithfulness to God in the face of suffering and shame.

But Mark does not just want his audience *to remember* Jesus's faithfulness; he also wants them *to be motivated to emulate it*. And Mark's intention to motivate his audience is most clearly indicated by two elements within his narrative. First, Mark's purpose of motivating loyalty to Jesus is indicated by his concern that the audience understand the true identity of Jesus. He is not just a "good teacher" (10:17); he is the Messiah (1:1; 8:27-30; 14:61-62)! But even this messianic identity must be nuanced. Mark's purpose is to demonstrate that loyalty to Jesus is nothing less than loyalty to God himself (e.g., 2:1-12; 10:21-22; 12:1-12, 28-37). Those who oppose, reject, or abandon Jesus cannot claim faithfulness to God. Mark's identification of Jesus with the God of Israel at various points throughout his Gospel provides a powerful motivation for enduring suffering and shame for his sake.

A second indication that Mark's purpose is to motivate loyalty among his audience occurs in the way he portrays different models of faithfulness. Mark frequently casts the twelve disciples as negative

---

11. See the section "What Does the Text Indicate about Its Occasion?" in chapter 2 (pp. 26-27).

examples of what it means to follow Jesus. Through the many failures and misunderstandings of the Twelve (e.g., 4:10-13; 6:49-52; 8:14-21; 10:35-41; 14:50), Mark's audience sees the pitfalls of confused discipleship and how a mind focused on the things of men rather than the things of God (8:33; 10:42-45) can lead, eventually, to abandoning Jesus altogether (14:50). At the same time, the steady faithfulness of Jesus (esp. 8:31-33; 14:36, 48-49, 61-63), along with occasional cameos from faithful minor characters like the Syrophoenician woman (7:24-30), blind Bartimaeus (10:46-52), and the woman who anoints Jesus (14:3-9) provides positive examples of what true devotion to God looks like.[12] The motivation to remain loyal to Jesus is further undergirded by Mark's inclusion of repeated exhortations to prepare for the prospect of shame and suffering so that they are not led astray (e.g. 8:34, 38; 13:5, 9, 13, 21-23, 33-37).

The purpose we have offered for Mark's Gospel carries explanatory power with respect not only to its genre and content but even to the arrangement of this content (as we will show in chapter 5). And this purpose ultimately supports our thesis that 10:45 is key to understanding this Gospel. After all, if Mark 10:45 truly is a key to Mark's Gospel, then we would expect this verse to be intimately related to Mark's purpose for writing—and we believe it is. Mark 10:45 synthesizes the topics of Jesus's identity and his suffering, specifically, within the context of Jesus's own teaching on true discipleship, that slow and difficult process during which we learn to shift our focus from the things of men to the things of God (10:42-45; cf. 8:31). Moreover, as we will show in the next chapter, 10:45 provides the *rationale* for this expectation of a loyalty to Jesus that is willing to deny oneself, take up one's cross, and follow in Jesus's footsteps (8:34). If Jesus is to be identified with the God of Israel, then he has every right to demand complete devotion

---

12. Joel F. Williams offers a compelling case for the positive role of these and several other minor characters in Mark's Gospel in *Other Followers of Jesus: Minor Characters as Major Figures in Mark's Gospel* (Sheffield: Sheffield Academic, 1994).

and faithfulness. However, Mark does not present this demand by fiat.
He seeks to *motivate* his audience's devotion by showing that Jesus has
not simply commanded their loyalty but earned it. He has earned it by
coming "to serve and to give his life as a ransom" *for them.*

Mark wants his audience to know that true discipleship means
following Jesus—the Son of God and Son of Man—along the path of
shame and suffering.[13] When his audience is tempted to abandon Jesus,
Mark wants them to remember that "whoever is ashamed of [Jesus]
and [his] words ... , the Son of Man will also be ashamed of him when
he comes in the glory of his Father with the holy angels" (8:38). But
Mark also wants his audience to remember that even the exalted and
authoritative Son of Man "did not come to be served, but to serve, and
to give his life as a ransom for many" (10:45). It is in this sense that 10:45
is such a key verse for Mark's Gospel. Mark 10:45 reveals the inseparable connection that the author has made between Jesus's atoning
death and the mandate of servant-minded discipleship. If "even the
Son of Man" endured suffering and shame for the sake of his people,
then how much more should those who follow him be willing to give
up everything for his sake! This verse does not just communicate the
reason the Son of Man came; it also epitomizes Mark's strategy for
encouraging his audience's loyalty to Jesus. Mark motivates his audience by reminding them who it is they are following. He writes this
story to remind his audience of *Jesus's identity*—they are following the
authoritative "Son of Man" (10:45; cf. 2:10), who will come with the

---

13. For discussions of discipleship as an important theme in Mark's Gospel,
see David E. Garland, *A Theology of Mark's Gospel: Good News about Jesus the
Messiah, the Son of God* (Grand Rapids: Zondervan, 2015), 388–454; Robert
Tannehill, "The Disciples in Mark: The Function of a Narrative Role," *Journal of
Religion* 57 (1977): 386–405; Ernest Best, *Following Jesus: Discipleship in the Gospel
According to Mark*, JSNTSS 4 (Sheffield: JSOT Press, 1981); John R. Donahue, *The
Theology and Setting of Discipleship in the Gospel of Mark* (Milwaukee: Marquette
University Press, 1998); Suzanne Henderson, *Christology and Discipleship in
the Gospel of Mark*, Society of New Testament Studies Monograph Series 135
(Cambridge: Cambridge University Press, 2005).

clouds of heaven (14:62) in the glory of his Father with the holy angels (8:38). And he writes to remind them *what Jesus has done for them*—he has given his life as a ransom for many (10:45). These two topics are the core contents of Mark's "gospel of Jesus Christ" (1:1), and they are the means by which he seeks to inspire and reinvigorate their dedication to Jesus. While Mark underscores the authority of Jesus, he is careful to highlight Jesus's commitment to use that authority not for his own glory but for the benefit of others. It is *through* this message about who Jesus is and what he has done that Mark accomplishes his purpose, which is *to motivate his audience to remain faithful to Jesus despite the shame and suffering* that come with following Jesus on the path of discipleship, to remain loyal to him even if it costs them everything (8:34; 10:29). Mark has skillfully structured his narrative so that his audience is able, like the disciples, to walk alongside Jesus, observing his ministry, witnessing the wonders, the controversies, the hostility, and the resolve with which Jesus faithfully embraces his mission to serve and to give his life as a ransom for many.

MARK'S COMPETENCE AS AN AUTHOR[14]

Before we survey the content of Mark's Gospel and how it serves his purpose for writing, it will be helpful to note Mark's literary and rhetorical competence as an author. The examples of compositional proficiency that we will discuss below indicate an intentionality behind the organization and structure of Mark's narrative. And this intentionality bolsters our confidence in our inferences about the purpose of his "gospel of Jesus Christ." Since Willi Marxsen's groundbreaking study, *Mark the Evangelist*,[15] scholarship has recognized Mark's capabilities as a theologian. This awareness has advanced through literary and narrative studies on the Gospels, in which scholars have

---

14. The germ of this section was presented earlier in a brief subsection of John J. R. Lee, *Christological Rereading of the Shema (Deut 6.4) in Mark's Gospel*, WUNT 2.533 (Tübingen: Mohr Siebeck, 2020), 244-47.

15. Marxsen, *Mark the Evangelist*.

demonstrated the value of treating each Gospel's narrative as a unified and integrated whole.[16] This section will utilize the insights of literary- and narrative-critical studies to offer several observations about Mark's competence as an author who exercises intentionality and control over his narrative.

First, Mark's ability as an author is clearly demonstrated in the central section of his Gospel (8:22–10:52).[17] This section portrays a transition from the Galilean locale of Jesus's ministry to his journey toward Jerusalem (leading to his death on the cross). It details three cycles of passion predictions (8:27–9:29; 9:30–10:31; 10:32–45).[18] Each of these cycles presents a prediction of Jesus's suffering, death, and resurrection (8:31; 9:31; 10:33–34), some misunderstanding from the disciples

---

16. Regarding a narrative-critical approach, see David M. Rhoads, Joanna Dewey, and Donald Michie, *Mark as Story: An Introduction to the Narrative of a Gospel*, 2nd ed. (Minneapolis: Fortress, 1999) and works cited therein. As for the unity of Mark's narrative, see, e.g., Norman R. Petersen, "'Point of View' in Mark's Narrative," *Semeia* 12 (1978): 97–121; Robert C. Tannehill, "The Gospel of Mark as Narrative Christology," *Semeia* 16 (1979): 57–95; Joanna Dewey, "Mark as Interwoven Tapestry: Forecasts and Echoes for a Listening Audience," *Catholic Biblical Quarterly* 53 (1991): 221–36.

17. This section is often referred to as the "Journey" or the "(On the) Way" section due to the repetition of the phrase ἐν τῇ ὁδῷ in it (8:27; 9:33–34; 10:32, 52) and Jesus's somewhat indirect journey from Galilee to Jerusalem.

18. Holly J. Carey has helpfully warned against an inordinate deemphasis of resurrection and its importance within Mark's Gospel that can result from describing these predictions merely as "passion predictions" without reference to the resurrection. Holly J. Carey, *Jesus' Cry from the Cross: Towards a First-Century Understanding of the Intertextual Relationship Between Psalm 22 and the Narrative of Mark's Gospel*, LNTS 398 (New York: T&T Clark, 2009), 46–48. We agree that the theme of resurrection is important in Mark's Gospel and that it is probably more prominent than is often realized. However, we believe that the reference to the resurrection in these predictions is deliberately ambiguous—at least to the characters before whom Jesus makes these predictions (e.g., 9:10)—compared to the description of Jesus's passion. Our use of the term "passion prediction" should be understood more as a synecdoche or a metonym for the suffering, death, and resurrection of Jesus, which we believe are components of a unified experience in Mark's Gospel.

(8:32; 9:32–34; 10:35–41), and Jesus's corrective teaching (8:33–38; 9:35–37; 10:42–45). These three elements appear in the same order in each cycle. This middle section of Mark's Gospel also contains seven occurrences of ὁδός ("way"), each likely associated with Mark's concept of discipleship (i.e., following Jesus on his way to Jerusalem, the location of his suffering and death). These three cycles are bookended by two separate healings of blind men, one in 8:22–26 and the other in 10:46–52. These are the only two healing passages in Mark's narrative in which Jesus restores a person's sight, and the latter (10:46–52) represents the final healing in the entire Gospel. These features indicate that Mark is a skilled and intentional author who has given great care and attention to the order of his narrative.

Second, several literary arrangements and structures demonstrate Mark's capacity to maintain control over his narrative. At the micro level, Mark often employs a two-step progression. The first step communicates something generally, while the second step reiterates the first with more specificity and detail.[19] Mark 1:32, for example, adds the description "when the sun had set" to "evening," emphasizing the fact that the crowds began bringing their sick to Jesus the moment the Sabbath had ended (see also 1:28, 45; 6:53; 7:26; and 14:3).[20] Another micro-level literary structure is Mark's use of intercalation, instances in which he places one story or narrative element inside another (see, e.g., 3:20–35; 5:21–43; 6:7–32; 11:12–25; 14:1–11; 14:53–65). This arrangement indicates some connection or relationship between the separate elements. One well-known example is the clearing of the temple placed between the cursing and withering of the fig tree (Mark 11:12–25). Each story illuminates the other; in this instance, Jesus's curse of the fig tree highlights God's judgment on the temple and its authorities.[21]

---

19. Garland, *A Theology of Mark's Gospel*, 93.

20. Garland, *A Theology of Mark's Gospel*, 93.

21. Mark L. Strauss, *Mark*, Zondervan Exegetical Commentary on the New Testament (Grand Rapids: Zondervan, 2014), 493.

Moving to a macro level, we find literary structures such as "allusionary repetitions"[22] and framing. Allusionary repetitions occur when
the author employs similar language between two separate pericopes
to provide additional meaning or depth.[23] Dean Deppe cites Mark 11:1–6
and 14:13–16 as examples. Each of these passages contains several iden-
tical words in the same order: ἀποστέλλει δύο τῶν μαθητῶν αὐτοῦ (11:1
and 14:13); καὶ λέγει αὐτοῖς ὑπάγετε εἰς τὴν κώμην ... καὶ ... ἀνθρώπων/
ον (11:2 and 14:13); εἴπατε ... ὁ (11:3 and 14:14); καὶ -ἦλθον καὶ εὗρον (11:4
and 14:16); καθὼς εἶπεν (11:6 and 14:16).[24] This repetition, Deppe argues,
closely ties the Last Supper to Jesus's triumphal entry and indicates
that Jesus's death would occur just as much according to plan as his
triumphal entry did. Both events are part of God's plan and purpose.[25]

Another noteworthy literary structure that Mark employs is framing. This structuring method is similar to intercalation, but framing
extends over a much broader section. The example that bookends the
three cycles of passion prophecy, the two separate healings of the blind
men (8:22–26 and 10:46–52), was discussed above. Another instance
of this technique is Mark's framing of Jesus's passion by reference
to women caring for his crucified body (14:3–9 and 16:1–6).[26] In fact,
Mark appears to frame the entirety of Jesus's ministry with instances
of "tearing" (see the uses of σχίζω in 1:10 and 15:38) immediately followed by a declaration of Jesus's divine sonship (a heavenly voice in
1:11 and a Roman centurion in 15:39); the revelatory "tearing" facilitates

---

22. This expression, "allusionary repetitions," is taken from Dean B. Deppe,
*The Theological Intentions of Mark's Literary Devices: Markan Intercalations, Frames,
Allusionary Repetitions, Narrative Surprises, and Three Types of Mirroring* (Eugene,
OR: Wipf & Stock, 2015), especially chapter 4.

23. Deppe, *The Theological Intentions of Mark's Literary Devices*, 204.

24. Deppe, *The Theological Intentions of Mark's Literary Devices*, 205–6.

25. Deppe, *The Theological Intentions of Mark's Literary Devices*, 207; for more
examples of allusionary repetitions, see 6:41//8:6–7//14:22–23; 13:21–37//14:32–
42; and 1:10–11//9:7//15:38–39//12:6 (Deppe, *The Theological Intentions of Mark's
Literary Devices*, 207–24).

26. Garland, *A Theology of Mark's Gospel*, 91.

the disclosure of Jesus's divine sonship in each passage.[27] These literary structures and arrangements indicate Mark's competence to control how and what he narrates.

Third, Mark's use of dramatic irony demonstrates his skill as a narrator. For example, in 2:7 ("Why does this man speak like this? He is blaspheming! Who is able to forgive sins except God alone?"), Mark uses Jesus's opponents (the scribes) to confirm his Christology, specifically, the confession of Jesus as the one with divine authority to forgive sins. Though the scribes in the story condemn Jesus for violating God's unique prerogative, their opposition to Jesus and their accusation that he is blaspheming reinforce Jesus's inseparable connection and coequality with Israel's God (2:1-12; cf. 1:2-3), since Mark most likely expects his audience to believe that Jesus did forgive the sins of the lame man (see 2:9-12).[28] By the question, "Who is able to forgive sins except God alone?" (2:7), the scribes, as characters of Mark's story, are shown to exalt Jesus unwittingly. Other clear examples of dramatic irony occur in the passion narrative. Jesus is mocked as "king of the Jews" (15:18; cf. v. 26) and "the Christ, the king of Israel" (15:32), yet such mockery ironically reflects the christological belief of the Evangelist and his original audience (for more examples, see also 3:4-6; 6:14-29; 7:9, 24-30; 8:27-33; 10:46-47).[29] As Jerry Camery-Hoggat notes, "the wide distribution of irony suggests that it was born of the author's conscious intent,"[30] and the repeated use of dramatic irony described

27. See, e.g., Strauss, *Mark*, 72.

28. For a discussion of the inseparable connection and coequality between Jesus and Israel's God in Mark's Gospel, see Lee, *Christological Rereading of the Shema (Deut 6.4) in Mark's Gospel*, esp. 153-74, which discusses Mark 2:1-12.

29. Deppe, *The Theological Intentions of Mark's Literary Devices*, 484-88; also, Ernest Best, *Mark: The Gospel as Story*, Studies of the New Testament and Its World (Edinburgh: T&T Clark, 1985), 18-20; Edwards, *Mark*, 12. For a helpful study of the Markan use of irony, see Jerry Camery-Hoggatt, *Irony in Mark's Gospel: Text and Subtext*, Society for New Testament Studies Monograph Series 72 (Cambridge: Cambridge University Press, 1992).

30. Camery-Hoggatt, *Irony in Mark's Gospel*, ix.

above indicates Mark's competency as a narrator and his capability in controlling and utilizing his material to deliver the intended message.

Fourth, Mark's use of Greek style for literary effect demonstrates his skill as an author. For example, Mark foregrounds events by use of the historical present, as in 3:20, where his use of the present-tense forms ἔρχεται and συνέρχεται gives vividness to the crowd's disruption.[31] Mark's use of the historical present often appears in key passages, such as those focusing on the person of Jesus or his salvific acts.[32] Another example is Mark's use of asyndeton (the omission of a conjunction between clauses) to increase tension. In Jesus's exchange with his disciples in 8:14-21, for instance, the first four sentences start with καί ("and"), but after the disciples fail to comprehend, Jesus's questioning drops the καί altogether (17-20a), creating the strong impression of tension.[33] This use of the historical present and asyndeton for literary effect implies Mark's competence as an author.

Fifth, Mark's interspersing of the passion motif throughout his entire narrative (see, e.g., 2:7, 19-20; 3:6, 19; the three passion prediction cycles in 8:27-9:29; 9:30-10.31; 10:32-45; and the passion narrative itself in chaps. 14-15) reveals his intentionality and competency in structuring his Gospel as an integrated story.[34] Relatedly, it is the charge of "blasphemy" early on in the narrative (2:7) that becomes the reason for Jesus's being handed over to the Romans for crucifixion later in the passion narrative (14:64). Much of Jesus's conflict with the

---

31. James W. Voelz, *Mark 1:1-8:26*, Concordia Commentary (St. Louis: Concordia, 2013), 15.

32. Voelz, *Mark 1:1-8:26*, 15; for more examples of Mark's use of the historical present in key passages, see Voelz's list: 2:1-12; 3:31-35; 4:35-41; 5:22-23, 35-43; 11:27-33; 14:32-42; 15:16-24. Voelz, 15.

33. Voelz, *Mark 1:1-8:26*, 17; for more examples of Mark's use of asyndeton, see Voelz's list: 1:24; 2:8b-9; 8:1; 9:43b, 45b, 47b; 10:28; 12:14b, 15b, 16b, 17b; 14:8. Voelz, 4.

34. For the pervasiveness of Mark's passion theme (and authority theme), see Demetrios Trakatellis, *Authority and Passion: Christological Aspects of the Gospel According to Mark* (Brookline: Holy Cross Orthodox Press, 1987).

religious authorities from 2:7 onward (including 2:1–3:6 and 11:27–12:44, which counterbalance each other within the narrative) ultimately leads to the charge of blasphemy at Jesus's trial (14:61–64, esp. v. 64). Trakatellis notes in his study on Mark's Christology, "The passion is not the terrible reality which is suddenly thrust at the end of a long course, but a reality which marks this course at every step, at every stage."[35] Consistent references and allusions to the passion of Jesus the Messiah across Mark's Gospel can hardly be considered coincidental. Rather, these references and allusions demonstrate the careful and intentional construction of the narrative by the Evangelist.

Other examples could further illustrate Mark's capabilities as an author, such as his use of "the Son of God" (see esp. 1:11; 9:7; 15:39) in highly strategic points of the narrative[36] or his consistent use of specific themes within his plot, such as Jesus's identity and authority. Mark also skillfully incorporates two collections of controversies over the validity of Jesus's authority, one in 2:1–3:6 (part of the Galilee section) and the other in 11:27–12:37 (part of the Jerusalem section), in such a way that each counterbalances the other. By this point, though, Mark's ability to produce a highly controlled and coherent narrative should be obvious.[37] This conclusion rests on his careful construction of the Journey section, his use of dramatic irony, the interspersion of

---

35. Trakatellis, *Authority and Passion*, 149.

36. See, e.g., Garland, *A Theology of Mark's Gospel*, 227–32. See also Gabi Markusse, *Salvation in the Gospel of Mark: The Death of Jesus and the Path of Discipleship* (Eugene, OR: Pickwick, 2018), 27–43, who argues for a compelling relationship between this phrase and the structure of Mark's Gospel.

37. Concerning Mark's reliability as a narrator, see Tannehill, "Disciples in Mark," 386–405; Petersen, "'Point of View' in Mark's Narrative," 97–121; Robert M. Fowler, *Loaves and Fishes: The Function of the Feeding Stories in the Gospel of Mark*, Society of Biblical Literature Dissertation Series 54 (Chico, CA: Scholars Press, 1981), 229n23; Edwards, *Mark*, 2–3, 10–12; cf. Deppe, *The Theological Intentions of Mark's Literary Devices*. Although Mark's Greek constructions may appear clumsy at some points and simple at others, the relative constructional clumsiness or the relative lack of polish does not necessarily mean that his overall literary/rhetorical skills are unsophisticated.

various motifs and themes throughout the narrative, and other structuring techniques that add depth and meaning to the story. As Martin
Hengel aptly notes, Mark "uses a very deliberate process of selecting
and ordering material in which hardly anything is left to chance."[38] If
Mark showed no discretion over the material included in his narrative, it would be presumptuous to suppose that we could determine
his purpose from his writing. But it is precisely through each of these
features and techniques that we do see an intentional hand at work.
Mark is crafting a story for his audience to remind them who it is that
they are following and what he has done for them so that they too will
be motivated to remain faithful as they deny themselves, take up their
crosses, and follow Jesus on the path of shame and suffering.

READING MARK'S GOSPEL
WITH HIS PURPOSE IN MIND

We have argued above that Mark's primary purpose for his Gospel
is to motivate his audience to remain loyal to Jesus even in the face
of shame and suffering. And Mark's strategy for accomplishing this
purpose is to tell the story of Jesus's own faithfulness as he endured
shame and suffering for the sake of God's people. We have already discussed how the general themes of persecution and discipleship relate
to our understanding of Mark's purpose, but below we will show that a
detailed survey of the content of Mark's Gospel supports our proposal
for Mark's purpose. In this section we will survey the content of Mark's
Gospel with an eye toward his purpose for writing. This survey will
provide two benefits. First, it will supply context for our discussion of
the meaning and significance of Mark 10:45 in the next chapter. Second,
it will demonstrate how each section of Mark's Gospel relates to the
author's purpose for writing. For our investigation, we will survey

---

38. Hengel, *Studies in the Gospel of Mark*, 38.

each of the major sections of Mark's Gospel as follows: 1:1–13; 1:14–8:21; 8:22–10:52; and 11:1–16:8.[39]

SURVEY OF MARK 1:1–13

We could easily include Mark 1:1–13 within a larger discussion of 1:1–8:21 as a whole, but this prologue—considering its proportion to the whole of Mark's Gospel—provides outsized value for an inquiry into the author's purpose. In the prologue, the author has his first opportunity to influence the thoughts and expectations of his audience. For this reason, a careful examination of Mark's prologue will offer great insight into his purpose. We will, as a result, designate these thirteen verses as a separate section and give them special attention.[40]

From the very first verse, Mark intends to communicate to his audience something about precisely *who* this Jesus is. The opening words contain a bold statement about the identity of Jesus by applying to him the title "Messiah, Son of God" (Χριστοῦ υἱοῦ Θεοῦ, our translation).

---

39. Scholars of Mark's Gospel disagree on where the middle "Journey" section begins, but 8:22 and 8:27 are the two most common suggestions. Those who opt for 8:22 as the beginning usually see 8:22–26 serving as an inclusio with 10:46–52 around the Journey section. For those who prefer 8:27 as the beginning, 8:22–26 is better understood as illustrating the "blindness" of the disciples in 8:14–21, especially vv. 17–18. See the discussion of Mark's structure in chapter 4 below.

40. There is disagreement about where this prologue ends. Various suggestions include ending at v. 8, v. 13, and v. 15. We believe v. 13 concludes the introduction. The focus of the introduction is the ministry of John the Baptist preparing the way for Jesus. While Jesus is introduced in v. 9, John the Baptist is still active in his ministry in 1:9–11 by the simple fact that he is the one baptizing Jesus in this portion of the text. Some scholars (e.g., Marcus, *Mark 1–8*; Adela Yarbro Collins, *Mark: A Commentary*, Hermeneia [Minneapolis: Fortress, 2007]) view 1:1–15 as a unit. A difference of views on the demarcation of Mark's prologue is understandable, at least in the sense that verses 14–15 are transitional, moving from the ministry of John the Baptist (who was highlighted in vv. 4–8) to that of Jesus Christ. The decision on the demarcation of Mark's prologue does not have much bearing on our discussion here and is, therefore, not pursued further.

Though the authenticity of "Son of God" in this verse is sharply disputed, most Greek manuscripts include it.[41] Generally, it is more likely
that a scribe would intentionally *add* a title like this than intentionally
remove one already present, but it is quite possible that the phrase "Son
of God" was omitted by accident. The similarity among the endings
of the words in this verse may have caused the scribe's eyes to jump
over the final words. This sort of omission was a common phenomenon in the transmission of manuscripts, and it is not hard to imagine
a scribe unintentionally skipping over some of these letters.[42] Since
the reading that includes the title is early and well attested, and the
unintentional omission of this title is explainable, we suggest that the
title is authentic. If the title "Son of God" is original here, it is a good

---

41. The LEB omits the phrase, as does the TNIV (although both the NIV84
and NIV11 include it). It is bracketed in the NA28 text, indicating uncertainty
on the part of the editors. The United Bible Societies Fifth Revised Edition of
The Greek New Testament (UBS5) gives the reading a "C" rating on a scale of A-D
ranging from highest certainty to lowest.

42. There are several repetitions of the **OY** ending in this verse. In
Greek, the verse reads: APXHT**OY**EYAΓΓEΛI**OY**IHC**OY**XPICT**OY**YI**OY**ΘE**OY**
(similar endings in bold). The similarity is even starker in the case of
nomina sacra, where very common or sacred names are abbreviated:
APXHT**OY**EYAΓΓEΛI**OY**IY̅X̅Y̅Y̅Θ̅Y̅. Of the seven words in this verse, the last
six all have the genitive singular ending (OY). If *nomina sacra* were employed,
then six of the last nine letters may have been upsilon (Y). Philip Comfort notes
that the word for "Son" in this title (YIOY) is only inconsistently written as a
nomen sacrum; Philip Comfort, *New Testament Text and Translation Commentary:
Commentary on the Variant Readings of the Ancient New Testament Manuscripts
and How They Relate to the Major English Translations* (Carol Stream, IL: Tyndale
House, 2008), 92. Bart Ehrman has strongly argued that this sort of omission is
exceedingly unlikely in the very first verse of a transcription. However, Tommy
Wasserman and Max Botner have both offered strong challenges to Ehrman's
assumptions and argumentation, both defending the plausibility of an omission
here. See Bart Ehrman, *The Orthodox Corruption of Scripture: The Effect of Early
Christological Controversies on the Text of the New Testament* (New York: Oxford
University Press, 1993), 72–75; Tommy Wasserman, "The 'Son of God' Was in the
Beginning (Mark 1:1)," *Journal for Theological Studies* 62, no. 1 (2011): 20–50, esp.
44–50; Max Botner, "The Role of Transcriptional Probability in the Text-Critical
Debate on Mark 1:1," *Catholic Biblical Quarterly* 77, no. 3 (2015): 467–80.

indication that the status or relationship designated by this title plays a significant role in Mark's purpose for writing. Considering the other notable locations in Mark where equivalent phrasing appears (1:11; 3:11; 5:7; 9:7; 12:6; 13:32; 14:61; 15:39), it does not seem out of place here in the opening verse.[43]

It is important to note that the Hebrew concept of God's son or "son of God" did not *necessarily* imply divinity.[44] The Old Testament utilizes father-son terminology to describe the relationship between God and his appointed human king in several places (e.g., 2 Sam 7:14; 1 Chron 17:13; 22:10; 28:6; Pss 2:6–7; 89:26–27). For this reason, the title "Son of God" naturally pairs with "Messiah" (Χριστός) in 1:1. Nevertheless, Mark is likely writing for a Greek-speaking audience that is broadly non-Jewish and located in Rome, where the title "son of God" would have implied some level of (potential) divinity.[45] While Mark's use of this title throughout his Gospel should determine what it means here, we can at least say that, already in the opening verse, the author is concerned with describing the identity of Jesus: he is Messiah, Son of God.

This interest in the identity of Jesus continues in the prologue. It is significant that in the composite Old Testament quotation of 1:2–3, the phrases "before your face" and "prepare your way" refer to the "face" and "way" of Jesus. In verse 2, "before your face" comes from Malachi 3:1 and Exodus 23:30, but neither of these texts completely matches the wording in Mark 1:2. Malachi 3:1 says that God is sending

---

43. Even if the title υἱὸς θεοῦ ("Son of God") is not original in 1:1, it is frequently applied to Jesus throughout the narrative, as early as 1:11.

44. See, e.g., the discussions in Adela Yarbro Collins and John J. Collins, *King and Messiah as Son of God: Divine, Human, and Angelic Messianic Figures in Biblical and Related Literature* (Grand Rapids: Eerdmans, 2008), esp. 1–74; Garrick V. Allen, et al., eds., *Son of God: Divine Sonship in Jewish and Christian Antiquity* (Winona Lake, IN: Eisenbrauns, 2019), esp. Max Botner's essay, "'Whoever Does the Will of God' (Mark 3:35): Mark's Christ as the Model Son," 106–17.

45. After his death, Julius Caesar was given the title *divus Iulius* ("deified Julius"), thereby making his adopted son and successor, Octavian (Augustus Caesar), *divi filius* ("son of the deified one"). Nero similarly was referred to as *divi Claudi filius*.

a messenger who "will clear the way before *my* face" (our translation). In the Malachi passage, both the MT and the LXX have a first-person pronoun ("before my face"), and the pertinent Hebrew and Greek pronouns refer to the LORD, that is, Yahweh, who is mentioned in Malachi 2:17 and 3:1 But as Mark appropriates this verse, he uses second-person pronouns instead. As a result, the "face" and "way" of Yahweh in Malachi 3:1 become the "face" and "way" of Jesus in Mark 1:2. Mark is somehow incorporating Jesus into his understanding of Yahweh, though the relationship between the two is not entirely clear at this point in the narrative.

Exodus 23:20 matches Mark 1:2 with respect to these pronouns ("*I am sending ... before your face* [our translation]). However, the *task* of the messenger in Exodus 23:20 differs slightly from Mark 1:2. In Mark, the messenger "prepare[s] your way," but in Exodus 23:20, the messenger will "watch over you on the way" (our translation).[46] In Exodus 23:20, the relevant pronoun ("you") refers not to Yahweh, as in Malachi 3:1, but to Israel. So in this one composite quotation from the Old Testament, Mark is applying to Jesus language that referred to Yahweh and language that referred to Israel in their respective contexts. Though the connection to Yahweh is more prominent here, the parallel between Jesus and Israel is still present and surfaces again in Mark 1:12–13, where Jesus is sent into the wilderness for forty days of testing with angels attending him (cf. Exod 23:20–33).

Mark 1:3 describes this messenger as "a voice crying in the wilderness, 'Prepare the way of the Lord! Make straight his paths!'" This description comes directly from the LXX of Isaiah 40:3, but here in Mark 1:3, "his paths (τὰς τρίβους αὐτοῦ)" has replaced "the paths of our God (τὰς τρίβους τοῦ θεοῦ ἡμῶν)," and once again, Mark applies to Jesus language referring to Yahweh in its original context. Mark is connecting the identity of Jesus in some way with that of Yahweh, the God of Israel.

---

46. The reading of LXX differs slightly from MT: καὶ ἐπιβλέψεται ὁδὸν πρὸ προσώπου μου ("and he will watch over [the] way before your face").

Mark reveals in verses 4-8 that John the Baptist is the messenger who announces the coming of the Lord. He then introduces the arrival of Jesus of Nazareth from Galilee (v. 9). Without any explanation (unlike Matt 3:13-15), Mark tells of the greater baptizer (v. 8) being baptized by the lesser (v. 9), after which the skies are ripped open (using the verb σχίζω), and the Holy Spirit descends and rests on Jesus (v. 10). Then a heavenly voice declares, "You are my beloved Son" (v. 11).[47] We discussed the identification of Jesus with Yahweh in 1:2-3 above. Here we see elements of an identification between Jesus and Israel. Jesus's baptism in the waters and the terminology of "beloved Son" remind the reader of Israel passing through the waters in the exodus from Egypt (Exod 14) and Yahweh's description of Israel as "my firstborn son" (Exod 4:22; cf. Gen 22:2; Ps 2:7; Isa 42:1). Similarly, in Mark 1:12-13, Jesus is sent into the wilderness by the Spirit for forty days to be tested, paralleling the forty years of testing that the Israelites endured on the way to the promised land.

In this short introductory portion of Mark's Gospel, several voices testify to the identity of Jesus. The voice of the author declares that Jesus is "Messiah, Son of God" (1:1, our translation). The voice of the prophet implies that this Jesus is, in some way, identified with Yahweh and Israel (1:2-3, cf. vv. 12-13). The voice of John proclaims that Jesus is "one ... more powerful than I, ... of whom I am not worthy to bend down and untie the strap of his sandals" (v. 7) and that "he will baptize you with the Holy Spirit" (v. 8). The voice from heaven announces that Jesus is the "beloved Son" of God (v. 11). Each of these testimonies about Jesus's identity will be confirmed, developed, and supplemented throughout Mark's Gospel. But from the prologue, this much seems clear: part of Mark's rhetorical strategy for motivating his audience to remain loyal to Jesus is to say something about precisely *who* this

---

47. Here Mark employs the Greek verb σχίζω (1:10) before the annunciation of Jesus's sonship (1:11). As discussed above, the same sequence appears at the end of Mark's Gospel, where the temple curtain is ripped open (15:38) and the Roman centurion declares, "Truly this man was God's Son!" (15:39).

Jesus is. Jesus is Messiah, Son of God, whose identity corresponds in some way to both Yahweh and Israel. In the next section (1:14-8:21), Mark will begin to fill out this picture of Jesus's identity by narrating Jesus's proclamation of God's kingdom and its arrival through his words and his works.

SURVEY OF MARK 1:14–8:21

We turn now to the next major section of Mark's Gospel, in which Jesus proclaims the arrival of the kingdom of God (1:14-15, 38-39; 3:14-15, 4:1-34) by demonstrating his power and authority in and around Galilee. A dominant theme in this section is Jesus's authority expressed through his mighty works and his teaching. Jesus demonstrates his authority over sickness and disease (1:29-31, 32-34, 40-45; 2:3-12; 3:1-5, 9-10; 5:21-43; 6:56; 7:32-37), the forces of nature (4:35-41; 6:48-51), sin and unrighteousness (2:5-12, 15-17), and even over the power of unclean spirits and Satan (1:23-26, 32-34, 39; 3:11-12, 23-27; 5:1-20; 7:29-30). He also demonstrates his authority to call and send apostles to proclaim the gospel of God's kingdom (1:16-20; 2:13-14; 3:13-19; 6:7-13; cf. John 15:16). In this section, Mark highlights Jesus's authority as superior to that of the religious leaders (1:21-22; 27-28; 3:22-30) and their traditions (2:18-22, 23-28; 3:2-6; 7:1-23).[48] This focus on Jesus's authority is not unrelated to his identity; they are two sides of the same coin. As Mark narrates the authoritative words and works of Jesus, it becomes evident that these demonstrations of authority are a commentary on Jesus's identity. When we see Jesus forgive sins (2:5), Mark wants us to ask along with the scribes, "Who is able to forgive sins except God alone?" (2:7).

Jesus's divine authority is indeed an expression of his divine identity, but that identity is not immediately apparent to every character in the story. Though the voice from heaven in 1:11 has clearly identified Jesus as "my beloved son," human voices offer conflicting appraisals.

---

48. The theme of controversy between Jesus and the religious leaders is prominent throughout 2:1-3:6 and 11:27-12:44.

Those who see Jesus cast out unclean spirits marvel at his authority (1:27-28). But the scribes from Jerusalem accuse Jesus of being "possessed by Beelzebul ... the ruler of the demons" (3:22). Jesus responds that it is by the Holy Spirit, not the spirit of Satan, that he casts out unclean spirits (3:29). When the disciples see Jesus calm the wind and the sea, they can only respond, "Who then is this?" (4:41), but the people of Jesus's hometown know him only as "the carpenter, the son of Mary and brother of James and Joses and Judas and Simon" (6:3). Jesus faces rejection from his family (3:21) and his hometown (6:1-6a). Herod fears that Jesus is John the Baptist raised from the dead (6:16). And in 8:14-21, Jesus's own disciples still seem unaware of his heavenly identity—or at least his power to provide for their needs—when they realize they have no bread with them. The *human* response to Jesus's works and teachings throughout Mark 1:14-8:21 is quite confused.

On the other hand, voices from the *spiritual* realm are not confused about Jesus's identity. The man in the Capernaum synagogue with an unclean spirit announces Jesus as "the Holy One of God" (1:24). Mark explains that the demons whom Jesus cast out "knew him" (1:34). The unclean spirits who see him cry out, "You are the Son of God!" (3:11). When the man possessed by Legion sees Jesus from afar, he falls down and cries out, recognizing him as "Jesus, Son of the Most High God" (5:7).

The only explicit comment in 1:14–8:21 that Jesus himself offers regarding his identity is the term "prophet" (6:4) and the phrase "the Son of Man" (2:10, 28).[49] However, the narrator also provides subtle clues to guide his audience's understanding of Jesus's identity. For example, in 5:19, Jesus commands the man possessed by Legion to tell his friends "how much the Lord [κύριος]" had done for him. The mention of "the Lord" here from the mouth of Jesus would have most likely caused Mark's audience to think of the God of Israel, whom the LXX

---

49. The meaning of the phrase "the Son of Man" in Mark 10:45 will be discussed in detail in chapter 4 below. Metaphorically, Jesus also refers to himself as a "physician" (2:17) and a "bridegroom" (2:19).

frequently calls "Lord" (κύριος). But in the next verse, the narrator tells us that the man "went away and began to proclaim in the Decapolis all that *Jesus* had done for him" (5:20, emphasis added). In this story, Mark seems to present Jesus as parallel to the God of Israel in a meaningful way, a parallel that appears at several places throughout this Gospel.

As we saw in the prologue, Mark applies Old Testament language about God to Jesus (see 1:2-3). A similar phenomenon appears in 6:30-44, where Jesus miraculously provides food for a large crowd that has followed him into the wilderness. This feeding is reminiscent of the way Israel's God faithfully provided food for his wandering people as they journeyed through the wilderness toward the land of promise.[50] This connection to Yahweh's provision for the wandering Israelites is strengthened if we read the following passage, where Jesus walks on water (6:45-52), as another allusion to the story of Israel's God guiding his people through the wilderness. Indeed, the comment in 6:52 ("they did not understand concerning the loaves") directly connects this story with 6:30-44. In 6:45-52, Mark uses concepts and vocabulary reminiscent of Yahweh's glory passing before Moses in Exodus 33:19-23 and 34:5-8 (and a similar incident in 1 Kings 19:11). As Yahweh did before his servant Moses, Jesus intends to "pass by" his disciples, who are proceeding ahead of him in a boat (Mark 6:48).[51] These connections are subtle, but their cumulative weight is worth consideration.

The authority and identity of Jesus are important topics in Mark 1:14-8:21. Mark highlights the authority of Jesus as superior to that of the religious leaders and natural and spiritual evil. Mark even describes Jesus with language reserved for God in the Hebrew Scriptures. This dramatic presentation has a polarizing effect, and human opinion

---

50. For the connection between Mark 6:34 and Numbers 27:17, see Rikki E. Watts, "Mark," in *Commentary on the New Testament Use of the Old Testament*, ed. G. K. Beale and D. A. Carson, 111–237 (Grand Rapids: Baker Academic, 2007), 158–61.

51. See Lee, *Christological Rereading of the Shema (Deut 6.4) in Mark's Gospel*, 205–7 for a discussion of the connections between 6:45-52 and OT descriptions of Yahweh's glory.

about Jesus is diverse. Some believe that he is Elijah or a prophet (6:15; cf. 8:28). Others think he is a blasphemer performing works by the power of Satan (2:7; 3:22). Even Jesus's own disciples are not always sure what to make of him (6:49–52). But the testimony from those with spiritual insight is unanimous. In agreement with the heavenly voice at Jesus's baptism (1:11), even the unclean spirits acknowledge him as the Son of God (1:24; 5:7). And so we can see from this section that part of Mark's strategy for urging his audience to remain faithful to Jesus is to depict and describe Jesus's unique power and authority—an authority that elicits questions about his identity and provokes hostility from those who do not embrace the kingdom of God. The authority that Jesus displays in this section is a comment on his identity. He exercises the authority of God himself. And Mark's narration of the controversy over Jesus's authority effectively forces his audience to choose for themselves who they say Jesus is. For Mark, the answer is clear. Jesus is not some blasphemer who works by the power of Satan. Mark wants his audience to understand that Jesus is the Son of God and Son of Man who controls both the storms and the spirits and who forgives sins as only God can. This is the Jesus whom they follow.

SURVEY OF MARK 8:22–10:52

The poor spiritual perception of the disciples in 8:14–21 seems to fore-shadow their blindness throughout 8:27–10:45, which is bracketed by Mark's only two stories of Jesus healing blind men (8:22–26; 10:46–52). The specific arrangement of this material discussing physical and spir-itual blindness reflect the intentionality of the author. Mark wants his audience to see the disciples' actions and misunderstandings as an example of spiritual blindness, a negative example of what it means to follow Jesus. Jesus's rebuke of Peter in 8:33 highlights this pervasive theme within 8:27–10:45, the conflict between a mind set on the things of God and a mind set on the things of men.

The interest in Jesus's identity that was so prominent in 1:14–8:21 carries over into 8:22–10:52, and we find in 8:29 Peter's reiteration of the narrator's opening statement (1:1) that Jesus is the Messiah

(Χριστός). Now that the disciples—and especially Peter—better understand *who* Jesus is, the focus of Mark's Gospel shifts to *what* Jesus has come *to do*. This middle "Journey" section[52] of Mark's Gospel is structured around a threefold cycle in which Jesus teaches his disciples that he must face rejection and suffering and ultimately die at the hands of the Jerusalem leaders and the gentile rulers. Each passion prediction also includes a brief but clear note that Jesus will rise from the dead after three days. However, the disciples do not understand what this means (9:10), and each prediction leaves them confused in some way (8:32; 9:32-34; 10:35-41).

Most of the material in 8:22-10:52 is didactic. When Jesus is not teaching his disciples what it truly means for him to be the Messiah— most specifically, that he must "give his life as a ransom for many" (10:45)—he is teaching them what it looks like for them to follow him faithfully. Even the narrative material in this section (e.g., the healing of a demon-oppressed boy in 9:14-27 and the question from the Pharisees in 10:2-9) provides opportunities for Mark to describe the difference between a mind focused on the things of God and one focused on the things of men (e.g., 9:28-29; 10:10-12). For the Evangelist, discipleship is the difficult process of *learning* to see things from the perspective of God rather than men.

Each of the three passion prediction cycles (8:27-9:29; 9:30-10:31; 10:32-45) contains some misunderstanding from the disciples about what it means to follow Jesus in the kingdom of God. In response to Jesus's first prediction (8:31), Peter pulls Jesus aside and begins to scold (ἤρξατο ἐπιτιμᾶν) him (v. 32). Peter's action parallels Jesus's warning (ἐπιτίμησεν) that the disciples should not speak to anyone about him (v. 30), but there is an important difference between these two scenes. Whereas Jesus eschews honor in verse 30 (as he has done repeatedly throughout the previous section [1:43-45; 3:12; 7:36]), here Peter wants

---

52. As noted earlier, this section is often referred to as the "Journey" or "(On the) Way" due to the repetition of the phrase ἐν τῇ ὁδῷ in it (8:27; 9:33-34; 10:32, 52) and Jesus's somewhat indirect journey from Galilee to Jerusalem.

Jesus to eschew shame (v. 32). Jesus responds sharply, rebuking Peter as "Satan," and then calls attention to the distinction that frequently surfaces throughout this Journey section, the difference between a mind set on the things of God versus one set on the things of men (v. 33).

Peter's misunderstanding provides an opportunity for Mark to emphasize the importance of dying to self and taking up one's cross in order to follow Jesus (8:34). A mind set on the things of men will not take up one's cross and follow Jesus down the path of suffering and shame. A mind set on the things of men will seek to save one's own life (8:35-36) rather than laying it down for the sake of others (10:45). And most importantly, although a mind set on the things of men may be willing to endure suffering to gain a greater reward (10:35-39), it is *not* ready to embrace rejection and shame the way Jesus will for the sake of his people (8:34; 10:45; 14:24). The mind set on the things of men is not ready to accept the difficult path by which the kingdom of God comes (cf. 9:1)—the path of suffering and shame that Jesus will walk. So Jesus calls the crowds together, announcing that "whoever loses his life on account of me and of the gospel will save it" (8:35), but also that "whoever is ashamed of me and my words in this adulterous and sinful generation, the Son of Man will also be ashamed of him when he comes in the glory of his Father with the holy angels" (8:38). In 8:35 and 38, Mark is providing his audience with a sort of "carrot and stick" motivation to remain loyal to Jesus. Those who lose everything for Jesus will actually lose nothing, but those who are ashamed of him will face even greater shame.

Just a few days after this warning, Jesus takes Peter, James, and John up to a high mountain, where he is transfigured in radiant glory before their eyes (9:2-3). Here the heavenly voice once again calls Jesus "my beloved Son" and directs the disciples to "listen to him" (9:7; cf. 1:11). Mark may be using this divine exhortation to address the disciples' misunderstanding and to encourage his audience to take seriously the necessity of Jesus's suffering and death. Jesus does not want his glory public until he has first suffered and been rejected. So as Jesus and the disciples are still coming down from the mountain, he commands them not to discuss what they had seen with anyone until he has been raised (9:9).

In the second cycle (9:30–10:31), Jesus again teaches his disciples about the rejection and suffering that await him, but they still do not understand (9:32). In 9:33–37, we discover the disciples had been arguing about who was the greatest, presumably, *as* Jesus was teaching them about his suffering. Mark uses this confusion to clarify again the difference between a mind set on the things of men and a mind set on the things of God (cf. 8:33). For the mind that is set on the things of God, greatness is measured by service (9:35). Jesus chooses to be represented not by the honored and powerful but by the vulnerable and powerless (9:37). The didactic material (9:38–50) that follows this passage serves as a corrective to the disciples' spirit of rivalry. Jesus assures his disciples, "Whoever is not against us is for us" (9:40) and urges them to "be at peace with one another" (9:50). The mind that is set on the things of men focuses on greatness, rivalry, and selfish ambition (9:34, 38). But the mind set on the things of God focuses on servanthood (9:35), welcoming others (9:39–41), and keeping peace (9:50). The subsequent stories (10:1–12, 13–16, 17–31) provide an opportunity for Mark to build on this foundation of a mindset focused on serving, welcoming, and caring for the weak and the vulnerable.

In the third and final cycle (10:32–45), Mark presents Jesus's most detailed and climactic passion prediction, which specifies Jerusalem as the exact location of his suffering and death. In the details of this final prediction, the weight of Jesus's fate sets in fully. The striking description of his rejection, suffering, and death (10:33–34) creates a stark contrast with the folly of James and John in 10:35–37. James and John—still focused on the things of men rather than the things of God, still seeking their own honor and glory, and still not understanding that whoever wants to be first will be last of all and servant of all (9:35)—ask Jesus to grant to them places of highest honor (10:37). Jesus's immediate response is to connect his glory and honor with his "cup" and "baptism," metaphors for suffering and death (10:38). When the other disciples begin to express their indignation toward James and John (10:41), Jesus calls the Twelve together and clarifies for them the distinction between greatness in this world (10:42) and greatness in the kingdom of God (10:43-44). And by pointing the disciples toward his own example and the mission he has been sent to accomplish, Jesus clarifies again the incongruency between a mindset focused on the things of men and one focused on the things of God. The mindset focused on the things of God is one that has "not come to be served, but to serve, and to give his life as a ransom for many" (10:45).

Following this third correction of the disciples, Mark offers the story of blind Bartimaeus at the end of the Journey section as a contrast to the Twelve and an image of true faithfulness (10:46-52). In this story, Bartimaeus is not confused about Jesus's identity; he knows exactly who Jesus is (10:47, 48). Bartimaeus's plea to Jesus is not a request for honor but a cry for mercy. When opposed by those who try to shame him into silence, Bartimaeus is undeterred. He cries out for Jesus even louder (v. 48). And when Jesus calls him, Bartimaeus does not hesitate to leave behind even his cloak, perhaps his only possession (v. 50; cf. Exod 22:26-27). Jesus tells Bartimaeus, "Go, your faith has healed you," but having received his sight, Bartimaeus does not "go" (Mark 10:52). Instead, he begins to follow Jesus "on the road" (ἐν τῇ ὁδῷ, 10:52), a phrase used repeatedly in the discipleship-focused Journey section (e.g., 8:27; 9:33, 34; 10:32), toward Jerusalem. This picture of undeterred trust and faithfulness motivates the audience to emulate Bartimaeus's determination and loyalty to Jesus.

Throughout the Journey section (8:22-10:52), Mark illustrates the distinction between faithful discipleship, which focuses on the things of God, and a mindset that remains focused on the things of men. He wants his audience to know that loyalty to Jesus requires a radical reordering of priorities and values. In this section, the demands of following Jesus are most clearly laid out (see esp. 8:34-38; 9:33-37; 10:42-45). Jesus's stern warning in 8:38 provides forceful motivation for Mark's audience to remain loyal to Jesus despite any shame and suffering they may face. But in 10:45, Mark explains the rationale for *why* they should do so—because "even the Son of Man did not come to be served, but to serve, and to give his life as a ransom for many." In this way, these important verses, located toward the beginning and the end of this section, respectively, support Mark's purpose of inspiring loyalty to Jesus among his audience. This section also contains several episodes in which Mark characterizes the disciples as an example of confused devotion to Jesus. Mark's portrayal of the disciples and the corrections that Jesus offers provide further motivation for the audience to faithfully follow Jesus, even when it costs them everything. The disciples are slow to understand what it means to follow Jesus. But despite their confusion and blunders, they are still hanging in there. And, even more importantly, Jesus has not given up on them. Mark does not want his audience to assume that shame and suffering are evidence that Jesus has abandoned them. On the contrary, these trials and hardships indicate that they are, in fact, following in Jesus's footsteps, so long as they stay on the difficult path of discipleship. The disciples may come off as thick-headed and slow to learn, but the gradual and sometimes painful process of discipleship, by which their values and mindset are transformed, does not happen overnight. And the narrative space of this middle section "on the way" to Jerusalem symbolically illustrates that difficult but necessary process.

SURVEY OF MARK 11:1–16:8

The final section of Mark's Gospel centers around the escalating tension between Jesus and the religious leaders and institutions in Jerusalem. While Jesus's authority has been challenged throughout Mark's Gospel (e.g., 2:7, 24; 3:2; 8:11), it is in Jerusalem that this conflict boils over and reaches its climax; Jesus is arrested (14:46), charged with blasphemy (14:64), and handed over to the Roman authorities to be crucified (15:1). Having spent the previous section (8:22–10:52) *illustrating* the difference between a mind focused on the things of God and one focused on the things of men, Mark now describes Jesus *embodying* this difference as he confronts opposition and hostility from the religious leaders in

Jerusalem and faithfully and obediently pursues the will of God, even in the face of death (14:36).

Mark 11:1–16:8 begins with those who followed Jesus on his journey to Jerusalem hailing him as the Davidic king and ushering him into the royal city (11:9–11; cf. Ps 118:25, 26). The human response to Jesus's identity seems to be growing. When Jesus enters the city, his final conflict with the religious leaders and institutions begins. His clearing of the temple (Mark 11:15–17) elicits questions about the source of his authority to do such things (11:27–33). Mark narrates this conflict through a series of conversations in which Jesus's opponents question him, hoping to find a charge against him so that they can arrest him (12:13–14, 18–23). Each time, Jesus responds by exposing their folly and undermining their authority (12:15–17, 24–27). Having silenced his opponents (v. 34), Jesus then puts a question to them that subtly raises the debate from whether Jesus's *authority* is from heaven (cf. 11:28) to whether Jesus *himself* is from heaven (12:35–37). Then, in Mark 13, at the prompting of one of his disciples, Jesus seals the fate of the temple he had previously cleared, declaring that not a single stone would be left upon another (13:1–2). Sitting across from the temple on the Mount of Olives and surrounded by his closest disciples, Jesus then begins one of the most extended discourses in Mark's Gospel, warning his disciples to remain alert so as not to be deceived by the tumultuous events to come (13:5–37). Though Jesus's suffering and death indeed have unique significance (10:45; 14:24), Mark makes it clear throughout this discourse that those who follow Jesus also must be willing to face a similar fate (13:13).

This discussion in Mark 13 of suffering for Jesus's sake naturally leads into the subsequent narration of Jesus's own suffering (Mark 14–15), about which he has been openly warning the disciples since Peter's confession that Jesus is the Messiah (8:27–31). Beginning with Mark 14:1, which explicitly mentions the Passover festival, the pace slows, and the narrative wheels are set in motion as we begin to see Jesus's predictions about his abandonment, rejection, suffering, and death (8:31; 9:31; 10:33–34) realized. Mark describes these events in vivid detail to show that everything Jesus had predicted about his death was fulfilled. By mentioning the Passover as he begins to narrate Jesus's passion (14:1), Mark connects the significance of Jesus's death with this foundational Israelite festival. Though Jesus's actual suffering does not begin until Gethsemane (14:32–34), the theme is foreshadowed by the plotting of the religious leaders (14:1–2) and the anointing in anticipation of his burial (14:3–9). During the Passover meal, Jesus teaches his disciples the atoning significance of his death, in which he will offer his body and blood in a covenant "for many" (14:22–24; cf. 10:45). The mention of "my blood ... poured out for many" is reminiscent of Jesus's words in 10:45, where he explains the significance of his death as "a ransom for many" (cf. Isa 53:10–12).

After the Passover meal, Jesus and the disciples head back to the Mount of Olives, where he had earlier warned them about the affliction they should expect to face for his sake (13:9–13). Once there, Jesus announces that they will all abandon him (14:27–31) despite his previous warning. At Gethsemane, Mark portrays Jesus becoming "distressed and troubled" (14:33). Jesus tells Peter, James, and John, "My soul is deeply grieved, to the point of death" (v. 34), but the disciples repeatedly fail him by falling asleep while he is praying (vv. 37, 40–41). Their failure reaches its lowest point when Judas betrays Jesus with a kiss (vv. 43–46) and all his disciples flee and abandon him (v. 50). Again, Mark is demonstrating that everything Jesus said about his suffering and death was fulfilled as predicted (14:17–21, 27, 49).

Jesus is then led before the Sanhedrin, where false witnesses testify against him, and the high priest questions him, asking if he is "the Christ, the Son of the Blessed One" (vv. 53–60, 61). In something of a climax to Mark's presentation of Jesus's identity, Jesus himself acknowledges this identity directly for the first time: "I am, and you will see the Son of Man sitting at the right hand of the Power and coming with the clouds of heaven" (14:62; cf. Ps 110:1; Dan 7:13–14). This declaration combines imagery from Psalm 110:1 and Daniel 7:13–14 in a way that dramatically implies the divine identity of Jesus. The implication is not lost on the high priest, who responds by accusing him of blasphemy (Mark 14:63-64; cf. 2:7), and those present condemn him to death and begin spitting on him, beating him, and mocking him (vv. 64-65; cf. 10:33-34). Mark juxtaposes Jesus's resolve as he is questioned by the high priest with Peter's shame and denial in 14:66-72. While Jesus is being beaten and mocked, Peter is questioned by a servant girl in the courtyard just outside, where he denies even knowing Jesus, fulfilling Jesus's prediction that Peter would deny him three times (14:30). Jesus had repeatedly prepared his disciples for shame and suffering during the Journey section:

"Let him deny himself and take up his cross." (8:34)

"Whoever is ashamed of me ... the Son of Man will also be ashamed of him." (8:38)

"If anyone wants to be first, he will be last of all and servant of all." (9:35)

"There is no one who has left house or brothers or sisters or mother or father or children or fields on account of me ... who will not receive a hundred times as much ... *with persecutions*— and in the age to come, eternal life. But many who are first will be last, and the last first." (10:29-31, emphasis added)

And the disciples had dismissively insisted that they were ready:

"We are able." (10:39)

"Surely not I?" (14:19)

"'If it is necessary for me to die with you, I will never deny you!' And they all were saying the same thing also." (14:31)

But when Jesus's predictions of his arrest are finally fulfilled, "they all abandoned him and fled" (14:50). And when accused of being associated with Jesus, Peter "began to curse and to swear with an oath, 'I do not know this man whom you are talking about!'" (14:71). Mark sets the

disciples' failures against the backdrop of repeated warnings, creating
in his audience a heavy disappointment with such disloyalty. The story
catches the audience in the same hubris that seized Peter: "Even if they
all fall away, certainly I will not!" (14:29). It is as if Mark is warning
his audience, along with the Apostle Paul, "the one who thinks that he
stands must watch out lest he fall" (1 Cor 10:12).

Jesus is then handed over to the Roman governor, just as he predicted (Mark 15:1; cf. 10:33). When given the option of having Jesus
or Barabbas released, the crowd rejects Jesus and calls for him to be
crucified, so Pilate concedes and orders that Jesus be scourged and
crucified (15:15). The soldiers mock him, beat him, spit on him, and
humiliate him before leading him to be crucified in abject shame and
suffering (15:16–20; cf. 10:33–34). Jesus dies on the cross and is buried
in a tomb just before the Sabbath begins (15:33–47). These and other
details Mark includes in this passion narrative (esp., 14:32–15:41) allude
to both Jesus's own predictions of his suffering (8:31; 9:31; 10:33–34;
14:27; cf. Zech 13:7) and certain Old Testament Scriptures (esp. Ps 22
[Mark 14:34]; Ps 118:22 [Mark 8:31]).[53] These allusions confirm for the
reader that indeed "it was necessary" for Jesus to suffer all these things
(8:31) and imply a sovereign hand working behind the scenes, even in
Jesus's (and the disciples') darkest hour.

Finally, we have the peculiar ending to Mark's Gospel (16:1–8). While
the manuscript evidence shows various readings for the final verses,
most scholars agree that the original form ended with the fearful
response of the women at the tomb in 16:8, with other endings added
later to fill out an admittedly abrupt conclusion.[54] Compared to the

---

53. For a discussion of the relationship between Psalm 22, specifically, and
Mark's narrative, see Carey, *Jesus' Cry from the Cross*. See also Joel Marcus, *The
Way of the Lord: Christological Exegesis of the Old Testament in the Gospel of Mark*
(New York: T&T Clark, 2004), 172–84, for a discussion of this and other righ-
teous sufferer psalms as related to Jesus's passion.

54. In addition to the ending at 16:8, the most common ending is an addition
of 12 verses immediately after v. 8. Other endings include an extended v. 8
("So they promptly reported all the things they had been commanded to those

resurrection narratives in the other canonical gospels, Mark's ending at 16:8 seems, for various reasons, unfinished (cf. Matt 28:9–20; Luke 24:13–53; John 20:11–21:25; also Acts 1:3–11). The chapter division at 16:1 is unfortunate because it may create an artificial sense of separation between Jesus's suffering and death and his resurrection.[55] In some ways, 16:1–8 can almost feel tacked on as an afterthought. It is understandable, then, that other endings may have been added to provide a sense of resolution. However, when we think about Jesus's own predictions of his resurrection, they too may strike the reader as brief and unexplained and even as an afterthought (8:31; 9:31; 10:34; cf. 9:9).[56] The narrative value of 16:1–8 is in Jesus's promise of his resurrection indeed being fulfilled. It is this fulfillment that connects 16:1–8 both to

---

around Peter. And after these things, Jesus himself also sent out through them from the east even as far as the west the holy and imperishable proclamation of eternal salvation. Amen.") before the longer ending and an addition between vv. 14 and 15 of the longer ending: "And they excused themselves, saying, 'This age of lawlessness and unbelief is under Satan, who does not allow the truth and power of God to prevail over the unclean things of the spirits [or, does not allow what lies under the unclean spirits to understand the truth and power of God]. Therefore reveal your righteousness now'—thus they spoke to Christ. And Christ replied to them, 'The term of years of Satan's power has been fulfilled, but other terrible things draw near. And for those who have sinned I was handed over to death, that they may return to the truth and sin no more, in order that they may inherit the spiritual and incorruptible glory of righteousness that is in heaven'" (translation here quoted from Roger L. Omanson and Bruce Manning Metzger, *A Textual Guide to the Greek New Testament: An Adaptation of Bruce M. Metzger's Textual Commentary for the Needs of Translators* [Stuttgart: Deutsche Bibelgesellschaft, 2006], 105).

55. We believe that 16:1–8 would be better labeled as 15:48–55 to maintain stronger continuity with the passion narrative. Then again, it is unlikely that Mark intended for his Gospel to be read in chapters at all rather than as one unified story.

56. To be clear, the mention of the resurrection in Jesus's predictions is no afterthought at all. But considering the explanation and detail given to Jesus's suffering, the brevity of these resurrection references is remarkable. It should not be surprising, then, if later readers also felt that the discussion of the resurrection in 16:1–8 was also a little too brief.

Jesus's passion and to the rest of 11:1–15:47, not to mention the passion and resurrection predictions of 8:31–10:45. This fulfillment validates the divine origin of his power and authority. The vindication of Jesus's divine authority (cf. 11:27–33), in contrast to the supposed authority of the religious leaders, is evidence of his divine identity.

There are several ways the content of this final section serves Mark's purpose of motivating his audience to remain loyal to Jesus even in the face of shame and suffering. First, as we discussed above, the specificity and detail with which Mark narrates the broader passion narrative (14:1–16:8) serve to remind his audience that everything Jesus faced not only was part of God's plan but also "was necessary" (8:31). Second, the overarching conflict between Jesus and the Jewish leadership throughout this final section exemplifies the difference between a mind focused on the things of God and one focused on the things of men. This is a distinction that Jesus has noted (8:33), explained (8:34–38; 9:35–37, 39–41; 10:5–16, 29–31, 42–45), and now embodied (11:15–19; 12:15–17, 26–27; 14:6–9, 32–42) for his disciples. Third, as Mark dramatically narrates Jesus's commitment to endure the shame and suffering of desertion by his followers, rejection by his people, and crucifixion by the Romans, the reader finds a model of what true loyalty and faithfulness to God look like. In Mark's Gospel, one's faithfulness to God is measured by loyalty to Jesus. Those who reject the Son are ultimately rejecting the Father who sent him (1:11; 9:7; cf. 12:1–11). And those who disdain Jesus's mission to serve and to give his life as a ransom for many (10:45) have despised the things of God in favor of the things of men (8:33). Finally, the discovery of the empty tomb reminds the audience that despite the expectation of shame and suffering on the path of discipleship, Jesus's journey does not end on the cross—and neither does theirs. Those who follow Jesus to the end can trust that he will not abandon them in death but will bring them with him to eternal life through resurrection (cf. 10:30). It is this hope that encourages Mark's audience to faithfully endure any measure of loss for the sake of following Jesus into the kingdom (cf. 9:43–48; 10:29).

CONCLUSIONS REGARDING
THE PURPOSE OF MARK'S GOSPEL

The identity and ministry of Jesus constitute the core content of Mark's Gospel. Mark begins his Gospel by asserting that Jesus is the Messiah, the Son of God. This assertion is affirmed throughout the Gospel despite diverse human reactions and opinions about Jesus. In the short prologue (1:1-13), Jesus's identity is introduced. He is heralded with language used for Yahweh in the Old Testament (vv. 2-3) and described as "one who is more powerful than" John the Baptist (v. 7). Mark 1:14-8:21 unpacks Jesus's power and authority as the Son of God and Son of Man, which he expressed through his mighty works and teaching.

Mark 8:22-10:52 clarifies the purpose of Jesus's coming and, relatedly, the call that those who follow him must answer. Peter acknowledges the messianic identity of Jesus (8:29), but his recoil at the thought of a rejected and dying Messiah demonstrates that the disciples still do not "see" clearly who Jesus is supposed to be (cf. 8:22-26). He is not the sort of Messiah that they are expecting. These misguided expectations set the stage for the didactic material in the Journey section (esp. 8:31-10:45), in which Jesus repeatedly clarifies his mission as one of servanthood and sacrifice rather than honor and domination, distinguishing between a mind focused on the things of God and a mind focused on the things of men. This distinction is most clearly explicated in Jesus's declaration that he has "not come to be served, but to serve, and to give his life as a ransom for many" (10:45). Jesus has not come to receive honor and glory but to serve and to give his life. And so those who follow after Jesus must also become a "slave of all" (10:44) and be willing to give up their lives for the sake of Jesus and the gospel (8:35; 10:29).

Having illustrated the differences between greatness in the kingdom of God and greatness in the kingdoms of this world, Jesus, the *servant* Messiah, enters Jerusalem, where the conflict between human authority and divine authority will climax in the crucifixion of the Son of God. And in Jesus's resurrection from the dead, his identity as the exalted Son of Man and his claim to divine authority are confirmed and vindicated. In this final section (11:1–16:8), the theme of Jesus's authority (highlighted in 1:14–8:21) and the theme of Jesus's suffering (developed in 8:22–10:52) find their denouement when the conflict between Jesus and the religious authorities culminates in the charge of blasphemy and the sentence of death (14:64). It is in this final section that the disciples exemplify the mind that is set on the things of men, seeking to save their own lives while abandoning their Lord (14:50). And it is here that Jesus fully personifies the mind that is set on the things of God through his complete obedience and utter devotion to the will of the Father (14:36).

Once again, the most important source for determining Mark's purpose is the text of the Gospel itself. The reconstructed historical occasion in which this Gospel arose can inform our understanding but only as a supplement to the evidence of the text. Though Mark's Gospel contains no explicit statement of its purpose, Mark is a skillful storyteller. And he has structured his story in such a way that certain themes and intentions become obvious. His principal focus seems to be demonstrating the identity of Jesus and describing what he came to do. And the *reason why* he is so preoccupied with the topics of Jesus's identity and ministry is to remind his readers precisely who it is that they are following. In terms of identity, Jesus is the glorious, authoritative Son of Man and Son of God. And in terms of ministry, this Jesus has come not to be served but to serve and to give his life as a ransom for many as he announces the arrival of God's kingdom. The purpose of Mark's Gospel is to offer this story about who Jesus is and what he has done as a model of servanthood and loyalty to God in the face of even the most extreme shame and suffering, encouraging followers of Jesus to faithfully persevere, just as Jesus did. Mark uses this story about who Jesus is and what he has done *to encourage those facing rejection and persecution to remain loyal to Jesus.* If even the glorious and exalted Son of Man was willing to serve and to give his life, then how much more should those who follow him be willing to do the same! In this way, Jesus's statement in Mark 10:45 is central both to the purpose and to the structure of Mark's Gospel. The next chapter will focus on the centrality of this important statement and examine what Mark intends for us to understand by it.

IV

THE MEANING
AND SIGNIFICANCE OF MARK 10:45

I N THE PREVIOUS CHAPTERS, WE concluded that Mark likely wrote his Gospel for Roman Christians around the time of Nero's persecution. We also argued that Mark's purpose for writing his Gospel was to motivate his audience to remain faithful to Jesus even in the face of suffering and shame. The primary means by which Mark motivates his audience is by telling them the story of who Jesus is and what he willingly endured for their sake. Mark paints the picture of Jesus's determined faithfulness on the way to the cross—a faithfulness that remained steady when those dearest to him stood in his way (8:32), when a friend betrayed him (14:43-46), and when his disciples abandoned him, leaving him to finish the journey alone (14:50). Mark uses each of these episodes to capture the hearts and minds of his audience as he reassures them that they are *not* alone when they walk the path of shame and suffering. Jesus has gone before them, and he is with them along the way.

The question now is how Mark 10:45 itself contributes to Mark's purpose. To understand this relationship, we must first understand the meaning and significance of this verse within its context. We admit that Mark 10:45 does not strike most readers as cryptic or confusing. Some may understandably wonder, "What exactly is there to dig into here?" It is apparent enough that "the Son of Man" refers to Jesus and that Jesus came not for his own benefit but to give his life for others.

But if we stop here, with a facile awareness of Jesus's mission to die for others, we miss the depth of this verse. We miss why there would even be a choice between serving and being served. We miss why anyone needs to be ransomed at all. Most importantly, if we satisfy ourselves with a hasty impression of Mark 10:45, we miss why exactly Mark would place this statement at such a strategic location in his story. And we risk misreading the message that Mark would offer to us who follow Jesus today.

This chapter aims to properly interpret Mark 10:45 within its context so that (in the next chapter) we can better understand its function within and contribution to Mark's Gospel as a whole. We will argue that in this verse and its immediate context, Mark reminds his readers that the Jesus whom they follow is the glorious Son of Man who laid aside everything, even his own life (cf. 10:29–30), to redeem them from the power of sin and death. Of course, this message surfaces at various places throughout Mark's Gospel, but its most prominent and explicit presentation is in Mark 10:45. Here Jesus explains the *rationale* for his expectation that the disciples must faithfully follow him, even through shame and suffering. And with this verse, Mark offers his readers further *motivation* to do the same. Several themes within the Second Gospel converge in this single verse, in which Jesus explains the purpose and significance of his death. And in the broader context of Jesus's instruction (10:42–45), this verse epitomizes the difference between a mind focused on the things of men and one focused on the things of God (8:33). Those who would follow after Jesus must be willing to follow him *to the cross* (8:34), where God is redeeming his people.

We will begin our study by outlining and discussing the literary structure of Mark's Gospel so we can appreciate the context of Mark 10:45. We will then investigate the grammatical, syntactical, and lexical features of this important verse in a phrase-by-phrase study. In this way, we will clarify the relationship of Mark 10:45 to the rest of Mark's Gospel and to the purpose of its author.

THE LITERARY CONTEXT OF MARK 10:45
WITHIN THE STRUCTURE
OF MARK'S GOSPEL

One question we may begin with is *how Mark 10:45 fits into the over-arching literary structure of the Second Gospel.* If we hope to grasp the meaning and significance of Mark 10:45 (the goal of this chapter) and to understand its function and contribution to Mark's message (the purpose of the next chapter), we must answer this question. Typical outlines of Mark's Gospel divide the literary structure into three major geographical units:

1. Jesus's northern ministry (Mark 1–8)[1]

2. Jesus's journey toward Jerusalem (Mark 8–10)

3. Jesus's activity in Jerusalem (Mark 11–16)

But even these major literary divisions are a bit artificial. For example, though the structure of a threefold passion prediction cycle within the middle section (Mark 8:27–10:45) appears obvious, it is less clear where Jesus's journey to Jerusalem actually begins. Some locate the boundaries of the Journey section at 8:22–10:52, incorporating the two healings of blind men (8:22–26; 10:26–52) as an inclusio around 8:27–10:45.[2] Others begin the cycle at 8:27, which sets the scene for Peter's confession that Jesus is the Christ.[3] A few interpreters even start this

---

1. Most interpreters find a major section break in Mark 8, but there is disagreement about the exact location of this break. The most common suggestions are between vv. 21 and 22, between vv. 26 and 26, or between vv. 30 and 31.

2. For example, Eugene Boring, *Mark: A Commentary* (Louisville: Westminster John Knox, 2006); R. T. France, *The Gospel of Mark: A Commentary on the Greek Text* (Grand Rapids: Eerdmans, 2002), 11; Garland, *A Theology of Mark's Gospel*; Marcus, *Mark 1–8*; Marcus, *Mark 8–16* (New Haven: Yale University Press, 2009); Stein, *Mark.*

3. For example, Yarbro Collins, *Mark*; Morna D. Hooker, *The Gospel according to Saint Mark* (Peabody: Hendrickson, 1991); Edwards, *Mark*; Craig A. Evans,

section at 8:31 with the first passion prediction.[4] However, the precise location where the middle Journey section begins does not significantly impact our interpretation of Mark 10:45.

Regarding the larger context of Mark's narrative, we believe the key to its structure is the intentional positioning of the threefold passion prediction cycle (8:27–10:45) surrounded by the only two healings of blindness in Mark's Gospel (8:22–26; 10:46–52). This arrangement is reinforced if we read these healing stories in light of the spiritual "blindness" of the disciples that Jesus rebukes in the immediately preceding passage (8:14–21). There Jesus asks the disciples, "Why are you discussing that you have no bread? Do you not yet perceive or understand? Have your hearts been hardened? *Although you have eyes, do you not see?* And although you have ears, do you not hear? And do you not remember?" (vv. 17–18, emphasis added).[5] Reading 8:22–10:52 as a unit highlights the theme of the disciples' blindness throughout the passion prediction cycles (e.g., 8:32; 9:32–34, 38; 10:13, 35–41) as another example of intercalation within Mark's Gospel.[6]

Structurally, each of the passion prediction cycles consists of three elements. The cycles (1) begin with Jesus predicting his suffering, death, and resurrection (8:31; 9:31; 10:33–34); (2) describe some misunderstanding on the part of the disciples about what it means to follow Jesus in the kingdom of God (8:32; 9:32–34; 10:35–41); and (3) feature

---

Mark 8:27–16:20 (Nashville: Thomas Nelson, 2001); Robert Guelich, *Mark 1–8:26* (Dallas: Word, 1989).

4. For example, William L. Lane, *The Gospel According to Mark*, New International Commentary on the New Testament (Grand Rapids: Eerdmans, 1974), 30–32; Sharyn Dowd, *Reading Mark* (Macon, GA: Smyth & Helwys, 2000).

5. As evidence for reading 8:22–26 as part of the middle section rather than as part of what precedes it, Garland further argues for three cycles of summary (1:14–15; 3:7–12; 6:6b), calling/commission (1:16–20; 3:13–19; 6:7–13), and opposition (3:6; 6:1–6a; 8:14–21) within 1:14–8:21. Garland, *A Theology of Mark's Gospel*, 99–101.

6. See the discussion in "Mark's Competence as an Author" in chapter 3 (p. 41) for other examples of intercalation or "sandwiching."

corrective teaching by Jesus in response to the confusion of the disciples (8:33–38; 9:35–37; 10:42–45). Though these cycles contain additional narrative material that does not fit neatly into one of these three categories (e.g., 9:14–29; 10:1–12), each cycle contains *at least* these three elements in the given order. It is within the third and final iteration of these passion prediction cycles that our text, Mark 10:45, appears. Properly interpreting Mark 10:45 requires attention not only to its immediate context (10:32–44) but to the broader context of the entire Gospel as well. Accordingly, the following sections will examine the context and literary structure of Mark's Gospel as a whole and then consider the function of this final passion prediction (10:32–45) within the literary context of the Journey section (8:22–10:52).

THE CONTEXT OF MARK'S GOSPEL
AS A WHOLE

Context exerts significant influence over how we interpret a text—at least it should. But it is no rare circumstance to see people, even Christians, misappropriate a verse by ignoring its literary and historical context. Context is a pesky thing. It can prevent us from (mis) using Scripture the way we might like. And so, a proper reading of Mark 10:45 must understand how it relates not only to its immediate context but also to the context of Mark's Gospel as a whole. Some of the discussion below will incorporate conclusions from the previous chapter, but here we offer our understanding of the literary and thematic features of Mark's Gospel in order to accurately relate 10:45 (and its immediate context) to the rest of Mark's story.

The first several verses of Mark's Gospel act as a prologue focused on John the Baptist, who sets the stage for Jesus's ministry (esp. 1:2–9). Verses 14 and 15 present a definite change in topic from John to Jesus, and they introduce the theme for the next major unit of Mark's Gospel: "Jesus went into Galilee proclaiming the gospel of God" (v. 14). The primary focus of Mark 1:14–8:21, then, is on Jesus demonstrating his authority in and around Galilee as he proclaims the gospel of the kingdom of God and performs works of power. As we discussed above, there is disagreement over where this new section narrating Jesus's ministry in and around Galilee transitions into the Journey section (e.g., 8:22, 8:27, or 8:31). If the structure of Mark is based solely on geography, one might even extend this transition to 10:1, where Jesus moves into Judea and Perea.[7] But Mark's structure is not exclusively geographical; it is also thematic. And throughout 1:14–8:21, Jesus, by his works and teachings, demonstrates that the kingdom of God has, in fact, come near (cf. 1:15).

Of course, these works and teachings are not the only reason that Jesus has come. The topic of Jesus's identity, which is so prominent in the first several chapters of Mark's Gospel, develops in a new way in the middle section (8:22–10:52) when Peter becomes the first human character to declare, "You are the Christ" (8:29). Opposition to Jesus had been mounting throughout 1:14–8:21, and now Jesus begins to teach his disciples that he must suffer and die (8:31). This scandalous news creates a tension between Jesus and his disciples that will build throughout the rest of this middle section (esp. 8:32; 9:10, 32; 10:38–40).

In 11:1–16:8, the predictions of Jesus's rejection, suffering, and death find their fulfillment through his escalating conflict with the Jerusalem authorities, culminating in his arrest and crucifixion. This final section concludes with a description of the empty tomb so brief that it almost feels like an afterthought tacked onto the story. But Jesus has been planting this seed since the very first passion prediction ("and after three days rise" [8:31, ESV; cf. 9:31; 10:34]). Just as it was necessary for the Son of Man to suffer many things and be rejected and killed, it was also necessary that he rise again.

These major units within Mark's Gospel weave together thematically, and each organically develops from what precedes it. It should not be too surprising, then, to find disagreements over which specific

---

7. For example, Charles Hedrick has argued for a major division at 10:1 against the understanding that the threefold prediction cycle forms a unified section; Charles W. Hedrick, "What Is a Gospel? Geography, Time and Narrative Structure," *Perspectives in Religious Studies* 10, no. 3 (1983): 255–68.

verses should mark the divisions within so cohesive a narrative. Here we offer our understanding of how the general structure of Mark's Gospel fits together:

OUTLINE OF MARK'S GOSPEL

I. Prologue (1:1–13)

    A. The Coming of the Messenger (1:1–8)

    B. The Coming of the Lord (1:9–13)

II. Jesus Demonstrates His Power and Authority in and around Galilee (1:14–8:21)

    A. Jesus Openly Proclaims the Gospel of the Kingdom of God by Teaching, Healing, and Casting out Demons (1:14–3:6)

    B. Jesus Selectively Continues His Ministry throughout Galilee and the Surrounding Areas (3:7–8:21)[8]

III. Jesus Teaches His Disciples the Differences between a Mind Focused on the Things of God and One Focused on the Things of Men (8:22–10:52)

    A. Healing of the First Blind Man (8:22–26)

    B. First Passion Prediction Cycle (8:27–9:29)

    C. Second Passion Prediction Cycle (9:30–10:31)

    D. Third Passion Prediction Cycle (10:32–45)

    E. Healing of the Second Blind Man (10:46–52)

---

8. Many scholars break Mark 3:7–8:21 into the smaller subsections 3:7–6:6a and 6:6b–8:21. There may be good structural reasons for this—for example, Garland, *A Theology of Mark's Gospel*, sees both 3:7–6:6a and 6:6b–8:21 (as well as 1:14–3:6) as beginning with a summary (1:14–15; 3:7–12; 6:6b) and a calling or commissioning of the disciples (1:16–20; 3:13–19; 6:7–13) and closing with disbelief or resistance to Jesus (3:6; 6:1–6a; 8:14–21). But changes to the overarching theme between 3:7–6:6a and 6:6b–8:21 usually seem a bit arbitrary. We believe that the shift from Jesus's open proclamation and ministry in 1:14–3:6 to a more reserved and selective proclamation and ministry in 3:7–8:21 is much clearer than a shift between 3:7–6:6a and 6:6b–8:21.

IV. Jesus Embodies the Differences between a Mind Focused on the Things of God and One Focused on the Things of Men (11:1–16:8)

    A. Confronting the Religious Leaders in the Temple (11:1–13:37)

    B. Preparing for the Passion (14:1–42)

    C. Fulfilling the Passion Predictions (14:43–16:8)

Focusing specifically on the Third Passion Prediction Cycle (10:32–45), we can outline the immediate context of Mark 10:45 as follows:

OUTLINE OF MARK 10:32–45

I. Jesus's Third Passion Prediction (10:32–34)

II. The Misguided Ambition of the Disciples (10:35–41)

    A. James and John Request Positions of Honor and Authority (10:35–37)

    B. Jesus Challenges Their Request (10:38–40)

    C. The Other Disciples React to the Request (10:41)

III. Jesus's Correction (10:42–45)

    A. Jesus Describes Worldly Honor and Authority (10:42)

    B. Jesus Describes True Honor and Authority (10:43–44)

    C. Jesus Explains Why True Honor and Authority Should Serve Others (10:45)

In this outline, we suggest that Mark 10:45 provides the *explanation* for Jesus's teaching that anyone who would follow him must "deny himself and take up his cross" (8:34). True honor and authority lie in denying oneself to serve others (10:43–44) and taking up one's cross to face shame and suffering for the sake of Jesus (10:38–39). Furthermore, the contrast in 10:42–45 between worldly honor and authority and true honor and authority is an *illustration* of Jesus's distinction between a mind focused on the things of God and one focused on the things of men (8:33). This final prediction cycle integrates the theme of suffering introduced in the first cycle (esp. 8:31–38) with the theme of servanthood discussed in the second cycle (esp. 9:35–37). In this way, 10:45 presents a climactic point not only within the third passion prediction cycle (10:32–45) but within the entire Journey section (8:22–10:52) as well.[9] With this literary structure in mind, we can now focus on how this third passion prediction cycle connects to the rest of Mark's Gospel.

CONNECTIONS BETWEEN MARK 10:32–45 AND THE REST OF MARK'S GOSPEL

Mark 10:32–45 presents the third and final iteration of Jesus's prediction that he will suffer, die, and rise again (vv. 33–34). This final passion prediction is the most explicit and detailed of the three predictions around which the Journey section is structured.[10] After Jesus's prediction (10:33–34), Mark relates yet another example of the disciples' persistent failure to recognize that the road ahead is one of suffering and shame (10:35–41; cf. 8:17–18, 21). This lack of understanding results in the self-seeking request of James and John to sit in the places of highest honor next to Jesus (10:37). The other ten disciples also seem to fall into a similar error when they "began to be indignant" at the boldness of the request (v. 41). Verses 42–45 contain Jesus's corrective teaching, in which he distinguishes between how one achieves honor in the kingdom of God versus in the nations of this world. Verse 45 then presents Jesus's mission of servanthood and self-sacrifice both as the *ultimate example* of what true honor and authority look like in the kingdom of God and as the *rationale* for sacrificial and servant-minded discipleship among those who follow him.

This third cycle (10:32–45) connects thematically with the previous cycle (9:31–10:31), in which the disciples had exposed their misunderstanding of true discipleship as they argued among themselves about

---

9. The function of Mark 10:45 within Mark's narrative and its contribution to our reading of the Second Gospel will be developed further in the next chapter.

10. Alberto Kaminouchi argues from what he terms the "echo principle" that this third cycle and the teaching it contains are central to Mark's Gospel in both a narrative and theological sense. See Alberto Kaminouchi, *'But It Is Not So Among You': Echoes of Power in Mark 10.32–45* (New York: T&T Clark, 2003), esp. 10, 57–71.

who was the greatest (9:34). In 10:35-37, James and John seem determined to settle that dispute by asking Jesus directly to grant that they,
rather than any of the other ten disciples, sit at his right and his left
"in your glory" (ἐν τῇ δόξῃ σου).[11] The concept of sitting at someone's
right, especially someone of honor or authority, commonly implies
participation in the honor or authority of that person (e.g., 1 Kgs 2:19;
Ps 110:1). References to sitting at the left of someone are far less frequent, but Josephus may provide a parallel in *Antiquities* 6.11.9, in which
he recounts a situation when King Saul sat down to supper with his
son, Jonathan, sitting at his right (ἐκ δεξιῶν) and Abner, the captain
of Saul's army, sitting at his other side (ἐκ τῶν ἑτέρων), presumably
at his left.[12] The collocation with δόξῃ ("glory") in 10:37 supports the
idea that James and John are requesting the highest places of honor,
and the analogy of gentile rulers in 10:42 provides context for sharing
in Jesus's authority.[13] James and John's desire for honor and power was
unmitigated by Jesus's previous correction that "if anyone wants to
be first [πρῶτος εἶναι], he will be last of all and servant of all [πάντων
διάκονος]" (9:35). So here, in 10:42, Jesus reiterates and intensifies his
admonition from 9:35. He points to "those who are considered to rule
over the Gentiles," who "lord it over them," and to "their people in

---

11. It is noteworthy that the prisoners who are crucified on the right and
left of Jesus are also described as "one on his right and one on his left" (ἕνα ἐκ
δεξιῶν καὶ ἕνα ἐξ εὐωνύμων αὐτοῦ [15:27]). What is most interesting about the
phrasing in 15:27 is that it seems to amalgamize the request of James and John
(specifically the use of εἷς) with the response of Jesus, in which he replaces
their use of ἀριστερῶν with the euphemism εὐωνύμων.

12. See Lane, *Mark*, 279.

13. Cf. the references to eschatological "glory" in 8:38 and 13:26. For a discussion of the similarities between 10:35-45 and the Qumranic Rule of the
Congregation, see John K. Goodrich, "Rule of the Congregation and Mark
10:32-52: Glory and Greatness in Eschatological Israel," in *Reading Mark in
Context: Jesus and Second Temple Judaism*, ed. Ben C. Blackwell, John K. Goodrich,
and Jason Maston (Grand Rapids: Zondervan, 2018), 166-73.

high positions," who "exercise authority over them" (10:42), as negative examples that the disciples must reject.[14]

Narry Santos notes the significance that "lord it over" (κατακυριεύουσιν) may have had for a reader who has only heard the word "lord" (κύριος) used for Jesus and God to this point in the narrative: "[The readers would] find it ironic that Gentile rulers, who do not deserve the designation 'lord', are the ones described in Mk 10:42 as lording it over other people, and that Jesus, who is rightfully ascribed that designation ["Lord"], is the one consistently seen in the narrative

---

14. The word for "those who are considered" (δοκοῦντες) in 10:42 is interesting. Some interpreters see no nuance or qualification at all in this participle. Among them, Robert Gundry translates the phrase as "the ones recognized to be ruling the Gentiles" (Gundry, Mark, 579; cf. Yarbro Collins, Mark, 499). It is true that these "rulers" do indeed rule, and the presence of the participle δοκοῦντες does not negate this fact. But it is unlikely that this word in no way qualifies the sense of rulership here. We should not push the significance of this participle too far, but it is reasonable that "those who are considered" may imply (or even emphasize) the ultimate rulership of God—without denying the reality of mediating "rulers." See Hooker, Mark, 247. For the subtle sense of irony in Mark's use of δοκοῦντες (10:42), see Kaminouchi, 'But It Is Not So Among You', 118-23. Mark's portrayal of two notable figures who seem to be powerful but, ironically, are powerless (i.e., Herod and Pilate) is in line with the use of irony in δοκοῦντες (10:42). Despite their powerful positions, both Herod (6:14-29) and Pilate (15:1-15) are controlled by others surrounding them—in the case of Herod, by Herodias (and his own oath before his guests), and in the case of Pilate, by the chief priests and the crowd. For further discussion of these two instances of Mark's narrative in relation to 10:42-45, see Kaminouchi, 'But It Is Not So Among You', 163-97. Alternatively, "those who are considered" (δοκοῦντες) may indicate that to "lord it over" (κατακυριεύουσιν) is behavior distinctive of gentile rulers. That is, this sort of "lording over" one's subjects is what makes one seem like a ruler among the gentiles. Mark Moore suggests this phrase implies that James and John are the ones who "consider themselves" to be rulers; Mark E. Moore, Kenotic Politics: The Reconfiguration of Power in Jesus' Political Praxis (New York: T&T Clark, 2013), 66. See also Adam Winn, "Tyrant or Servant? Roman Political Ideology and Mark 10.42-45," JSNT 36, no. 4 (2014): 325-52, for a discussion of recusatio and popular Roman political ideology and how they relate to Mark 10:42-45. See the section, "Pervasiveness of Irony," in the next chapter for further discussion of this phrase.

as a humble servant."[15] Santos further comments on the parallelism in Jesus's corrective teaching here: "[T]he intensification in [v. 43-44] appears to have reached a climax: from wishing to be 'great' to wishing to be the 'first,' which is the highest form of greatness, and from being 'your servant' to being 'slave of all,' which is the highest form of daily servanthood. This obvious intensification alerts the readers to the great importance of [vv. 43-44]."[16] Jesus's response to the desire for power and glory is starker here in the third cycle (10:42-45) than it was in the second cycle (9:35). Intensifying from "servant" (διάκονος, cf. 9:35) to "servant" *and* "slave" (δοῦλος, 10:44), Jesus dramatically declares that whoever would desire the highest honor must be *slave of all*. These literary and lexical features signal that Jesus's correction to his disciples in this third passion prediction cycle is climactic within the Journey section.

This final prediction cycle also contains parallels with other passages in Mark's Gospel. Jesus's response to James and John in 10:36, "What do you want that I do for you?" (τί θέλετέ [με] ποιήσω ὑμῖν), parallels his response to blind Bartimaeus in 10:51, "What do you want me to do for you?" (τί σοι θέλεις ποιήσω). This parallel may indicate that Mark wants his readers to compare the desires of James and John, who see Jesus as a source of honor and power for themselves, with the desire of Bartimaeus, who sees Jesus as a source of mercy, healing, and rescue. There is also a grammatical parallel between the request of James and John in 10:35, "We want you to do for us whatever we ask you" (θέλομεν ἵνα ὃ ἐὰν αἰτήσωμέν σε ποιήσῃς ἡμῖν), and the conversation between Herod Antipas and the daughter of Herodias in 6:22-23. Herod offers, "Ask me for whatever you want" (αἴτησόν με ὃ ἐὰν θέλῃς) and "whatever you ask me for I will give you" (ὅ τι ἐάν με αἰτήσῃς δώσω σοι). The phrase ὃ (τι) ἐάν ("whatever") and an aorist form of αἰτέω ("request")

---

15. Narry Santos, *Slave of All: The Paradox of Authority and Servanthood in the Gospel of Mark* (New York: Sheffield Academic, 2003), 205. The Greek terms for "lord" and "lord it over" are related to the same Greek root.

16. Santos, *Slave of All*, 205.

each appear in 6:22-23 and 10:35. And in both 6:23 and 10:35, the aorist form of αἰτέω ("request") is subjunctive. Mark Moore suggests that these parallel constructions emphasize the failure of James and John to understand that Jesus's rule will be different from that of earthly rulers like Herod Antipas.[17] The parallelism that permeates this passage is evidence of the care with which the author composed it and further proof of its significance within Mark's Gospel.[18]

Jesus's corrective teaching in this final prediction cycle *connects* his glory with his suffering and death (cf. 8:34-38; 9:9; 14:32-15:41) — a connection epitomized in 10:45, where Jesus explains that the reason for his coming was "to serve and to give his life as a ransom for many." Jesus's serving and giving his life for others illustrates the sort of sacrificial service that corresponds to true honor and authority in the kingdom of God. Jesus connects James and John's request for honor to his suffering and death via the metaphor of his "cup" and "baptism" in 10:38. The resolve with which Jesus confronts his fate is striking in contrast with his disciples' rivalry and self-interest. Biblically, both "cup" and "baptism" can refer to overwhelming distress or suffering. This is particularly true in contexts of judgment.[19] In Mark's Gospel, and especially the threefold passion prediction, there is little doubt that these metaphors refer to the suffering and, ultimately, the death that awaits Jesus in Jerusalem (cf. the "cup" in 14:36). The phrase "in your glory" (ἐν τῇ δόξῃ σου) is quite ironic considering the very misguided

----

17. Moore, *Kenotic Politics*, 64. Jesus exposes the disciples' worldly misunderstanding of his mission in 8:33 when he rebukes Peter for standing between him and his suffering: "You are not thinking the thoughts of God but those of men."

18. See the discussion in "Mark's Competence as an Author" in chapter 3 (pp. 39-46) for more examples of the Evangelist's literary proficiency.

19. For references to "cup," see Psalm 11:6 (10:6 [LXX]); 75:8 (74:9 [LXX]); Isaiah 51:17, 22; Jeremiah 25:15, 17, 28 (32:15, 17, 28 [LXX]); 49:12 (30:6 [LXX]); Habakkuk 2:16; Ezekiel 23:31-33. Regarding baptism, see Job 9:31, where Aquila reads και τοτε εν διαφορα βαπτισεις με. Origen's Hexapla cites Symmachus as reading ἐβαπτίσθην εἰς ἀπεράντους καταδύσεις at Psalm 68:3 (69:2 [LXX]). Cf. Luke 12:50.

conception that the disciples have of Jesus's glory. This confusion about true glory is why Jesus tells them that they do not understand what they are asking (10:38). James and John see glory in authority and rule, but the true glory we find in Jesus demands his service and submission, even to the point of death on a cross (10:45; cf. Phil 2:8). In this ultimate contrast between a mind focused on the things of God and one focused on the things of men, Mark reminds his audience that they have not understood Christ's true glory and authority *unless* they have embraced Christ's mission to give his life for others.

We have seen how the third passion prediction cycle functions as a climax within the Journey section. The prediction within this third cycle is the most detailed and explicit, and it is here in the third cycle that Jesus reveals his ultimate destination and purpose, dying on a Roman cross to redeem God's people. The literary parallels between this third cycle and the previous two, not to mention the connections to other sections of the narrative, demonstrate the cohesiveness of Mark's Gospel and the unity of its message. But to fully grasp that message, we must dig deeper into what we believe is both structurally and thematically a key verse of Mark's Gospel. Mark 10:45 is key for understanding Mark's message in the specific sense that it integrates the following core emphases of the Second Gospel: (1) Jesus's divine identity as the Danielic Son of Man, (2) the atoning nature of Jesus's death, and (3) the example that Jesus's faithfulness sets for his disciples, not least Mark's intended audience. The integration of these emphases in Mark 10:45 confirms that a better understanding of this verse will enhance our understanding of the entire Gospel. The next section of this chapter provides a phrase-by-phrase exegetical analysis of this key verse in hopes of discovering its meaning and significance.

DIGGING INTO MARK 10:45

The climax of the third passion prediction cycle (10:32–35), if not the entire Journey section in Mark's Gospel (8:22–10:52), is the statement made in 10:45. Narry Santos describes the climactic nature of Mark 10:45 well:

As the readers reflect on the significance of Jesus' giving his life as a ransom, they make more sense of Mark's effort to present the three passion predictions of Jesus. In these three predictions, Mark always includes the death of Jesus. In fact, in 8:31, he specifies that Jesus "must" (δεῖ) suffer, implying divine necessity. Up until 10:45b, he gives no reason why Jesus must suffer and be killed in the hands of God's enemies. Only in Mk 10:45b have they first seen that the reason for Jesus' death is to give his life a ransom for many. This unveiling of the reason for Jesus' death alerts the readers rhetorically to its climactic position and role for the entire central section of 8:22–10:52.[20]

In what follows, we will analyze the words and phrases of Mark 10:45 to unearth as much information as possible for interpreting this verse and understanding how it contributes to the message of Mark's Gospel.[21] We will establish that Mark 10:45 provides the rationale for the radical expectations Jesus has of his disciples (e.g., 8:34; 9:35; 10:21, 25–26, 29–31, 43–44) by revealing the radical sacrifice that Jesus himself has made to redeem God's people. Those who want to follow the Son of Man in his glory must first be willing to follow him to the cross, where God is redeeming his people, through Jesus's death, from their own sin and death. Our focus will be on the text of Mark's Gospel as it stands, which undoubtedly attributes the saying to Jesus, and not on the historical questions of sources and their transmission and redactions. We confine ourselves here to the text Mark has given us: "For even the Son of Man did not come to be served but to serve and to give his life as a ransom for many."

---

20. Santos, *Slave of All*, 208. See also our discussion of the climactic force of Mark 10:45 in chapter 5 below.

21. See Appendix II for additional studies on this verse.

"FOR EVEN"

These two words clarify the relationship of verse 45 to the rest of Jesus's teaching in verses 42-44. "For" (γάρ) is a conjunction that usually introduces an explanation of what precedes it. Consider a familiar example in John 3:15b-16: "So the Son of man must be lifted up, that everyone who believes may have eternal life in him. For God so loved the world that he gave his one and only Son" (NIV, emphasis added). The word "for" indicates that verse 16 is providing some explanation of the preceding statement in verse 15. God loving the world and giving his Son is not necessarily the *cause* or *reason* that "everyone who believes may have eternal life in him"—though "for" (γάρ) can function this way. But John 3:16 does provide background information that helps *explain* the clause, "everyone who believes may have eternal life" (v. 15, NIV). God's love for the world, by which he gave his Son (v. 16), clarifies the significance and meaning of verse 15. The same is true in Mark 10:45. The "for" (γάρ) clause in Mark 10:45 explains and clarifies the *rationale* for the principle that "whoever wants to become great" and "most prominent" must be servants and slaves (vv. 43-44). Jesus, and Mark through him, are arguing from the greater to the lesser. Jesus is the greater; the disciples are the lesser. If Jesus, the greater, gave even his life for others, then how much more must the disciples, the lesser, be willing to do so as well! Why should we be servants and slaves? Because *even* the Son of Man came to serve and to give his life.[22]

In this way, we must read Mark 10:45 in relation to 10:42-44. We saw above that 10:42-45 contains Jesus's corrective teaching to the disciples after their thick-headedness is put on full display (10:35-41). They

---

22. R. T. France comments on the function of καὶ γάρ connecting v. 45 to the preceding verses: "The conjunction καὶ γάρ and the repetition of the theme of service link this declaration closely with what precedes. The υἱὸς τοῦ ἀνθρώπου provides the *supreme model* of status reversal in that he whose destiny it was διακονηθῆναι (Dan 7:14 LXX: πάντα τὰ ἔθνη τῆς γῆς κατὰ γένη καὶ πᾶσα δόξα αὐτῷ λατρεύουσα; Theodotion: πάντες οἱ λαοί, φυλαί, γλῶσσαι αὐτῷ δουλεύσουσιν) was instead to become πάντων διάκονος." France, *The Gospel of Mark*, 419, emphasis added.

still do not understand Jesus's initial call in the first prediction cycle (esp. 8:34–35) to suffer for his sake. And they still do not comprehend his clear warning in the second cycle that "many who are first will be last, and the last first" (9:35). Now, in the third cycle, James and John continue to ignore the shame and suffering that come with following Jesus. They are blinded by the honor and glory they hope to gain from him (10:37). And so, in 10:42–44, Jesus corrects the disciples' understanding of what it means to "rule" in God's kingdom:

> You know that those who are considered to rule over the Gentiles lord it over them, and their people in high positions exercise authority over them. But it is not like this among you! But whoever wants to become great among you must be your servant, and whoever wants to be most prominent among you must be the slave of all.

Within God's kingdom, "whoever wants to be most prominent ... must be slave of all" (10:44). So in 10:45, Jesus clarifies *why* those seeking prominence must serve as slaves. If *even the Son of Man* came not to be served but to serve, then those following him must be willing to serve as well.[23] The example of Jesus's own life explains why the path of humble servanthood is the only way to prominence in God's kingdom.

The word translated "even" (καί) in this verse can serve a variety of functions.[24] Quite often, it is a conjunction joining two or more words, phrases, or clauses—in which case it translates as "and." But καί can also *emphasize* a word, phrase, or clause. In this case, it is often

---

23. See also Gundry, *Mark*, 581.

24. The phrase καὶ γάρ occurs twice in Mark's Gospel (10:45; 14:70). BDAG treats the instance here and several others as a phrase, but as J. K. Elliott notes, "At both places [in Mark] each particle seems to retain its full force"; J. K. Elliott, *The Language and Style of the Gospel of Mark: An Edition of C. H. Turner's "Notes on Marcan Usage" Together with Other Comparable Studies*, Supplements to Novum Testamentum 71 (New York: Brill, 1993), 182. Other instances where this phrase occurs and where καί seems to have the intensive additive function include 2 Chron 24:7; 4 Macc 2:16; Ps 40:10 (LXX); Matt 15:27; Luke 6:32; Rom 15:3.

translated as "even" or "indeed" depending on the context. The καί in this verse indicates an intensified example of the principle laid out in 10:43-44 that true greatness is a result of sacrificial service.[25] This construction indicates that the statements "must be your servant" (v. 43) and "must be the slave of all" (v. 44) should be true among the disciples because the Son of Man has made an even starker sacrifice. *Even* the exalted Son of Man, who receives "dominion and glory and kingship" (Dan 7:14),[26] *even he* has come to serve. If even this exalted, authoritative figure has come to serve, then so must those who would follow him. With the words "for even," Jesus points to himself as the ultimate illustration of sacrificial servanthood and the ultimate example of a mind focused on the things of God rather than men.[27]

---

25. Other examples of καί with this function include Matt 5:46-47; 10:30; Mark 1:27.

26. An allusion to Dan 7:14 in this verse is disputed, but evidence for this connection will be given in the discussion of the phrase "the Son of Man" below.

27. Some may argue that the intensification indicated by καί in Mark 10:45 is due not to a difference in relative authority or greatness between a disciple and the exalted Son of Man (Dan 7) but rather to a difference in the extent of service and submission between a disciple—who is instructed to become a slave—and Jesus, who came not just to serve but even "to give his life as a ransom for many." Such a reading might undermine the evidence for a Danielic background to the Son of Man expression in this verse. However, if the point of emphasis or intensification were on the extent of service, the word καί would likely not precede the phrase "the Son of Man." Furthermore, throughout 8:22–10:52, we learn that while the lives of the disciples do not serve as a ransom, disciples are nevertheless expected to be willing to give their lives (esp. 8:34; 10:38-39; 13:9-13). Therefore, the contrast in this parallel between what the disciples are called to do and what Jesus is called to do more appropriately centers not in their respective fates but rather in the respective position from which each steps down to serve. While giving one's life is truly a great sacrifice, it is not as great as the sacrifice of the glorious and exalted Son of Man who gave his life as a ransom for many (Matt 10:24; John 13:16; 15:20).

"THE SON OF MAN"

There is significant debate about precisely how the phrase ὁ υἱὸς τοῦ ἀνθρώπου should be read in this verse.[28] W. J. Moulder's comments are indicative of the difficulty that this phrase presents: "No single problem is of more central importance in New Testament studies than the Son of Man question. ... [A]mong the many important Son of Man logia to be found in the Gospels, one of the most critical to be reckoned with is Mark x.45."[29] Though Moulder was writing decades ago, his comments are still relevant as we interpret Mark 10:45 today. Most contemporary interpreters understand the phrase "Son of Man" in this verse in one of two basic categories. Scholars like Geza Vermes and Maurice Casey view this phrase as carrying no connotation of honor or exaltation at all. Vermes argues that this phrase is used simply as a euphemism of modesty,[30] while Casey argues that the phrase refers to humans in general. Alternatively, the phrase "the Son of Man" in

---

28. See the divergent interpretations in Maurice Casey, *The Solution to the 'Son of Man' Problem* (New York: T&T Clark, 2009), 131–34; Geza Vermes, "The Son of Man Debate Revisited (1960–2000)," *Journal of Jewish Studies* 61, no. 2 (2010): 205–6; Yarbro Collins, *Mark*, 500; Marcus, *Mark 8–16*, 74. Morna D. Hooker, *The Son of Man in Mark: A Study of the Background of the Term and Its Use in St. Mark's Gospel* (London: SPCK, 1967), 5–7, discusses the failure of source, form, and tradition criticisms to provide a singular solution to the historicity of Jesus's use of the term. Likewise, see Delbert Burkett's dismissal of many such attempts to understand the phrase in its broader NT usage; Delbert Burkett, *The Son of Man Debate: A History and Evaluation* (New York: Cambridge University Press, 2000), 13–21.

29. W. J. Moulder, "Old Testament Background and the Interpretation of Mark X.45," *NTS* 24, no. 1 (1977): 120.

30. Vermes summarizes his understanding of this convention: "A circumlocutional self-reference is a statement made by a speaker about himself, framed in the third person form with 'son of man' as the surrogate. In circumstances of modesty, self-effacement, fear or awe, this speaker uses roundabout talk because he does not want to call a spade a spade. Understood in this meaning, the 'son of man' idiom makes full sense and can be applied to all the Gospel passages that display the corresponding Greek phraseology"; Vermes, "The Son of Man Debate Revisited," 199. See also Vermes, *Jesus the Jew* (London: Collins, 1973), 137–65; Vermes, *The Authentic Gospel of Jesus* (London: Penguin, 2004), 234–65.

Mark 10:45 may refer to the exalted human-*like* figure in Daniel 7:13-14. Whether the phrase conveys connotations of humility or honor, both interpretations agree that Mark employs it as a designation that Jesus uses for himself.

Does "Son of Man" Simply Mean "Human Being"?

Those who read "Son of Man" in Mark 10:45 as referring only to a human being will find corroborating evidence in the frequency with which the phrase is used this way in the Old Testament, especially in Ezekiel. The book of Ezekiel contains over ninety occurrences of the phrase, and each seems to emphasize the relative humility or frailty of humankind in contrast to God. As such, the NRSV regularly translates the phrase as "mortal" in Ezekiel. Psalm 8:5 (υἱὸς ἀνθρώπου, LXX) and several other Old Testament passages also express a similar concept.[31]

From a slightly different angle, Vermes has argued that the Aramaic equivalent (א)נש(א) בר, from which the Greek phrase was translated, would have been understood as a euphemistic self-reference expressing *modesty*. Vermes asserts that this euphemism would be especially appropriate when discussing taboo topics like death or fear or situations that call for modesty, such as bold claims of honor or authority.[32] In this case, the reason for Jesus using "the Son of Man" to refer to himself may be to obscure the taboo reference to his own death.[33] Vermes further argues that this phrase is never used in Aramaic as a title.[34] If we take Vermes's suggestion that "the Son of Man" in Mark 10:45 is only a modest euphemism, then Jesus is using this phrase simply to point to himself as an example of sacrificial service that his disciples should follow, with no allusion at all to the "one like a son of man" in Daniel 7:13. There is nothing objectionable about this reading in isolation; most interpretations of "the Son of Man" in Mark 10:45 do see it

---

31. See, e.g., Num 23:19; Isa 51:12; Ps 146:3; Job 25:6; 35:8.
32. Vermes, "The Son of Man Debate Revisited."
33. Vermes, "The Son of Man Debate Revisited," 198.
34. Vermes, "The Son of Man Debate Revisited," 195.

as self-referential. But our question is whether the broader context of Mark's Gospel indicates that the self-referential phrase in this verse should be read as a simple circumlocution, modest or otherwise, or as an indication of Jesus's exalted status.

Mark's utilization of "the Son of Man" within his Gospel seems deliberate rather than casual and haphazard. If Mark has a reason for incorporating the phrase where he does, then what is that reason? If the expression is *merely* a self-referential circumlocution, a strangely translated Aramaism, as Casey suggests, then why is it so sporadic? The phrase occurs only fourteen times in Mark's Gospel, while Jesus uses first-person singular pronouns to refer to himself numerous times in Mark's Gospel and no less than six times in 10:35–45 alone (10:36, 38 [2x], 39 [2x], 40). And why does this phrase refer to no one else in Mark? Was Jesus the only person who knew about or felt compelled to use this idiom? If the expression is a euphemism used to express *modesty*, as Vermes suggests, then it is surprising how often Jesus also uses first-person pronouns both in the contexts where he uses "the Son of Man" (2:11; 8:38; 14:18, 20, 42) and in conversations about death (8:34–35; 10:38–39; 14:24, 28), shame (8:38; 14:18; 14:30; 9:42; 13:9, 13) and divine authority or characteristics (6:50; 7:14–15; 11:29–30, 33; 13:31; 14:6–8)—topics apparently requiring modesty.[35] We believe there is a better way to account for Jesus's use of "the Son of Man" in 10:45, one that accommodates the use of this phrase throughout Mark's Gospel.

"The Son of Man" Identifies Jesus as the Figure in Daniel 7:13–14

There are several details within 10:45 and Mark's Gospel as a whole that support reading this reference to "the Son of Man" in connection with the exalted human-like figure of Daniel 7:13–14:

---

35. Vermes, "The Son of Man Debate Revisited," 198. If Vermes is correct, it may be unrealistic for us to expect this euphemistic phrase to occur in every instance of a taboo topic. Even so, the usage as a euphemism seems sparse and inconsistent within Mark's Gospel.

I continued watching in the visions of the night, and look, with
the clouds of heaven one like a son of man was coming, and he
came to the Ancient of Days, and was presented before him.
And to him was given dominion and glory and kingship that all
the peoples, the nations, and languages would serve him; his
dominion is a dominion without end that will not cease, and
his kingdom is one that will not be destroyed.

We will discuss the evidence for the connection between Mark 10:45
and Daniel 7 below, but the foundation for this connection is Mark's
use of "the Son of Man" throughout his Gospel. Therefore, a closer
examination of the use of this phrase throughout Mark is in order.

The Use of "the Son of Man" throughout Mark's Gospel

Modern New Testament scholars have noted that Jesus tends to use the
phrase "the Son of Man" in three different contexts within the Gospel
narratives, namely, Jesus's present earthly authority, his future eschatological glory, and his passion.[36] But these categories must be viewed
as broadly descriptive and often overlapping rather than prescriptive
and discrete. Furthermore, these categories describe the context in
which the phrase occurs, not its meaning or referent. In Mark's Gospel,
"the Son of Man" occurs fourteen times (2:10, 28; 8:31, 38; 9:9, 12, 31; 10:33,
45; 13:26; 14:21 [2x], 41, 62).[37] Throughout the Gospel, Jesus seems to be
the only one who uses this phrase. Mark never explains what it means
or from where it comes. He simply indicates that Jesus used it as a way

---

36. See Rudolf K. Bultmann, *Theology of the New Testament*, 2 vols. (London:
SCM Press, 1952), 1:30, for a classic description of these categories.

37. In 3:28, a similar phrase refers to human beings ("the sons of men"),
reflecting a common usage in the LXX (esp. Psalms). However, both "sons" and
"men" are plural (τοῖς υἱοῖς τῶν ἀνθρώπων) in 3:28, so this instance should not
determine the meaning of "the Son of Man" in its singular form elsewhere. See,
e.g., the following LXX references: (with the article present for both terms)
Gen 11:5; Pss (LXX) 10:4; 11:2, 9; 13:2; 30:20; 32:13; 35:8; 44:3; 48:3; 52:3; 57:2; 61:10;
65:5; 106:8, 15, 21, 31; 113:24; 144:12; (with the article missing) 1 Kgdms 26:19; 2
Kgdms 7:14; 3 Kgdms 8:39; 2 Chron 6:30; Pss (LXX) 4:3; 20:11; 56:5; 89:3; 145:3.

of referring to himself. Mark seems to assume his readers are already familiar with the expression and its significance. But two particular passages are essential for understanding the significance of "Son of Man" in Mark's Gospel, especially in Mark 10:45. These passages are the healing of the paralytic in 2:1–12 and Jesus's conversation with the high priest in 14:61–65. These are the first and final occurrences of the "Son of Man" expression in Mark's Gospel. Each passage contains the phrase along with a claim that Jesus is doing something blasphemous in the eyes of the religious authorities.

We begin with Mark 2:1–12:

> And when he entered again into Capernaum after some days, it became known that he was at home. And many had gathered, so that there was no longer room, not even at the door, and he was speaking the word to them. And they came bringing to him a paralytic, carried by four of them. And when they were not able to bring him to him because of the crowd, they removed the roof where he was. And after digging through, they lowered the stretcher on which the paralytic was lying. And when Jesus saw their faith, he said to the paralytic, "Child, your sins are forgiven." Now some of the scribes were sitting there and reasoning in their hearts, "Why does this man speak like this? He is blaspheming! Who is able to forgive sins except God alone?" And immediately Jesus, perceiving in his spirit that they were reasoning like this within themselves, said to them, "Why are you considering these things in your hearts? Which is easier to say to the paralytic, 'Your sins are forgiven,' or to say 'Get up and pick up your stretcher and walk'? But so that you may know that the Son of Man has authority on earth to forgive sins,"—he said to the paralytic—"I say to you, get up, pick up your stretcher, and go to your home." And he got up and immediately picked up his stretcher and went out in front of them all, so that they were all amazed and glorified God, saying, "We have never seen anything like this!"

In this very first Markan occurrence of "the Son of Man," Jesus refers to himself as "the Son of Man," who "has authority on the earth to forgive sins" (v. 10). The setting is his conflict with a group of scribes who considered Jesus's claim to forgive sins (v. 5) to be blasphemous (v. 7). It is possible that Jesus uses "the Son of Man" as a humble euphemism here—especially since he is making the bold claim to forgive sins.[38] However, the mention of "authority" (ἐξουσία) in 2:10 ("the Son of Man has authority on earth to forgive sins") also supports a connection to the "one like a son of man" in Daniel 7:13-14, who "was given dominion" (ἐξουσία in LXX). This context indicates that "the Son of Man" is employed here as a designation of authority rather than modesty. The connection to Daniel 7:13-14 in Mark 2:1-12 is not as direct as it seems to be in other passages, but Jesus's appropriation of a divine prerogative (authority to forgive sins) and the accusation of blasphemy paired with the phrase "the Son of Man" support the likelihood of a Danielic background.[39]

---

38. Vermes discusses this possibility in "The Son of Man Debate Revisited," 198.

39. Daniel Boyarin, *The Jewish Gospels: The Story of the Jewish Christ* (New York: The New Press, 2012), 57–59. One objection to reading "the Son of Man" as a reference to the exalted human-like figure of Dan 7 in Mark 2:10—and in the other Markan occurrences, for that matter—is that the author gives no indication that the characters who hear this phrase connect it with the figure in Dan 7. After all, it would be quite a claim for Jesus to identify himself with the exalted figure of Dan 7, who receives dominion and power and a kingdom and eternal authority (ἐξουσία αἰώνιος, Dan 7:14 LXX). R. H. Fuller concludes that "it is impossible to account for these sayings [in which "Son of Man" refers to Jesus's earthly ministry] within the framework of Jewish apocalyptic, where the Son of man is a transcendent figure coming on the clouds of heaven"; R. H. Fuller, *The Foundations of New Testament Christology* (London: Collins, 1969), 124. Fuller argues that if Jesus would have used this title to refer to the apocalyptic "one like a son of man" from Dan 7, it would have immediately evoked images of a "transcendent figure coming on the clouds of heaven" (Boyarin, 124), and, of course, those present in the narrative of 2:1-12 do not react as if Jesus were making such a claim for himself. Even if we were to agree that Mark, as a narrator, has an obligation to record the sort of reaction that Fuller would expect given an allusion to Dan 7:13-14, we could easily note that the scribes

Just as necessary as 2:1–12 for our consideration is the final and most explicit use of "the Son of Man" in Mark's Gospel, Mark 14:61–65:

> But he was silent and did not reply anything. Again the high priest asked him and said to him, "Are you the Christ, the Son of the Blessed One?" And Jesus said, "I am, and you will see the Son of Man sitting at the right hand of the Power and coming with the clouds of heaven." And the high priest tore his clothes and said, "What further need do we have of witnesses? You have heard the blasphemy! What do you think?" And they all condemned him as deserving death. And some began to spit on him and to cover his face and to strike him with their fists, and to say to him "Prophesy!" And the officers received him with slaps in the face.

In 14:61, Jesus appears before the high priest, who directly asks whether he is the Messiah (Χριστός), and Jesus responds, "I am, and you will

---

have already reacted in surprise and offense at Jesus's claim to exercise the divine prerogative of forgiveness in 2:5. Does Mark really need to include an *additional* reaction of surprise and offense if Jesus were to connect himself to the Dan 7 figure? If Mark has already portrayed the scribes as shocked and surprised by Jesus's claim to forgive sins, indicated by their reaction that he is blaspheming (2:7)—the same reaction, by the way, as that of the high priest (14:63-64) when Jesus refers to himself as the Son of Man "coming with the clouds of heaven" during his trial (14:62)—then there is no need for Mark to record a second reaction when Jesus uses the title "Son of Man" in 2:10. Indeed, for Mark and his audience, the claim to forgive sins may well have been *more* controversial than appropriating a description of the Danielic "one like a son of man." While such an objection is more relevant to questions about the historicity of this phrase in the original life setting of Jesus, our focus is on how Mark intended his own audience to understand it. In this regard, Mark's narration does happen to include dramatic reactions, both positive and negative, to the words and actions of Jesus in this passage. Mark sets the general response from the crowd (astonishment in 2:12) over against the reaction of the scribes (offense in 2:7). Furthermore, Mark is writing from a life-setting in which the acceptance of Jesus as the Danielic Son of Man would have been far less objectionable than the original life-setting in which Jesus would have uttered this saying.

see the Son of Man sitting at the right hand of the Power and coming with the clouds of heaven" (v. 62). There are certainly instances of "the Son of Man" in Mark's Gospel in which the immediate context does not necessitate an allusion to Daniel 7. In fact, on its own, Mark 10:45 may not seem to require such a reference. But here in 14:62, the mention of "the Son of Man sitting at the right hand of the Power"⁴⁰ and "coming with the clouds of heaven" (ἐρχόμενον μετὰ τῶν νεφαλῶν τοῦ οὐρανοῦ) provides convincing support for interpreting at least this occurrence of "the Son of Man" in light of Daniel 7, where the one like a son of man is also "coming with the clouds of heaven" (μετὰ τῶν νεφαλῶν τοῦ οὐρανοῦ ὡς υἱὸς ἀνθρώπου ἐρχόμενος ἦν [v. 13, Theodotion]).⁴¹ This interpretation is further strengthened when the occurrence in 14:62 is considered together with the parallel eschatological language surrounding "the Son of Man" in 8:38 and 13:26-27.

> For whoever is ashamed of me and my words in this adulterous and sinful generation, *the Son of Man* [ὁ υἱὸς τοῦ ἀνθρώπου] will also be ashamed of him when *he comes in the glory of his Father with the holy angels* [ἔλθῃ ἐν τῇ δόξῃ τοῦ πατρὸς αὐτοῦ μετὰ τῶν ἀγγέλων τῶν ἁγίων]. (Mark 8:38, emphasis added)

> And then they will see *the Son of Man arriving in the clouds with great power and glory* [τὸν υἱὸν τοῦ ἀνθρώπου ἐρχόμενον ἐν νεφέλαις μετὰ δυνάμεως πολλῆς καὶ δόξης]. And then he will send out the angels, and will gather the elect together from the four winds, from the end of the earth to the end of heaven. (Mark 13:26-27, emphasis added)

---

40. The language here alludes to Ps 110:1, specifically. However, the idea of sitting at the right hand of "the Power" (a circumlocution for God) relates to supreme authority, honor, and glory, important themes in Dan 7:13-14.

41. Rahlfs's edition of the Old Greek is similar: ἐπὶ τῶν νεφελῶν τοῦ οὐρανοῦ ὡς υἱὸς ἀνθρώπου ἤρχετο; Alfred Rahlfs, *Septuaginta* (Stuttgart: Deutsche Bibelgesellschaft, 1996).

These three passages (8:38; 13:26–27; 14:61–65) seem to clearly connect the phrase "the Son of Man" with imagery from Daniel 7:13-14. And here in 14:63-65, the response of those who hear Jesus identifying himself with the "one like a son of man" from Daniel 7:13 who would come "with the clouds of heaven" parallels the reaction of the scribes in 2:7. The high priest tears his clothes and accuses Jesus of blasphemy, and others present begin to spit on him and strike him. Throughout Mark's Gospel, "the Son of Man" is often a climactic element to the passage in which it appears (2:10, 28; 8:38; 9:12; 13:26–27; 14:21, 41–42, 60–65), so Mark may have intentionally reserved the strongest reaction to Jesus's appropriation of Daniel 7 imagery until the climax of the conflict in his narrative (Mark 14:61-64).

Mark's first use of "the Son of Man" in 2:10 and, especially, his final use in 14:62, with the latter clearly indicating an allusion to Daniel 7, should guide our reading of this expression elsewhere. In both his early and later ministry, Jesus faces the accusation of blasphemy (2:1-12; 14:61-65). And each time, he uses the phrase "the Son of Man" for himself (2:10; 14:62). The question we must consider is this: regardless of the historical circumstances, the traditions, and the sources that Mark may or may not have used, *is it likely that Mark, as a careful and competent author, is employing this phrase with different meanings across his Gospel?*[42] No, we believe it is more likely that the phrase "the Son of Man" had already come to be understood by Mark's audience as identifying Jesus with the exalted figure of Daniel 7 and that Mark intends for his readers to make this identification as he uses this title throughout his Gospel. Our goal, once more, is not to explore the question of whether the so-called historical Jesus himself had Daniel 7 in view when he spoke this phrase. Instead, we are interested primarily in what the author meant by it and how his original audience would have understood it. We recognize that what Mark expresses about Jesus's identity may not settle questions about Jesus's own historical use of this phrase. But if

---

42. See the previous discussion, "Mark's Competence as an Author," in chapter 3 (pp. 39-46).

the function of "the Son of Man" in Mark 8:38; 13:26; and 14:62 is to allude to Daniel 7—and there is good reason to think it is—then it is likely that Mark would have had this allusion in view when incorporating the phrase elsewhere in his Gospel. It would be peculiar to assume that Mark utilized the Daniel 7 background for only *some* of these Son of Man references while muting that background for others. Instead, we believe Mark intends a consistent understanding of this phrase throughout his Gospel. Therefore, anyone who accepts an allusion to Daniel 7 in Mark 14:62 (or 2:10 or 8:38 or 13:26–27) should have no significant objection to Mark's audience inferring an identification between Jesus and the "one like a son of man" in Daniel 7. A sharp distinction between the use of this phrase in 10:45 and 14:62, thus, is not tenable.

The Use of "the Son of Man" in Mark 10:45

Turning to Mark 10:45, we recognize a few potential objections to a Daniel 7 allusion in this verse. First, Mark 10:45 does not exhibit the similarities with Daniel 7 that Mark 14:61–65 does. There is, in fact, no lexical overlap between the LXX text of Daniel 7:13–14 and Mark 10:45 apart from "(the) son of man" ([ὁ] υἱὸς [τοῦ] ἀνθρώπου) and the verb "came" or "coming" (ἔρχομαι). Even in these two similarities, the Daniel 7 (LXX) passage lacks the definite article(s) for "son of man" (υἱὸς ἀνθρώπου) and uses a different tense for the verb "coming" (ἔρχομαι).[43] Additionally, a Daniel 7 background may seem to contradict Jesus's statement that he came "not to be served" (Mark 10:45). In Daniel 7:14, this "one like a son of man ... was given dominion and glory and kingship that all the peoples, the nations, and languages would *serve* him" (emphasis added). Daniel 7 describes this figure as being served, but "the Son of Man" in Mark 10:45 did not come to be served.

---

43. Rahlfs's edition of the LXX presents the Old Greek reading as ἤρχετο (imperfect tense) and the Theodotion reading as a paraphrastic present participle (ἐρχόμενος) with the imperfect ἦν. Mark 10:45 uses the aorist indicative ἦλθεν.

Therefore, some may suggest that Daniel 7 does not make sense as a background for Mark 10:45.

But these objections are not convincing. If we consider the features of Mark 10:45 and its immediate context (esp. 10:42-44) in light of our previous discussion of 2:10 and 14:62, then the plausibility of Daniel 7 as a background for 10:45 is significantly strengthened. First, the intensifying function of "for even" (καὶ γάρ) described in the previous section indicates a literary parallelism between the greater (Jesus) and the lesser (disciples) that makes more sense if "the Son of Man" has an exalted rather than humble connotation. In 10:43-44, Jesus has juxtaposed the notions of glory and honor with humility and service. Here, in the climactic discourse of the Journey section (10:32-45), Jesus explains the necessity of humility and service on the part of the disciples. He teaches them that *even* the Son of Man—portrayed with "human" glory and honor *par excellence* in Daniel 7—*even he* came not to be served but to serve and to give his life as a ransom for many. In this way, Mark 10:45 connects the pinnacle of glory and honor (represented by this Son of Man) with the highest expression of service (giving his life). Reading "the Son of Man" in 10:45 with the sense of human frailty we find in Psalms or Ezekiel or as referring to humanity in general does not seem to fit the context of Mark 10:43-45. Even Vermes's understanding of the phrase as a modest or euphemistic circumlocution contradicts both the intensifying "even" (καί) that begins this statement and the connection between the height of honor and the height of service.

Further connections between Mark 10:45 and Daniel 7 become evident as we examine the broader context of each passage. Brant Pitre has observed that several parallels to Daniel 7 appear from James and John's request in 10:35-40.[44] Pitre notes the following similarities with Daniel 7:

---

44. Brant Pitre, "The 'Ransom for Many,' the Exodus, and the End of the Exile: Redemption as the Restoration of All Israel (Mark 10:35-45)," *Letter & Spirit* 1 (2005): 41-68, esp. 43-49.

At this point, the parallels are few, but strong: images of the disciples "sitting," presumably on thrones (Mark 10:37) [cf. Dan. 7:9], with a "Son of Man" (Mark 10:45) [cf. Dan. 7:13] who has been given "glory" (Mark 10:37) [cf. Dan. 7:14]—all of these make it reasonable to suggest that James and John appear to view Jesus as the royal "one like a Son of Man" [Dan. 7:13] and themselves as the (soon-to-be) exalted "saints of the Most High" [Dan. 7:18, 21–22, 25, 27]. Hence, their request establishes a theme of eschatological rule and glorification, and this theme is not completed until Jesus' explicit mention of the Son of Man in Mark 10:45 hearkens back to the thrones and glory of Daniel 7.[45]

Pitre argues Jesus's words in Mark 10:45 reveal that

the messianic Son of Man will give his life in the eschatological tribulation in order to release ("ransom") the scattered tribes of Israel (the "many") from their exile among the Gentile nations. That is, he will give his life, in a kind of new Passover [cf. 14:12–26], in order to bring about a New Exodus: the long-awaited return from exile.[46]

Some of the parallels Pitre cites may be more convincing than others, but the cumulative weight is noteworthy. Morna Hooker also finds in Daniel 7 a background both for the expression "the Son of Man" (whom she reads as a corporate entity in the context of Dan 7) and for the phrase "to give his life as a ransom for many":

Nevertheless, because the Son of man [in Dan 7:13] is a corporate figure, we must recognize that while the destiny of the saints as a whole is to move through suffering to glory [cf. Dan. 7:21–22], the destiny of particular individuals may vary considerably: for some it meant death, and if the author's hope were ever fulfilled, it would be truly said of them that they served their

---

45. Pitre, "The 'Ransom for Many,'" 44.
46. Pitre, "The 'Ransom for Many,'" 45.

fellows and gave their lives as a ransom that God might save his people. ... These are the few whose lives were given for the many, and whose deaths proved their obedience to God. ... If Jesus is now seen as fulfilling the role of the Son of man, the startling paradoxes of Mark 10.45 are, after all, comprehensible. As Son of man he is destined to pass through suffering and death [cf. Dan 7:21, 25] to glory and authority [cf. Dan. 7:14, 18, 22, 27]; but since he alone is the Son of man, it is part of his destiny also to serve others and to give his life as a ransom for them.[47]

Here Hooker shows how the concept of the Danielic "Son of Man" may have become associated with service and suffering.[48] To reject a Danielic background for Mark 10:45 altogether, one must dismiss not just some but all of these parallels. Furthermore, to reject such a background one must also downplay, it would seem, the evidence for an allusion to Daniel 7:13 in *any* of the Markan occurrences of "the Son of Man," including the most obvious references in Mark 13:26 and 14:62. But it seems unlikely that there is no allusion at all in any of these cases. It is far more plausible that Daniel 7 is relevant to Mark 10:45, at least as a background for Mark's use of "the Son of Man" across his narrative. Therefore, we believe that it is reasonable to read Mark 10:45 as clarifying the mission of the glorious human-like figure described in Daniel 7.

Though the phrase "the Son of Man" has proven controversial in several respects, the primary question for us is how Mark intended for his audience to understand the term, especially in 10:45. While

---

47. Hooker, *The Son of Man in Mark*, 142–43.

48. See, e.g., Jesus's statement in Mark 9:12 that "it [is] written concerning the Son of Man that he should suffer many things and be treated with contempt." Daniel 7 does not explicitly indicate that this "one like a son of man" will suffer and be treated with contempt, so some interpreters suggest that Jesus's statement in 9:12 must be referring to some other Scripture. But Hooker's observations about the connection between the suffering saints and the "one like a son of man" in Dan 7 suggest that a reference to another Scripture may not be necessary. Boyarin also finds references to the suffering Son of Man in 7:25–27. Boyarin, *The Jewish Gospels*, 135–45.

Jesus clearly uses this phrase to refer to himself throughout Mark's Gospel, the Evangelist also includes it in several contexts that share verbal and thematic parallels with Daniel 7. The two most obvious parallels are the phrase "coming in/with the clouds" (Mark 13:26; 14:62; cf. Dan 7:13) and the references to great authority, power, and glory (Mark 2:10, 12, 28; 8:38; 9:1; 13:26; 14:62; cf. Dan 7:14). Mark 10:45 itself contains neither parallel, but its immediate context (10:35–44) references both glory and places of honor (esp. 10:37). We cannot reject a Daniel 7 background for Mark 10:45 solely on the grounds that Daniel 7 makes no mention of the suffering of this Son of Man figure. Such a rejection would ignore the other parallels mentioned above between Daniel 7 and the other Markan contexts that employ the "Son of Man" expression. If the Evangelist intends for his readers to associate the label "the Son of Man" with Daniel 7 in *any* of its occurrences, is it not reasonable to expect that his audience would consider this background whenever the phrase appears? We believe it is. And given the themes of honor, glory, and greatness in the immediate context (Mark 10:35–44), Mark likely anticipated that the phrase "the Son of Man" in 10:45 would remind his audience of these themes in Daniel 7. We are not suggesting that those who read Mark 10:45 with no allusion to Daniel 7 cannot understand the verse at all. But we do believe that the vision of Daniel 7, in which "one like a son of man" receives authority and honor and glory and is given an eternal kingdom, clarifies and adds a richness to our appreciation of Jesus's teaching in 10:42–45 about how honor and authority work in the kingdom of God.

"DID NOT COME TO BE SERVED BUT TO SERVE"

Having understood what Mark intends to communicate with the phrase "the Son of Man," we find the reason *why* this "Son of Man" has come. The verb "did not come" (οὐκ ἦλθεν) is followed by a compound infinitive clause indicating purpose: "not ... to be served but to serve."[49] The

---

49. Simon Gathercole has argued that constructions like this ("I have come" + purpose) support the notion of the Christ's preexistence in the Synoptic

infinitives "not ... to be served" (οὐκ ... διακονηθῆναι) and "to serve" (διακονῆσαι) are contrasted by the conjunction "but" (ἀλλά). The point of this contrast, in view of Jesus's teaching in 10:42-45, is to correct the misconception that the rule of "the Son of Man" would follow the pattern of those who rule the nations. *Being served* was not the purpose for which the Son of Man came. The Son of Man came to serve others.[50]

Interestingly, every other occurrence of the verb for "serve" (διακονέω) in Mark's Gospel includes Jesus as the object of serving. In 1:13, angels *serve* Jesus while he is in the wilderness. In 1:31, the mother-in-law of Simon begins to *serve* Jesus and his disciples after being healed by Jesus. In 15:41, three women—Mary Magdalene, Mary the mother of James and Joses, and Salome—are said to have followed and *served* Jesus in Galilee. But these examples do not contradict Jesus's statement in 10:45. In none of these examples does Jesus *compel* the service rendered to him like the pagan rulers mentioned in 10:42. In 1:13, the angels, who are described elsewhere in the New Testament as "servant (λειτουργικά) spirits sent for ministering (διακονία)" (Heb 1:14, our translation), are simply doing their job. In Mark 1:31, the service rendered to Jesus is either a demonstration that the healing was effective (i.e., Simon's mother-in-law now resumes her regular activity, which in this setting would be to serve those she is hosting), or it is an expression of gratitude for how Jesus himself had first *served* this woman by healing her. Indeed, it may be both. And in 15:41, the mention of service rendered to Jesus in Galilee is probably a reference to material support (food and shelter) that Jesus received as he was

---

Gospels; Simon Gathercole, *The Preexistent Son: Recovering the Christologies of Matthew, Mark, and Luke* (Grand Rapids: Eerdmans, 2006). But Gathercole's argument has received significant criticism. Yarbro Collins and Collins, in *King and Messiah as Son of God*, esp. 123-26, argue, for example, that the meaning of these constructions is idiomatic rather than literal—an objection that Gathercole himself anticipates. For Gathercole's caveat about an idiomatic sense of the phrase, see *The Preexistent Son*, 87.

50. For the motif of servanthood in Mark, see Santos, *Slave of All*, chapters 3-5.

serving others through his preaching, teaching, and healing. None of these instances of service to Jesus conflict with the statement in 10:45 that he did not come to be served. Jesus at no point compels this service, nor does he indicate it is his goal. Instead, when others do serve Jesus in Mark's Gospel, this service is usually a response to Jesus's mission of helping others.

Mark has repeatedly demonstrated that Jesus's concern was to use his power for the benefit of others rather than for his own glory. He describes Jesus as being moved to help the leper in 1:38. Jesus has compassion for the crowds seeking him in 6:34. Jesus frequently redirects honor toward God (3:28–29, 35; 4:26, 30; 5:19; 9:37). Some scholars even suggest that the so-called "secrecy" motif, long noted as distinctive to Mark's story about Jesus, is evidence of Jesus's humility.[51] There is a real sense in which Jesus has not come to draw attention to himself. He has not come to proclaim his own kingdom but the kingdom *of God* (1:15). Jesus is, of course, central to the kingdom of God. In fact, Mark portrays him as the king (11:9–10; cf. 15:16–20, 32). But Jesus does not claim or request honor for himself, unlike the rulers among the nations (10:42). This emphasis on Jesus's mission to serve others is especially significant if Mark is writing in the shadow of the Neronian persecution, as we suggested in chapter 2. Mark's readers would then have a striking counterexample in the cruelty and self-indulgence of Nero to whom they could compare Jesus.[52]

In our discussion of the phrase "the Son of Man," we considered whether the statement that Jesus did not come to be served (Mark

---

51. Adam Winn, *Reading Mark's Christology under Caesar: Jesus the Messiah and Roman Imperial Ideology* (Downers Grove, IL: IVP Academic, 2018), 119–130; Winn, "Resisting Honor: The Markan Secrecy Motif and Roman Imperial Ideology," *JBL* 133, no. 3 (2014): 583–601; David Watson, *Honor Among Christians: The Cultural Key to the Messianic Secret* (Minneapolis: Fortress, 2010).

52. See Suetonius Tranquillus, *Suetonius: The Lives of Caesars, The Lives of Illustrious Men*, trans. J. C. Rolfe, The Loeb Classical Library vol. 1 (Cambridge, MA: Harvard University Press, 1914), 371–85, for some examples of Nero's atrocious behavior.

10:45) was inconsistent with a Danielic background (esp. Dan 7:14). We explained why the parallels between Daniel 7 and Mark 10:35–45 outweigh this apparent inconsistency, but there is more to be said about what "did not come to be served" means. The "one like a son of man" in Daniel 7:13 is a glorious and exalted human-like figure who is said to be served (יְפַלְחוּן; λατρεύουσα; Theodotion: δουλεύσουσιν) by the nations (v. 14). It is easy to point to the English word "serve" in most translations of both Mark 10:45 and Daniel 7:14 and infer a contradiction between these two figures. The Danielic "one like a son of man" is served by "all the peoples, the nations, and languages," yet the "Son of Man" in Mark 10:45 "did not come to be served." But there is no actual contradiction between Daniel 7:14 and Mark 10:45. The Aramaic verb פלח (Dan 7:14, MT) carries a different connotation from διακονέω in Mark 10:45. The Aramaic פלח usually translates into Greek with verbs like λατρεύω (Dan 7:14, LXX), ὑποτάσσω (Dan 7:27, LXX), or φοβέομαι (Dan 3:17, LXX) rather than διακονέω.[53] Each time פלח appears in Daniel (3:12, 14, 17–18, 28; 6:1, 20[MT]; 7:14, 27), it seems to have a cultic sense or imply reverence and honor directed toward God. The Greek verb in Mark 10:45 (διακονέω), on the other hand, usually conveys the idea of physical help, assistance, or support.[54] Mark 10:45 does not indicate that no one would ever serve, support, or help the Son of Man. Nor does this verse suggest that the Son of Man will not receive worship, reverence, or honor (Dan 7:14) when he comes "in the glory of his Father ... with the clouds of heaven" (Mark 8:38; 14:62; cf. 13:26). Instead, Jesus is clarifying here that the sort of honor and service described in Daniel 7:13–14 is not the *purpose* for which he has come. The *purpose* for which Jesus has come is to serve and to give his life. He is slave of all (cf. Mark 10:44). And *because of* this servanthood, he receives "dominion and glory and kingship that all the peoples, the nations, and languages would serve

---

53. The Theodotion version of Greek Dan 7:14 does use "they will serve him" (δουλεύσουσιν). However, the context seems to indicate a cultic connotation.

54. This is certainly the case in Mark's Gospel (1:13, 31; 10:45; 15:41). See the discussion of this verb in the section on "the Son of Man" above.

him" (Dan 7:14; cf. Phil 2:9). The disciples expect Jesus to be honored and served. James and John actually seek to participate in this honor (10:35–37). Reading Daniel's vision, it is hard to blame the disciples for this expectation. But their mistake, which Jesus corrects in 10:42–45, was to presume that the glory and honor and "service" (פלח) given to the one like a Son of Man (Dan 7:13–14) were the *goal* or *purpose* of his mission rather than the natural *outcome*. Jesus reorients his disciples' perspective on honor and service by clarifying, "For even the Son of Man *did not come to be served but to serve*." There is nothing wrong with receiving proper honor, but Jesus wants those who follow him to know that true honor in the kingdom of God presupposes denying oneself for the sake of others.

"AND TO GIVE HIS LIFE AS A RANSOM FOR MANY"

Having clarified that *even the Son of Man* did not come to be served but to serve, Jesus then specifies the ultimate extent of his serving: "to give his life as a ransom for many." This phrase unpacks and further describes the infinitive "to serve" (διακονῆσαι), highlighting the depth to which the Son of Man is willing to go in serving others. The word employed here for "life" (ψυχή) often refers to the individual self or person rather than someone's lifetime or lifespan.[55] That is, "to give his life" does really mean "to be killed" (cf. 8:31; 9:31; 10:34) and not simply "to dedicate his lifetime" to some cause or purpose, as we often use the phrase today.

The idea of "giving," "giving up," or "losing" of one's life occurs in a few places in Mark's Gospel, but 8:35–37 is one of the more notable instances because of its location after the very first passion prediction (8:31). There Jesus teaches that his followers must each be willing to "give up" or "lose" his "life" (ἀπολέσει τὴν ψυχὴν αὐτοῦ, 8:35). The

---

55. The preferred Greek root for the few instances in which a lifestyle or lifetime is spoken of seems to be either βίος or ζωή rather than ψυχή, sometimes used in the genitive with the headwords ἡμέραι or ἔτη (see, e.g., Wis 4:9; 5:4; 4 Macc 8:8; 1 Tim 2:2; Shepherd of Hermas, *Mandate* 11.7, 16 [43.7, 16]).

phrases for "lose his life" in 8:35 and "give his life" in 10:45 may not be enough on their own to indicate an inclusio, but they at least contribute to the unity of 8:27–10:45 around the theme of sacrificial service. Mark 10:45 further parallels 8:35–37 with the idea of "exchange." In Mark 8:37, Jesus asks, "What can a person give [δοῖ] in exchange [ἀντάλλαγμα] for his life [ψυχή]?" And in 10:45, Jesus declares that he will "give" (δοῦναι) his own life (ψυχή) as a ransom in exchange for (ἀντί) many.[56] These parallels speak to the literary cohesiveness and unity of Mark 8:27–10:45 and highlight the thematic significance of the passion prediction cycles for interpreting Mark's Gospel as a whole.[57]

The phrase "as a ransom for many" is a point of disagreement among interpreters. We could ask numerous questions about the implications of this phrase, but we must recognize that neither the content nor context of this verse provides direct answers to many of these questions.[58] The word for "ransom" (λύτρον) is relatively rare in the New Testament.[59] It occurs only here and in the Matthean parallel (Matt

---

56. The prepositional phrase ἀντὶ πολλῶν modifies the noun λύτρον rather than the infinitive δοῦναι, thus functioning adjectivally, as hinted by its distance from the infinitive δοῦναι and its proximity to the noun λύτρον. See Rodney Decker, *Mark 9–16: A Handbook on the Greek Text,* Baylor Handbook on the Greek New Testament (Waco, TX: Baylor University Press, 2014), 72.

57. We discussed the unity of 8:27–10:45 (and 8:22–10:52, if we incorporate the episodes of Jesus healing blind men as an inclusio around 8:27–10:45) in chapter 3 in the section, "Mark's Competence as an Author." There we also discussed the pattern within each of the passion prediction cycles (Jesus's prediction, the disciples' misunderstanding, Jesus's correction) and Mark's use of the word ὁδός throughout this section.

58. For example, the most common question asked about this metaphor is probably, "To whom is this ransom paid?" See Appendix II for a short survey of how interpreters have tried to answer some of these questions throughout history.

59. The word "as" in the phrase "as a ransom," which indicates an object-complement relationship between "his life" and "ransom," is not explicit in the Greek text (δοῦναι τὴν ψυχὴν αὐτοῦ λύτρον ἀντὶ πολλῶν) but is implied by the two direct objects "his life" and "a ransom." This object-complement construction is a relationship between two nouns where the complement

20:28), along with a compound form (ἀντίλυτρον) in 1 Timothy 2:6. The cognate noun λύτρωσις and its compound form ἀπολύτρωσις, both usually translated as "redemption," are more frequent, with thirteen occurrences in the New Testament.[60] If we consider the other cognates of λύτρον in the New Testament, we find twenty occurrences of its root in total.[61] All of these words are conceptually related. For example, a "ransom" (λύτρον) is what is usually paid or given to accomplish "redemption" (λύτρωσις). These meanings fit well with the usage of this root in the LXX (see, e.g., Exod 21:30; 30:11-16; Lev 25:51-52; Num 3:12; Prov 13:8). While λύτρον often translates as "ransom," it may be helpful to think of λύτρον more as the "redemption price" paid to redeem someone or something.

The *situation* of redemption, that is, the situation *from which* someone or something is redeemed, varies throughout the Old Testament. Slaves are redeemed from slavery (Lev 19:20),[62] land is redeemed from sale (Lev 25:23-28), Israelites are redeemed from hired service (Lev 25:47-55), tithes are redeemed from being offered to God (Lev 27:31), and the firstborn of Israel are redeemed from service to God (Num 3:12; 18:15). In the New Testament, on the other hand, the situation of redemption is seldom made explicit. Though the people of God are always the object of redemption (what is redeemed) in the New Testament, the text rarely mentions *from what* they are redeemed. Ephesians 1:7 and Colossians 1:14 explain redemption simply as "the forgiveness of sins." Titus 2:14 speaks of redemption "from all lawlessness." Hebrews 9:15 mentions "redemption of transgressions"

("ransom") predicates something about the direct object ("his life"). A quite literal translation of this phrase would be, "to give his life [to be] a ransom."

60. Occurrences of λύτρωσις are Luke 1:68; 2:38; Heb 9:12. Occurrences of ἀπολύτρωσις are Luke 21:28; Rom 3:24; 8:23; 1 Cor 1:30; Eph 1:7, 14; 4:30; Col 1:14; Heb 9:15; 11:35.

61. These other cognates include the verb λυτρόω ("I redeem, liberate," Luke 24:21; Titus 2:14; 1 Pet 1:18) and the noun λυτρωτής ("redeemer," Acts 7:35).

62. For the connection between "ransom" (λύτρον, 10:45) and slavery ("slave of all [πάντων δοῦλος]," 10:44), see Marcus, *Mark 8-16*, 749-50.

(ἀπολύτρωσιν τῶν … παραβάσεων). Finally, 1 Peter 1:18 mentions redemption "from your futile way of life." If we understand each of these verses as describing the *situation from which* people are redeemed, then the concept of redemption seems figurative rather than literal. In other words, the New Testament primarily uses the literal, Old Testament concept of *transactional* redemption as a metaphor for God redeeming his people from sins, lawlessness, transgressions, and a futile lifestyle.

Since the condition *from which* the "many" are ransomed or redeemed is not made clear in Mark 10:45, it seems safe to presume that it is figurative here as well. That is, the "ransom" in Mark 10:45 should not be thought of in a literal sense as if it were a literal price paid in a literal transaction. Instead, Mark shows Jesus employing the figure of ransom and redemption mainly to describe the effect of his death. Through his death, Jesus becomes the way that "the many" are redeemed—presumably *from* death and presumably *by* God. If the "ransom" in Mark 10:45 is a metaphor, then common questions like, "To *whom* is this ransom being paid?" probably miss the point. Mark's focus in this verse is not *to whom* the payment is made. Timothy Howerzyl summarizes the same conclusion after offering several chapters on the relationships among metaphor, reality, and the linguistic background of Mark 10:45: "[discussions] of the recipient of the payment [are] almost certainly beyond the intention of the metaphor as we find it in the Gospel accounts."[63] We should instead understand this metaphor to mean that the death (and rising again) of Jesus is how God's people can finally be released from the judgment and penalty for their sin and disobedience so that they can return to their rightful Master.

The preposition "for" (ἀντί) in this phrase naturally collocates with "ransom" (λύτρον) since both words include the connotation of "exchange" (recall ἀντίλυτρον in 1 Tim 2:6). This preposition is one of

---

63. Timothy Howerzyl, "Imaging Salvation: An Inquiry into the Function of Metaphor in Christian Soteriology, with Application to Mark 10:45 and the Metaphor of Ransom" (PhD diss., Fuller Theological Seminary, 2015), 244.

the rarest in the New Testament, occurring only seventeen times (Matt 2:22; 5:38 [2x]; 17:27; 20:28; Mark 10:45; Luke 11:11; John 1:16; Rom 12:17; 1 Cor 11:15; Eph 5:31; 1 Thess 5:15; Heb 12:2, 16; Jas 4:15; 1 Pet 3:9 [2x]) outside of the idiomatic ἀνθ᾽ ὧν ("because") construction. The primary senses of ἀντί in the New Testament are "in place of" or "in exchange for," two very similar ideas. Adding a slightly different connotation, BDAG lists Matthew 17:27; Mark 10:45 // Matthew 20:28; and Genesis 44:33 (LXX) as examples of ἀντί "indicating a process of intervention," presumably for the benefit of the object.[64] The connotation of benefit or intervention indicates that ἀντί is sometimes equivalent to ὑπέρ ("in behalf of, for the sake of"; cf. ὑπὲρ πολλῶν in Mark 14:24). The sense of benefit is a somewhat more abstract extension of substitution or exchange. However, the respective contexts of each of the biblical texts cited by BDAG (Matt 17:27; Mark 10:45 // Matt 20:28; Gen 44:33 [LXX]) do not demand this more abstract sense. Genesis 44:33 (LXX), in particular, seems to indicate substitution: "Now, then, I will remain with you as a servant instead of (ἀντί) the child." Concerning Matthew 17:27, Murray Harris argues that ἀντί simply stands in for the dative case to add grammatical variety and that ἀντί in this verse indicates substitution.[65] Regarding Mark 10:45, we have noted above that the use of "ransom" (λύτρον) implies a context of exchange, and so the broader meaning of benefit or intervention for ἀντί is not necessary here either. It seems clear, then, that the purpose toward which Jesus is marching "on the way" toward Jerusalem, at least in part, is to give up his own life in exchange for the lives of "many" others.

Who then are the "many" (πολλῶν) in Mark 10:45? The word πολύς may be used here in a Semitic manner, comparable to πᾶς, with its extensity in view. Rodney Decker observes the interchange between πᾶς and πολύς in Isaiah 53:6, 12 (LXX) as well as in Romans 5:12, 15.[66]

---

64. BDAG, 88, s.v. ἀντί.

65. Murray J. Harris, *Prepositions and Theology in the Greek New Testament: An Essential Reference Resource for Exegesis* (Grand Rapids: Zondervan, 2012), 51–52.

66. Decker, *Mark 9–16*, 72.

These examples show that when employed with attention to extensity, πολύς could mean something equivalent to πᾶς.[67] But even more prominent than the conceptual equivalence between πᾶς and πολύς is the *contrast* between the one person ("the Son of Man") who gives his life and the "many" who benefit.

Some interpreters find a connection in πολλῶν to the servant song of Isaiah 52:13–53:12, suggesting an Isaianic background for Jesus's mission to give his life as a ransom for many. The word "many" (πολύς, LXX) occurs three times in the final two verses of this Isaiah passage.

> From the trouble of his life he will see; he will be satisfied. In his knowledge, the righteous one, my servant, shall declare *many* (πολλοῖς) righteous, and he is the one who will bear their iniquities. Therefore, I will divide to him a portion among the *many* (πολλούς), and with the strong ones he will divide bounty, because he poured his life out to death and was counted with the transgressors; and he was the one who bore the sin of *many* (πολλῶν) and will intercede for the transgressors. (Isa 53:11–12, emphasis added).

It is not the word "many" alone but also the idea of a single servant acting for the sake of many others that connects this Isaianic text and Mark 10:45. In this passage, the singular servant will "declare many righteous" and will "bear their iniquities" (Isa 53:11). This singular servant "bore the sin of many," and he will "intercede for the transgressors" (v. 12). The servant also "poured out his life to death" (v. 12) for

---

67. The potential interchangeability and equivalency between these two words is attested even in Mark 10:44–45, as πᾶς (v. 44) and πολύς (v. 45) are employed in these two verses and both describe the beneficiary of service. Additionally, the phrases containing these two words ("slave of all" in v. 44, and "ransom for many" in v. 45) resonate with each other in that both phrases (especially the words "slave" and "ransom") have the practice of slavery in view, which was of part of everyday life for Mark's original audience (see Kaminouchi, *'But It Is Not So Among You,'* 208). Slavery terms and images (δοῦλος, διάκονος, and λύτρον) are repeatedly employed in vv. 42–45.

the many, which is strikingly similar to how Jesus will "give his life as a ransom for many" (Mark 10:45).

Another feature often cited to connect Mark 10:45 to Isaiah 52:13–53:12 is the "sin offering" (אָשָׁם; περί ἁμαρτίας in LXX) mentioned in 53:10 (cf. Lev 5:14–19; Num 5:5–8), which provides a conceptual parallel for the λύτρον in Mark 10:45.[68] On the conceptual parallels between Mark 10:45 and Isaiah, David Garland rightly notes, "The ransom saying in 10:45 weaves Isaian themes with Daniel 7:13–14 in much the same way Mark knits together biblical passages [viz., Exod 23:20; Isa 40:3; Mal 3:1] in 1:2–3 to interpret one another."[69] Admittedly, most parallels between Mark 10:45 and Isaiah 53 are conceptual rather than direct and verbal. Still, the similarity in the redemptive service of the singular servant for the sake of the many is striking. The sparsity of direct verbal parallels between Isaiah 53 and Mark 10:45 is the primary objection scholars like Morna Hooker and C. K. Barrett have raised against reading Mark 10:45 in light of Isaiah 53.[70] But this objection has been critiqued, rightly in our view, as too demanding of what constitutes a legitimate parallel.[71] We can at least say that Isaiah is a significant influence on

---

68. See Lane, *Mark*, 384. Murray Harris also lists Exod 30:11–16 and Ps 49:7–9 (in addition to Isa 52–53) as possible OT backgrounds for this saying; Harris, *Prepositions and Theology in the Greek New Testament*, 53–54.

69. Garland, *A Theology of Mark's Gospel*, 476.

70. Morna D. Hooker, *Jesus and the Servant: The Influence of the Servant Concept of Deutero-Isaiah in the New Testament* (London: SPCK, 1959); Hooker, *Mark*, 248–49; C. K. Barrett, "The Background of Mark 10:45," in *New Testament Essays*, ed. A. J. B. Higgins (Manchester: Manchester University Press, 1959), 1–18.

71. For responses to this objection, see R. T. France, "The Servant of the Lord in the Teaching of Jesus," *Tyndale Bulletin* 19 (1968): 26–52; Rikki Watts, "Jesus' Death, Isaiah 53, and Mark 10:45: A Crux Revisited," in *Jesus and the Suffering Servant: Isaiah 53 and Christian Origins*, ed. William Bellinger and William R. Farmer (Harrisburg, PA: Trinity, 1998), 125–51. In our section above on the phrase "the Son of Man," we discussed Brant Pitre's article ("The 'Ransom for Many,' the Exodus, and the End of the Exile"), which describes parallels between Dan 7 and Mark 10:35–45. In that article, Pitre also offers an interesting proposal rooted in Dan 9 that Jesus's life is a ransom paid to free the captive tribes of Israel who are still in exile; Pitre, "The 'Ransom for Many,' " 49–53.

Mark's Gospel (cf. Mark 1:2–3), and the conceptual similarities between Isaiah 53 and Mark 10:45 make it likely that the author would have had Isaiah 53 in mind when describing Jesus as suffering and dying for the sake of "many" others.

In the phrase "to give his life as a ransom for many," Jesus explains the depth to which his servanthood extends. Mark depicts Jesus's servanthood in many ways. He restores health (1:31; 1:40–45; 3:5, 10; 5:25–29; 6:56), casts out unclean spirits (1:25–26; 5:1–13; 9:25–27), heals disabilities (2:9–12; 7:32–35; 8:22–25; 10:46–52), and even raises the dead (5:35–43; cf. 9:27). Many of these works he accomplishes with little more than a word (e.g., 1:25; 5:41; 7:29, 34). But he does not stop there. He gives his very life. He holds nothing back; he keeps nothing to himself. He gives everything he has, everything he is. And by giving his own life, he provides the means by which God will redeem his people from sin and death, releasing them from the curse of disobedience to receive eternal life in his kingdom.

CONCLUSIONS REGARDING THE MEANING AND SIGNIFICANCE OF MARK 10:45

Examining the broader context of 10:45, we have seen that the overarching theme of Mark 10:32–45 is that honor and authority work very differently in the kingdom of God (and of his Messiah) than they do among the kingdoms of this world. The core of this contrast is the difference between a mind focused on the things of God and one focused on the things of men (8:33). Jesus has illustrated this contrast throughout the Journey section (8:34–38; 9:35–37; 10:5–9, 13–16, 23–31). The disciples will not grasp who Jesus truly is and what he has come to do until they accept that "it is necessary for the Son of Man to suffer many things ... and to be put to death" (8:31). And they cannot fully appreciate the glory of "the Son of Man" until they understand that he "did not come to be served, but to serve, and to give his life as a ransom for many" (10:45). Anyone who seeks to follow after the Messiah must go where he goes, and the "way of the Lord" that John prepared (1:2–8) leads straight to a cross. With these narrative and thematic contexts

in mind, we offer the following interpretive paraphrase of Mark 10:45:
[*If*] even the Son of Man [*in all his glory and authority*] came to serve
others and willingly laid down his life for the redemption of God's
people, [*then those who wish to follow him must also be willing to serve
others and even to endure a similar fate for his sake*]. We acknowledge that
this paraphrase carries the context of the preceding verses (10:42–44)
into verse 45, but we have already determined that it is impossible to
properly understand the meaning and significance of 10:45 apart from
this context.

Understanding Jesus's teaching about honor and service in the
kingdom of God, we must be careful not to read the correction of James
and John as an outright condemnation of glory and honor. Such a conclusion misses the point of the passage. Jesus does not reprimand James
and John for seeking places of honor and authority. Instead, Jesus is
reorienting their understanding of *how* these things must be achieved:
"whoever would desire to be great among you will be your servant,
and whoever would desire to be first among you will be slave of all"
(10:44). The proper path to honor is *through serving others*. While it
would be stretching the text too far to claim that honor is the inevitable result of service, Jesus is certainly delegitimizing the pursuit of
honor and power for its own sake. At the same time, the service and
suffering mentioned here are more than just hurdles on the path to
power. As Mark Moore has clarified, "Suffering is not the price one
pays on the way to achieving positions of power. *Rather, suffering, particularly through service, is the vocation of all leaders in the kingdom.*"[72]
The idea of achieving honor *through* service, though paradoxical in
the culture of the ancient Mediterranean world (and in ours), is nevertheless in accord with the guidance of the Torah's command to care
for one's neighbor as oneself (Lev 19:18). But the call to die—despite
the previous predictions (Mark 8:31; 9:31; 10:33–34) and the teachings
on discipleship (8:34–38; 9:33–50)—is a call that the disciples could
not yet understand. In Mark 10:42–45, at the climax of his journey to

---

72. Moore, *Kenotic Politics*, 65 (italics original).

Jerusalem, Jesus reveals to his disciples that the "glory" they anticipate will only come after he gives his life as a ransom for many. He further confirms that James and John will indeed share in his suffering and shame.[73] Those who want to share in Jesus's glory must be willing to give everything to follow him. It is one thing to serve (v. 43) and to be "a slave of all" (v. 44), but it is another thing altogether to lay down one's own life for the sake of others (v. 45).

In Jesus's correction of James and John's nearsighted request to take part in his glory, Mark presents Jesus pointing to the highest expression of honor and glory, that of the "one like a son of man" from the vision of Daniel. But even this glorious Son of Man is not too exalted to become a servant of those captive to sickness and disease (1:34), to those possessed by unclean spirits and demons (1:21-28, 34), to those bound in sin and unrighteousness (2:5, 17), and to those trapped in a mindset focused on the things of men (8:33). Even this glorious Son of Man is not too exalted to give his life as a ransom to release these captives to return them to God.

In Mark's Gospel, Jesus lays down his life in the loneliest of circumstances—betrayed by a friend (14:44-45), abandoned by his disciples (14:50), and "forsaken" by his God (15:34). But Mark wants his audience to know that this Jesus will not forsake those who follow him. Jesus has paved the path; he has faced the power of death and has overcome it. Each of the three passion predictions (8:31; 9:31; 10:33-34) and Mark's narrative itself end with a mention of the resurrection (16:1-8). It is because Jesus has defeated death in his resurrection that those who follow after him can walk the path of service and suffering—and even death itself—with the confidence that they will also follow him in glory

---

73. Acts 12:2 mentions the death of James by the sword of Herod Agrippa. Various traditions exist regarding the death of John, including Tertullian's comment that John survived boiling oil only to be exiled; Tertullian, "The Prescription against Heretics," in *Latin Christianity: Its Founder, Tertullian*, ed. Alexander Roberts, James Donaldson, and A. Cleveland Coxe, trans. Peter Holmes, *Ante-Nicene Fathers*, vol. 3 (Buffalo: Christian Literature Company, 1885), 260.

(13:24-27, 32-37; cf. 8:38).[74] Mark wants his audience to know that no shame, no suffering, not even death should deter them from following Jesus because this is the path that Jesus himself walked—this is "the way of the Lord" (1:3; cf. Isa 40:3). The path of a servant, the path of suffering—*this* is the path to glory and honor in God's kingdom because it is the path of Jesus, the Son of Man. And the glory of eternal life in resurrection, which awaits those who leave everything behind to follow him (10:29-30; cf. 8:38), far surpasses any worldly position of honor and authority. Mark wants his audience to know that those who follow Jesus on the path of service and suffering can take comfort both in the future hope of glory and in the present reality that this is the path that our Lord himself trod.

This chapter has attempted to understand the meaning and significance of Mark 10:45 in light of its content and context. Now we turn to examine the function of Mark 10:45 within the narrative of the Second Gospel and to explore its contribution to our reading and appreciation of Mark's story as a whole.

---

74. See, e.g., Robert Stein, *Jesus, the Temple, and the Coming Son of Man: A Commentary on Mark 13* (Downers Grove, IL: IVP Academic, 2014) for the discussion of 13:24-27 and vv. 32-37 as references to Christ's return.

THE FUNCTION
AND CONTRIBUTION OF MARK 10:45

I N THIS CHAPTER, WE WILL argue that Mark 10:45 serves as an indispensable key for unlocking the message of Mark's Gospel. The strategic function of 10:45 within Mark's narrative and its contribution to our appreciation and understanding of the Second Gospel are often underappreciated, despite the relative consensus that this verse is in some general sense important. Our goal in this chapter is to clarify both *why* and *how* Mark 10:45 is so crucial to our reading of Mark's Gospel.

Generally speaking, Mark 10:45 is key for understanding the message of the Second Gospel in that it encapsulates the core emphases of its narrative—Jesus's divine identity (especially as the Danielic Son of Man), the atoning nature of Jesus's death, and the example that Jesus's sacrificial service sets for his disciples (not least Mark's intended audience). Given such integration, we can say that understanding 10:45 properly will enhance our appreciation of Mark's overall message. All of this speaks to the critical importance of 10:45 within Mark's Gospel. But beyond a general discussion of its significance, we will point out three specific factors that indicate the *function* of 10:45 within Mark's Gospel: (1) its highly strategic location within Mark's narrative sequence, (2) its expression of Jesus's final and most explicit purpose statement, and (3) its explication of the purpose of Jesus's death. We should view these three specific factors in organic connection to one another rather than just independently. Ultimately, we must consider their collective weight in order to have a comprehensive understanding of our verse's function. In the preceding chapter, we offered a phrase-by-phrase analysis of Mark 10:45, so it is unnecessary to reiterate our exegetical conclusions here. However, when helpful and needed, some of those conclusions and related details will be revisited, in briefer form. After demonstrating *why* Mark 10:45 is key to understanding the message of the Second Gospel, we will then, in turn, describe *how* this verse *contributes* to our appreciation and interpretation of various components of Mark's narrative, such as the fundamental significance of Jesus's atoning death and of servant-minded discipleship as well as ramifications relating to Mark's narrative integrity, his pervasive use of irony, and the upside-down nature of God's kingdom.

WHY SHOULD WE CARE ABOUT MARK 10:45?

We begin with the claim that Mark 10:45 is key to grasping the message of the Second Gospel. Here we will consider three functions of 10:45 that support this claim: (1) the verse's strategic location within the narrative, (2) its declaration of Jesus's purpose, and (3) its explanation of the meaning behind Jesus's death. These three factors are not independent of one another but interlinked, so we should view them as reinforcing each other. However, for the convenience of the discussion, we will tackle them one by one and then briefly expound their integration.

MARK 10:45 IS STRATEGICALLY LOCATED
WITHIN MARK'S NARRATIVE SEQUENCE

The importance of a verse depends not only on its content but also on where and how it is situated within its larger context. Mark 10:45 is no exception in this regard.[1] This verse concludes the series of three elab-

---

1. See our discussion of how Mark 10:45 relates to its context in the section "Connections between Mark 10:32–45 and the Rest of Mark's Gospel" in the previous chapter, pp. 79–84. The present section builds upon and develops that previous discussion.

orately structured passion prediction cycles occurring across 8:27–
10:45 (8:27–9:29; 9:30–10:31; 10:32–45). Each cycle contains (1) Jesus's
prediction of his own death (8:31; 9:31; 10:33–34), (2) the disciples' failure to grasp the meaning of Jesus's prediction (8:32; 9:32–34; 10:35–41),
and (3) Jesus's corrective teaching on discipleship in response to the
disciples' failure (8:33–38; 9:35–37; 10:42–45)—in the same order in
each cycle. These three cycles are framed by the only two healings of
blindness in Mark's Gospel (8:22–26 and 10:46–52), which together form
an inclusio to the pivotal Journey section (8:22–10:52). These two stories symbolically anticipate the "healing" of the disciples' "blindness"
toward the nature of Jesus's messiahship.[2] The sequence of passion prediction, the disciples' error, and corrective teaching repeated within
each of the three cycles, together with the framing of the Journey section by the only two healings of sight in Mark's Gospel, implies an
intentional design on the part of the author. Within such a deliberately
designed Journey section, Mark 10:45 appears to consummate not just
the immediately preceding verses (10:35–44) but all three cycles (8:27–
10:44) and to provide a climactic moment within the entire Journey
section (8:22–10:52).

Two observations, in particular, support the point that Mark 10:45
is a climactic text within the Journey section. First, this verse finally
explains the reason for the *necessity* of Jesus's suffering and death
noted in the first passion prophecy (esp. "it is necessary" [δεῖ], 8:31).
Second, the rhetorical question near the beginning of the Journey section, "What can a person give in exchange for his life?" (8:37), prepares
the reader for the remarkable statement in this verse that Jesus came
to give *his* life in exchange "for many" (10:45).[3] The connections that
10:45 shares with 8:31 and 8:37, verses located closely together near

---

2. See Mark 8:14–21, especially vv. 17–18, in which Jesus's rebuke of the disciples links the imagery of sight with the notion of understanding: "*Do you not
yet perceive or understand?* Have your hearts been hardened? *Although you have
eyes, do you not see?* And although you have ears, do you not hear?" (emphasis
added). Refer also to Yarbro Collins, *Mark*, 394–95.

3. Hengel, *Studies in the Gospel of Mark*, 142n24.

the beginning of the very first passion prediction cycle (8:27–9:29), imply that Mark has deliberately constructed the whole Journey section in a way that points and moves—even from its outset—toward the ransom saying of Mark 10:45. These connections suggest not only that the three cycles of passion prediction are interlinked but that 10:45 offers a deliberate conclusion to those cycles. Thus, Mark 10:45 is critical for understanding not only the third passion prediction cycle (10:32–45) but also the entire Journey section.

Among these three cycles in the Journey section, the third appears to be the most climactic. There is, for example, more detail in its passion prediction (10:33–34) than in those in the first and the second cycles (8:31; 9:31). It is also in the third cycle that Jerusalem (10:33) is first identified as the location of Jesus's death. Similarly, the description of Jesus's passion is most vivid in this final prediction (vv. 33–34). The inclusion of verse 45 at the end of the third cycle, explicitly stating the purpose of Jesus's mission and the meaning of his death (see below), is another reason to think that among the three, the third one is climactic.[4] The pure and explicit focus on Jesus's suffering across the third cycle (10:32–45) further justifies viewing this last cycle as climactic. Unlike the first two cycles, which contain elements that do not directly and explicitly concern Jesus's passion (see, e.g., 9:14–19; 10:1–12), the third cycle concentrates on Jesus's suffering and death throughout. Within this climactic third cycle (10:32–45), verse 45 in particular presents the culminating moment as already noted above

---

4. For further discussion on the culminating nature of the third passion prediction cycle (10:32–45) within Mark's middle Journey section, see Kaminouchi, 'But It Is Not So Among You,' 42–71 (70–71 for summary). Kaminouchi examines echoes within the three-part pattern of repetition in Mark's middle section (8:27–10:45), which reveals Mark 10:32–45 to be in the climatic position of the Gospel (43). As these echoes are repeated, the slight differences between each echo "create a crescendo" and highlight Jesus's teaching on power and service (57). Kaminouchi's study, he claims, shows that Mark 10:42–45, in particular, culminates "Jesus' teachings in the section of the journey to Jerusalem" (209). For Kaminouchi's discussion of the unit of Mark 10:32–45 itself, see Kaminouchi, 88–156.

and as further indicated by the use of the ascensive καί ("even") at the very opening of the ransom saying, which usually signals some ultimate or emphatic statement that follows.[5]

We have described the critical importance of Mark 10:45 primarily in relation to the *preceding* context within the Journey section. There is, however, another direction to be considered. In addition to providing the climax of the central Journey section of Mark's Gospel, this concluding verse of the three passion prediction cycles also points *forward* to the final section in Jerusalem (Mark 11–16), which is the locus of Jesus's death as a "ransom" payment (10:45; cf. 14:24) and the very place where the details of Jesus's passion predictions (8:31; 9:31; 10:33–34; cf. 9:12–13) find their fulfillment.[6] The strategic function of 10:45 in relation to both its preceding and subsequent contexts in Mark's narrative implies that this verse is indeed a key to the Second Gospel.

MARK 10:45 DECLARES JESUS'S PURPOSE

Mark 10:45 is crucial for understanding the Second Gospel not only because of its strategic location and culminating function, as noted above, but also because it contains the ultimate purpose statement for Jesus's life and ministry. As Stein notes, 10:45 "reveals Mark's understanding of the purpose of Jesus, the Son of Man. The verse explains why he came ... and his God-given commission."[7] Witherington also states, "Unlike in the earlier passion predictions, we have not merely

---

5. Daniel B. Wallace describes the ascensive function of καί as "express[ing] a *final addition* or *point of focus*"; Daniel B. Wallace, *Greek Grammar Beyond the Basics: An Exegetical Syntax of the New Testament* (Grand Rapids: Zondervan, 1996), 670, italics original. See our discussion of the phrase "For Even" in chapter 4 (pp. 86–88).

6. For example, Jesus is betrayed into the hands of men (14:43–46; cf. 9:31; 10:33); suffers many things (14:65; 15:15, 16–20; cf. 8:31; 10:34); is rejected by the elders and the chief priests and the scribes (12:12; 14:1, 43–64; cf. 8:31; 10:33); is handed over to the gentiles (15:1; cf. 10:33); is mocked, spit on, flogged (15:15, 16–20; cf. 10:34), and killed (15:37–39; cf. 8:31; 9:31; 10:34); and rises after three days (16:1–8; cf. 8:31; 9:31; 10:34).

7. Stein, *Mark*, 489.

a statement of what will happen to the Son of Man but a statement of the purpose for his coming [in 10:45]."[8] Jesus, the Son of Man, expresses his purpose in 10:45—not "to be served, but to serve, and to give his life as a ransom for many." And it would be safe to assume that the Evangelist took this purpose statement seriously since he wrote this "Jesus book"[9] not as a neutral, objective historian but as a committed follower of Jesus, as reflected across his narrative (e.g., 1:1; 8:29, 34, 38; 9:41; 10:29-30; 14:61-62).[10]

As we argued in chapter 4, the identity of "the Son of Man," the grammatical subject of the purpose statement in Mark 10:45, seems to correspond to the "one like a son of man" depicted in Daniel 7:13-14. Although the background of this expression is a classic headache for New Testament scholars, the repeated coupling of Danielic imagery of coming with the clouds of heaven and the epithet, "the Son of Man," which is notably close in wording to the "one like a son of man" in Daniel 7 (Mark 13:26 and 14:62), supports this conclusion.[11] The "one like a son of man" is an authoritative figure in Daniel 7:13-14 who approaches "the Ancient of Days (τοῦ παλαιοῦ τῶν ἡμερῶν [7:13]; עַתִּיק יוֹמַיָּא [MT])" and receives universal sovereignty (v. 14). Daniel 7:14 stresses, "And to him was given dominion and glory and kingship that all the peoples, the nations, and languages would serve him; his dominion is a dominion without end that will not cease, and his kingdom is one that will not be destroyed." Early on in his narrative, Mark introduces "the Son of Man" as a figure with supreme power—one having "authority ... to forgive sins" like only Israel's God can (2:10 [cf. vv. 5, 7]) and as the "lord even of the Sabbath," a day consecrated by and for the biblical

---

8. Ben Witherington III, *The Gospel of Mark: A Socio-Rhetorical Commentary* (Grand Rapids: Eerdmans, 2001), 291, with reference to John Painter, *Mark's Gospel* (London: Routledge, 1997), 150.

9. The term is borrowed from Larry Hurtado, *Lord Jesus Christ: Devotion to Jesus in Earliest Christianity* (Grand Rapids: Eerdmans, 2003), chap. 5.

10. As Hengel aptly notes, "Mark only reports history which has undergone the deliberate reflection of faith." Hengel, *Studies in the Gospel of Mark*, 38.

11. See the discussion in the section "The Son of Man" in chapter 4 (pp. 91-98).

deity (v. 28; cf. Exod 20:10–11; Lev 23:3; Deut 5:14; Isa 58:13). In so doing, Mark inseparably links the authoritative "Son of Man" with Israel's one God. However, in Mark 10:45, just before Jesus enters Jerusalem, the Evangelist emphasizes that the mission of this supremely authoritative figure, the Son of Man, is not to receive service from others— even though "all the peoples, the nations, and languages would serve him" (Dan 7:14)—but to serve others and even to die as a ransom for many (Mark 10:45).[12] To serve and give his life as a ransom payment is the purpose of the Son of Man's mission.[13]

To be fair, Mark 10:45 is not the only saying in the Second Gospel that states the purpose of Jesus's mission. Mark 1:24 and 2:17 have the same construction as 10:45, employing ἔρχομαι ("to come") as the main verb followed by an infinitive of purpose:

> Saying, "Leave us alone, Jesus the Nazarene! Have you come to destroy us (ἦλθες ἀπολέσαι ἡμᾶς)? I know who you are—the Holy One of God!" (1:24)

> And when Jesus heard it, he said to them, "Those who are healthy do not have need of a physician, but those who are sick. I have

---

12. Cf. Hooker, *The Son of Man in Mark*, 141.

13. Some scholars (e.g., Winn, "Tyrant or Servant?") note that Mark's emphasis on servanthood as found in 10:42–45 aims to attack Rome and its power-driven rulership. Although such an attack could probably be part of Mark's intent, it appears to be the case that 10:42–45 is more against the Twelve than Rome. In Mark's portrayal, Jesus raises an issue with "Rome" that is lurking within the disciples (vv. 35–41; cf. 8:33, in which Jesus rebukes Peter as "Satan") rather than the empire itself. Some may say that it was a diplomatic way of attacking or negotiating with Rome, but once again, it should not be too quickly dismissed that in Mark's presentation here, Jesus's criticism is directed ultimately toward his disciples rather than the Roman authorities. In addition, we concur with Adela Yarbro Collins, who notes, "The theme of liberation from human tyrants is a minor and subtle one in Mark"; Adela Yarbro Collins, "Mark's Interpretation of the Death of Jesus," *JBL* 128, no. 3 (2009): 550. Yarbo Collins goes on to remark, "The liberation from demonic powers, in contrast, is a major theme" ("Mark's Interpretation," 550).

not come to call the righteous, but sinners (οὐκ ἦλθον καλέσαι δικαίους ἀλλὰ ἁμαρτωλούς)." (2:17)

Mark 1:38, which employs ἐξέρχομαι instead of ἔρχομαι, contains another purpose statement of Jesus, though without an accompanying infinitive: "Let us go elsewhere, into the neighboring rural towns, so that I can preach there also, because I have come out for this very reason (εἰς τοῦτο γὰρ ἐξῆλθον)." Here, the notion of purpose is communicated by the prepositional phrase εἰς τοῦτο (which literally means "for this"). This verse seems less significant than 1:24 and 2:17, however, in that it has more to do with Jesus's reason for "coming out" to the wilderness in a particular instance than the purpose of his overall ministry (see 1:35, which has the verb "depart/come out [ἐξέρχομαι]" in Greek just as v. 38). Nonetheless, given that the cause for Jesus's local ministry as referred to in 1:38 likely has some bearing on his overarching mission, we include 1:38 in this discussion.

Destroying the works of Satan (1:24), calling sinners (2:17), and proclaiming the message of the kingdom (1:38; cf. 1:14–15) each reveals meaningful aspects of Jesus's ministry. Nevertheless, these three purpose statements found toward the beginning of the Galilean section (1:14–8:21) do not have as strategic a location within Mark's narrative sequence as 10:45 (see above). Nor do they explicitly mention the passion of Jesus, one of the most dominant themes in Mark's Gospel, or define its meaning (see below). It is, in fact, not until 8:31 that Jesus begins to speak openly about his impending suffering and death. Thus, these three purpose statements (1:24; 1:38; 2:17) cannot hold the same weight and significance as 10:45. Jesus's statement in 10:45 is not the only purpose statement in the Second Gospel, but it is the most prominent one. When we consider this verse's explicit reference to Jesus's death and its explanation of *why* Jesus must die as well as its strategic placement with respect to both the preceding and subsequent portions of the narrative, it is fair to say that Mark 10:45 is the *ultimate* purpose statement for Jesus's mission within Mark's narrative. Along that line, we agree with Martin Hengel, who viewed Mark 10:45 as "the first passage to put the career of Jesus in the right light."[14] Furthermore, if Mark's Gospel is a form of ancient biography (*bios*), as many scholars today suggest,[15] then we might even say that since Jesus is the main character of this book, his ultimate mission statement in 10:45 comprises the core thrust of Mark's Gospel. And because Mark's intended audience encounters Jesus through the Evangelist's portrayal, the statement of Jesus in 10:45 also hints at the Evangelist's purpose for writing—Mark is encouraging and challenging his audience in trials and suffering to emulate the faithfulness of Jesus through sacrificial service, following their prototype, the supremely authoritative Son of Man who gave his life as a ransom for many.

We have presented so far two specific factors that demonstrate Mark 10:45 as key for understanding the Second Gospel, namely, the highly strategic location of the verse with its consummating function and its highly explicit content as the most outstanding, if not ultimate, purpose statement of Jesus within Mark's narrative. There is one other factor that indicates the critical function of Mark 10:45 within the Second Gospel.

MARK 10:45 ARTICULATES THE MEANING OF JESUS'S DEATH

Mark 10:45 is a key to understanding Mark's narrative because it explains precisely what Jesus will accomplish through his death on the cross. The death of Jesus is the event toward which Mark's narrative has explicitly been marching since the first passion prediction (8:31), and it is hinted from early on in the narrative (see, e.g., the accusation of Jesus as blasphemer in 2:7)—as Martin Kähler famously said, the New Testament Gospels, not least Mark, can be described as "passion

---

14. Hengel, *Studies in the Gospel of Mark*, 142n24.

15. For Mark's genre as a Greco-Roman biography (*bios*), see the discussions in Burridge, *What Are the Gospels?*; Keener, *Christobiography*; Bond, *The First Biography of Jesus*. As the given titles indicate, only Bond's work is focused specifically on Mark.

narratives with extended introductions."[16] With that said, it is interesting that the Evangelist does not reveal the meaning and significance of Jesus's death when it is first mentioned (8:31) or when it finally takes place (15:16–41). Instead, here at the climax of the Journey section, Mark explains why "it was necessary" (8:31) for the Son of Man to die, so his life could be given as "a ransom for many" (λύτρον ἀντί πολλῶν, 10:45). Jesus's death was foreshadowed from early in the narrative (2:7; 3:6, 19), and he announced his impending suffering repeatedly on his journey (8:31; 9:31; 10:33–34; cf. 9:12–13). But only as of 10:45 does he disclose the *reason* for his suffering and death. The three cycles of passion prediction conclude here with the mention of "a ransom for many" (10:45), and this concluding phrase not only foretells what is going to take place in Jerusalem but also specifies its significance. While the particular manner in which Mark utilizes the ransom metaphor is not specified by the Evangelist himself, we can probably agree with Narry Santos, who remarks, "This picture of ransom reveals to the readers that Jesus' passion and death are to be viewed as the price for the liberation of many."[17] Mark's decision to reveal the meaning of Jesus's death at this strategic point in the narrative suggests that he wants his audience to understand all that follows in Jerusalem (chaps 11–16) and especially Jesus's death (15:16–41) *in light of the statement in 10:45.*

Although 10:45 does not offer much in the way of literal correspondence to the Song of the Suffering Servant (Isa 52:13–53:12 LXX), the notion of someone's death benefiting an extensive number of people ("a ransom for many") combined with the servanthood theme and related terminology across verses 43–45 (e.g., the cognates διάκονος in v. 43 and διακονέω in v. 45), seems to point to that Isaianic passage.[18] The

---

16. Martin Kähler, *The So-Called Historical Jesus and the Historic Biblical Christ*, trans. Carl E. Braaten (Philadelphia: Fortress, 1964), 80n11. For the significance of Jesus's atoning death in Mark, see our discussion below.

17. Santos, *Slave of All*, 208. See also the discussion of the phrase "as a ransom for many" in chapter 4 (pp. 111–13).

18. See the discussion of the Isaianic background of Mark 10:45 in the section "To Give His Life as a Ransom for Many" (pp. 111–13). For the relevance and

fact that Mark's Gospel begins with the naming of "Isaiah the Prophet" (1:2) and the subsequent citation of Isaiah 40:3 (part of the opening section for Isa 40–55 where the Song of the Suffering Servant belongs; cf. Mark 1:3) lends further plausibility to the claim that Mark 10:45 alludes to Isaiah 52:13–53:12.[19] It seems that in the conclusion to the Journey section at 10:45, the Evangelist intertwines the Son of Man picture of Daniel 7:13–14 with the suffering servant imagery of Isaiah 52:13–53:12, something he has been doing since the first use of the "Son of Man" in the Journey section (8:31), where he links this Danielic epithet with the language and images of suffering reminiscent of Isaiah 52:13–53:12 (see Mark 8:31; 9:12, 31; 10:33; cf. 14:21, 41). In fact, Mark weaves Scriptures together from the beginning of his Gospel. In Mark 1:2–3, he integrates Malachi 3:1, Exodus 23:30, and Isaiah 40:3 under the label, "Isaiah the Prophet" (Mark 1:2). Shortly after, the author links, again, multiple Scriptures (Isa 42:1; Ps 2:7; Gen 22:2, 12, 17) in describing the heavenly voice at Jesus's baptism (Mark 1:11). Mark's composite citation of Old Testament Scripture also appears in 11:17, which references Isaiah 56:7 and Jeremiah 7:11 side by side. In light of Mark's blending of Scripture elsewhere, it is not too surprising to find something similar here at Mark 10:45.

---

importance of the Isaianic framework of New Exodus in understanding Mark 10:45, refer to Watts, "Jesus' Death, Isaiah 53, and Mark 10:45." For the Isaianic New Exodus paradigm in Mark, see Joel Marcus, *The Way of the Lord* (Louisville: Westminster/John Knox Press, 1992); Rikki E. Watts, *Isaiah's New Exodus and Mark* (Tübingen: Mohr Siebeck, 1997). Morten Hørning Jensen, "Atonement Theology in the Gospel of Mark," *Biblica* 100, no. 1 (2019): 84–104, also supports the Isaianic framework in Mark's Gospel yet gives primary attention to the notions of atonement and divine proximity.

19. Mark's references to different passages of Isaiah across his narrative (most clearly, Isa 6:9–10 quoted in Mark 4:12; the naming of "Isaiah" and the following quotation of Isa 29:13 in Mark 7:6–7; the allusion to Isa 66:24 in Mark 9:48; the quotation of Isa 56:7 in Mark 11:17; and the allusion to Isa 13:10/34:4 in Mark 13:24–25) add further weight to the plausibility of the allusion to Isa 52:13–53:12 in Mark 10:45.

Looking backward, Mark 10:45 brings clarity to the threefold passion prediction (8:31; 9:31; 10:33-34), explaining *why* Jesus must die. Looking forward, 10:45 contextualizes the passion that Jesus will face, describing the *significance* of his suffering and death that the Evangelist will narrate. Mark depicts Jesus's death on a Roman cross in great detail. In fact, no other section in the Second Gospel is more detailed or slower paced than the episodes surrounding the crucifixion of Jesus in chapter 15. And yet, *within* the crucifixion scene and the episodes immediately surrounding it, the Evangelist is silent as to the meaning and significance of Jesus's death. Only at the conclusion of the passion prediction cycles in 10:45 and in the Lord's Supper passage (especially 14:24: "This is my blood of the covenant which is poured out for many [τοῦτό ἐστιν τὸ αἷμά μου τῆς διαθήκης τὸ ἐκχυννόμενον ὑπὲρ πολλῶν]") do we find such an explanation.[20] Indeed, without Mark 10:45, the mention of "my blood ... poured out for many" in 14:24 would be relatively oblique. Given that the death of Jesus was already viewed with great significance among the followers of Jesus before Mark's composition,[21] it is most natural to think that the author intended to draw his audience's attention to the explicit statement on the meaning and significance of Jesus's death as found in 10:45.

THE COMPLEMENTARY ORIENTATION
OF THESE THREE FACTORS

We have shown so far that Mark 10:45 is key to understanding the message of the Second Gospel. The function of this verse has been discussed with respect to three particular factors: (1) its highly strategic location and culminating role within the narrative sequence, (2) its expression

---

20. Strauss, *Mark*, 19.

21. Pauline writings such as Romans and Galatians are clear examples of this. The fact that the passion theme penetrates the entire Gospel of Mark (see, e.g., 2:7; 3:6, 19; the threefold passion prediction cycles in 8:27-10:45; the passion narrative in 14-15) is further evidence as well. Regarding the pervasion of the passion theme across Mark's entire Gospel, see Trakatellis, *Authority and Passion*, 149 and *passim*.

regarding the purpose of Jesus's mission, and (3) its articulation of the significance of Jesus's death.[22] The weight of each of these factors is only magnified when they are considered in connection to one another. For instance, crucial components of Jesus's purpose and the meaning of his death obtain utmost significance because of their strategic location at 10:45. At the same time, the strategic location of this verse within the narrative sequence gains prominence because it accommodates the purpose of Jesus's mission and the meaning of Jesus's passion. Also, the explications of the reason for Jesus's mission and the significance of his death overlap, each amplifying the force of the other.

The crucial importance of Mark 10:45 for understanding the Second Gospel is evident given these three factors considered individually and collectively. Moreover, two further considerations add weight to the case above. First, to begin the statement in 10:45, Mark uses an ascensive καί ("even"), implying his intention to highlight the verse's subject matter.[23] Second, given that Mark has a habit of concluding various passages with an impactful statement from Jesus without further elaboration (see 2:17, 22, 28; 3:35; 7:23; 8:21, 26; 9:29; 9:50; 10:31; 11:25; 12:44; 13:37; 14:9), the lack of any subsequent explanation on the saying of 10:45 prior to the next episode suggests that the Markan author indeed regarded verse 45 as significant.

22. For the effect of the notions/images relating to atonement on Mark's original audience in light of their Hellenistic cultural milieu, see the discussions in Martin Hengel, *The Atonement* (Philadelphia: Fortress, 1981); Adela Yarbro Collins, "Finding Meaning in the Death of Jesus," *Journal of Religion* 78, no. 2 (1998): 175–96. For a study focused on Mark 10:45 and the λύτρον word group with a similar orientation, see Adela Yarbro Collins, "The Signification of Mark 10:45 among Gentile Christians," *Harvard Theological Review* 90, no. 4 (1997): 371–82. The cultural relevance and importance of the ransom/atonement concept for Mark's original audience would have likely led them to pay attention to a statement like Mark 10:45, and if so, the significance of the verse in the Second Gospel is further reinforced in connection to the audience's cultural context.

23. See the section "For Even" in the previous chapter (pp. 86–88).

In chapter 3, we discussed Mark's capabilities by considering various features across the narrative of the Second Gospel and concluded
that in the Markan narrative we find a competent author who controlled his story masterfully and efficiently.[24] Mark's competency
implies that integrating the explanation of Jesus's mission with the
meaning of his death at such a strategic location as 10:45 is not coincidental. The critical importance of Mark 10:45 as key to understanding
the message of the Second Gospel is not a conclusion imposed upon
the text. Rather, it reflects the Evangelist's intentional crafting and
structuring of his story. Mark did not employ the statement in 10:45
haphazardly or carelessly. He deliberately assigned critical significance
to this verse as indicated by its prominent content and its strategic
location within the narrative sequence.

HOW DOES MARK 10:45 ENHANCE
OUR READING OF THE SECOND GOSPEL?

We have just shown *in what specific sense* Mark 10:45 is key to understanding the message of the Second Gospel. Both its crucial content
and its strategic placement within the structure of Mark's narrative demonstrate the importance of this key verse. But why does this
matter? What do we gain if we allow 10:45 to guide our reading of
Mark's narrative? *How* does Mark 10:45 contribute to our appreciation
and interpretation of Mark's story centering on who Jesus is and what
he has done? We now intend to answer these questions and, in so doing,
will elaborate on the fundamental significance of Jesus's atoning death
and its inseparable connection to servant-minded discipleship within
Mark's narrative, among other points. So far, we have focused on this
verse's *function* within Mark's narrative arrangement. We draw our
attention now to the *contribution* of 10:45 for interpreting and appreciating Mark's message.

---

24. This discussion in chapter 3 is in the section "Mark's Competence as
an Author" (pp. 39-46).

THE SIGNIFICANCE OF JESUS'S MINISTRY
AND ATONING DEATH

Mark 10:45 contributes to our understanding of the Second Gospel by highlighting the purpose for which Jesus gives his life. We have already discussed above the importance of Jesus's atoning death in Mark's narrative. Mark 10:45 is the first of only two references to the soteriological significance of Jesus's death in the Second Gospel, along with 14:24. And 10:45 describes this significance explicitly at a highly strategic location within the sequence of Mark's narrative. Therefore, it is natural to conclude that the soteriological value of Jesus's death is indeed a crucial concept in Mark's Gospel. Admittedly, Mark does not discuss this concept as frequently as some other New Testament authors like Paul or the author of Hebrews. Nevertheless, he does situate its primary expression in the key location of 10:45 and arranges his narrative in a manner that highlights this verse and, as a result, the significance of Jesus's atoning death.

Mark's two explicit statements regarding the soteriological significance of Jesus's death (10:45; 14:24) are *both* in strategic locations. Mark 10:45, in particular, is placed at the conclusion of the carefully structured threefold passion prediction cycle (8:27–10:45) shortly before Jesus's entry to Jerusalem, the location of his death. Mark 14:24, which explains the significance of Jesus's death as "my blood of the covenant which is poured out for many," is situated at the high point of the Lord's Supper passage, where Jesus reinterprets and reformulates Israel's foundational meal, the Passover, around himself and his impending death. This verse reinforces the atoning significance of Jesus's death that 10:45 has already denoted,[25] thus together preparing for the pas-

---

25. The link between Mark 10:45 and 14:24 is seen from the similar phrases (ἀντὶ πολλῶν in 10:45 and ὑπὲρ πολλῶν in 14:24) and especially from the common notion that Jesus's atoning death benefits multitudes ("many"). At the narrative level, 10:45, as the first explicit statement about the meaning of Jesus's death, sets the tone for how the second of only two such statements in 14:24 should be understood. For discussion of Mark 14:24, see, e.g., Garland, *A Theology of Mark's Gospel*, 478–81.

sion narrative proper (the crucifixion account in 15:16–41), which itself contains no explanation or explicit mention of the soteriological character of Jesus's death. Given that Mark's only two direct comments about the atoning significance of Jesus's death are both located in strategic places within the narrative, it would be safe to conclude that the salvific nature of Jesus's suffering and death is a critical theme for the author. Concerning Mark's theology of atonement, *where* and *how* he highlights this theme is probably more important than his *frequency* in so doing.[26]

While the Markan author does not express the salvific nature of Jesus's death often, its significance is implied by several other elements across his narrative. When we examine these elements, it becomes clear that the Evangelist has arranged his material to underscore the atoning significance of Jesus's death. The following examples, though not comprehensive, demonstrate this point.

A Ministry of Repentance and Forgiveness

Mark's description of John's baptism (1:4) implies the significance of atonement in Jesus's mission. Toward the beginning of his narrative, Mark introduces John the Baptist, characterizing his ministry as a "baptism of repentance *for the forgiveness of sins*" (1:4; emphasis added; cf. v. 5). However, since John's ministry is that of the one preparing "the way of the Lord" (1:3 quoting Isa 40:3; cf. Mark 9:12–13), which in Mark's narrative development turns out to be Jesus's way toward the cross, the forgiveness of sins indicated by John's baptism should be seen as *preparatory* in nature, anticipating the *ultimate* forgiveness that the Lord, Jesus, will bring. In other words, just as the forerunner's ministry concerned forgiveness of sins, Jesus's mission is also related to forgiveness

---

26. See Hengel, *Studies in the Gospel of Mark*, 37–38, 142n24 (cf. 35, 44). Refer also to Evans, *Mark 8:27–16:20*, 125. For implicit references highlighting the importance of Jesus's atoning death in Mark's narrative with attention to the hints at the replacement of the temple by Jesus's death, see Garland, *A Theology of Mark's Gospel*, 481–506; cf. Robert Snow, *Daniel's Son of Man in Mark* (Eugene, OR: Pickwick, 2016), 92–125.

of sins—something that becomes explicit in 10:45. Moreover, Jesus's inaugural proclamation, which demands repentance from his audience (1:15), supplies added weight to this point. The mention of repentance in Jesus's preaching (1:15: "Repent and believe in the gospel!") should be linked to the description of John's ministry, which prepared the way for Jesus (1:2-8, especially v. 3 ["prepare the way of the Lord"]) and in that context offered a baptism of *repentance with reference to the forgiveness of sins* (v. 4). Given the explicit connection between repentance and forgiveness of sins in the forerunner's ministry (v. 4), the reference to repentance in Jesus's inaugural preaching (v. 15) would also connect to the forgiveness of sins. This link between repentance and absolution of sins in the ministry of Jesus is strengthened by the Isaianic background of Mark's opening. Mark's naming of "the prophet Isaiah" (1:2) and the subsequent quotation of Isaiah 40:3 (Mark 1:3), in particular, seem to hint at the relevance of atonement in Mark's Gospel. Isaiah 40:1-11, from which Mark quotes (1:3), concerns the pardoning of sins: "'Comfort; comfort my people,' says your God. 'Speak to the heart of Jerusalem, and call to her, that her compulsory labor is fulfilled, that *her sin is paid for,* that she has received from the hand of Yahweh double *for all her sins*'" (Isa 40:1-2; emphasis added). The notion of absolving sins occurs consistently across Isaiah 40-55 (see, e.g., 43:22-44:8; 44:21-28; 50:1-3; 52:13-53:12; 55:7).[27] Unless we assume that the Markan author disregarded the original context of the Scripture quoted in 1:3, the prominence of forgiveness across Isaiah 40-55 serves to affirm the relevance and significance of atonement within Mark's narrative.

---

27. For the link between the forgiveness of sins and the return from exile as well as application of such a link to understanding Jesus's ministry portrayed in the Gospels, see, e.g., N. T. Wright, *Jesus and the Victory of God*, Christian Origins and the Question of God 2 (London: SPCK, 1996), 268-274. Wright notes the link from Isa 40-55; Lam 4:22; Jer 31:31-34; 33:4-11; Ezek 36:24-26, 33; 37:21-23; Dan 9:16-19, among others.

The Authority to Forgive Sins

The conflict between Jesus and the scribes narrated in Mark 2:1–12 also contributes to the significance of atonement in Mark's Gospel. For one, this passage, which is the first of many controversies in Mark between Jesus and the religious authorities, pertains specifically to Jesus's authority to *forgive sins* (v. 7). Second, the scribes believe that, by claiming to forgive sins, Jesus is appropriating for himself a divine prerogative reserved solely for the God of Israel and that he is thus committing blasphemy (v. 7)—a charge that the religious leaders will later level against him as the grounds for condemning him to *death* (14:64). Furthermore, this pericope includes the very first occurrence of the title "the Son of Man," which is employed in the only two passages that explain *the meaning of Jesus's death* (see 10:45; and 14:21 in the immediate context of 14:24) and is also used in the second half of Mark's narrative predominantly in relation to Jesus's *passion* (e.g., 8:31; 9:9, 12, 31; 10:33, 45; 14:21, 41). Finally, *this very first occurrence of "the Son of Man" in Mark is associated directly with pardoning sins* (esp. 2:5, 10), which was clearly a divine prerogative in the Old Testament and Second Temple literature (Exod 34:6–7; Pss 32:1–5; 51:1–4, 9–10; 85:2; 103:3; 130:4; 2 Sam 12:13; Isa 43:25; 44:22; Dan 9:9; Micah 7:18; Zech 3:4; cf. 1QS 2:8–9; 11:14; CD 2:4–5; 3:18; 4:6–10). These factors, when considered collectively, imply a link between Jesus's death and the forgiveness of sins, the link explicated in 10:45 and confirmed in 14:24.

There are several other passages that deserve mention regarding the significance of atonement in Mark's Gospel. Mark 2:13–17, which immediately follows the episode just discussed (2:1–12) within the same collection of controversies between Jesus and Jewish authorities (2:1–3:6), shows that dealing with sins is at least one part of Jesus's mission, especially in light of his declaration, "I have not come to call the righteous, but *sinners*" (2:17; emphasis added; cf. vv. 15–16). The enigmatic saying of Mark 4:10–12, specifically verse 12 ("lest they turn and it be *forgiven* them" [emphasis added]) situated between Jesus's presentation of the parable of the sower (vv. 3–9) and its interpretation (vv. 13–20), signifies that embracing Jesus and his teaching (vv. 8, 20) has to do, in some way, with the pardoning of sins. And finally, the tearing of the temple veil (most likely the sanctuary veil, 15:38) as Jesus dies on the cross probably alludes to Leviticus 16, which describes the one occasion each year on which this veil would be opened for the Day of Atonement (cf. Heb 6:19; 9:3; 10:20).[28] Each of these passages adds further weight to the significance of atonement in Mark's Gospel.

Atonement and the Temple

Since the temple was the location and visible means of atonement in Israelite worship, replacing the temple would seem to anticipate a new and better means of atonement, specifically, the atonement provided by the Messiah's death (Mark 10:45; 14:24).[29] And indeed, several passages in Mark's narrative do imply the replacement of the temple: (1) the Evangelist's critical stance toward the temple institution and its authorities as seen in Jesus's cursing of the fig tree intercalated with his demonstration in the temple (11:12–25); (2) a series of conflicts between Jesus and the Jewish authorities situated in the temple precinct (11:27–12:37); (3) Jesus's blunt prediction of the temple's destruction (Mark 13, esp. vv. 1–23, 28–31); and (4) several other texts across the narrative (12:33, 38–40; 14:58, 61–65; 15:10–11, 29). Mark's repeated references to forgiveness without mention of the temple's sacrificial system (2:1–12; 11:25) have a similar force.[30] Regarding 11:27–12:37, in particular, one should not overlook the fact that Jesus's conflicts with

---

28. Hengel, *Studies in the Gospel of Mark*, 37–38, 142n24. For further discussion of the importance of Mark 15:38 for the Evangelist's atonement theology, see Jensen, "Atonement Theology in the Gospel of Mark," 99–102.

29. Garland states, "Ironically, it is at Golgotha, the place of the skull, not at the temple, that the ultimate sacrifice for the forgiveness of sins occurs"; Garland, *A Theology of Mark's Gospel*, 480. See also Jostein Ådna, "Jesus' Symbolic Act in the Temple (Mark 11:15–17): The Replacement of the Sacrificial Cult by His Atoning Death," in *Gemeinde ohne Tempel*, ed. Beate Ego, Armin Lange, and Peter Pilhofer, WUNT 2.118 (Tübingen: Mohr Siebeck, 1999), 461–75.

30. See Garland, *A Theology of Mark's Gospel*, 481–506, for further discussion. See also Jensen, "Atonement Theology in the Gospel of Mark"; Yarbro Collins, "Finding Meaning in the Death of Jesus," 176–78.

and refutation of Jewish authorities are located *in the temple* (note the
phrase "in the temple" [ἐν τῷ ἱερῷ] in 11:27 and, again, in 12:35). The
hostile questioning of Jesus by these authorities working in and around
the temple and Jesus's utter repudiation of them in the temple imply
not only their illegitimacy but also that of the temple institution in
and around which they play key roles.

The Necessity of Jesus's Death

The statements that portray Jesus's death as a matter of divine necessity
(δεῖ in 8:31) or scriptural inevitability (14:21, 49; cf. 9:12)[31] also demonstrate the importance of Jesus's atoning death in the Second Gospel.
Likewise, the series of passages foreshadowing, predicting, and por-
traying Jesus's death throughout Mark's narrative (e.g., 2:7; 3:6, 19; 8:31;
9:12-13, 31; 10:33-34; chaps. 14-15) increase the significance of Jesus's
atoning death *by supplementing* those passages that either express its
atoning significance (10:45; 14:24) or imply such significance (see, e.g.,
the passages listed in the preceding "Atonement and the Temple" section). Similarly, the Roman centurion's confession of Jesus as "Son of
God"—the first and only explicit human acknowledgment of Jesus as

---

31. Jesus's prophecy about the details leading to his crucifixion and their
subsequent fulfillment in Mark's narrative (see, e.g., Judas' betrayal [14:18-21,
vv. 43-46], Peter's denial [v. 30, vv. 66-72], and the disciples' abandonment of
Jesus [v. 27, v. 50]) are also noteworthy in relation to the inevitability of his
passion. Since Jesus's words are seen as supremely authoritative and trust-
worthy in Mark's Gospel (e.g., 1:25-28; 8:38; 13:31), Jesus's prediction of his
death and the specific details leading to it, when followed by their fulfillment,
further hint at the necessity of Jesus's passion. The fulfillment of particular
Scriptures in the passion narrative with reference to Jesus's capture and suffering (most explicitly, see Zech 13:7 in Mark 14:27; Ps 22:1 in Mark 15:34) has
a similar implication for the necessity of Jesus's death. Also, we suggest that
the references to Scriptures in the passion narrative serve not only to describe
and justify *how* Jesus died but also to link the related themes of the pertinent
OT Scriptures with the *atoning significance* of Jesus's passion, thus prompting
the interpretation of those Scriptures in light of Jesus's soteriological death

God's Son in Mark—is located *under the foot of the cross* (15:39).[32] The particular location of such a climactic christological confession provides *implicit* support for the significance of Jesus's death. To be clear, these passages do not express or allude to the salvific nature of Jesus's passion themselves, although they do indicate the importance of Jesus's passion in one way or another. Nevertheless, since they are inseparably bound with other components that either express the atoning significance of Jesus's passion (10:45; 14:24) or hint at it within Mark's narrative scheme, it is reasonable to say that these passages, too, ultimately serve to reinforce the significance of Jesus's atoning death, even if only indirectly.

All the above components contribute to Mark's presentation of Jesus's atoning death and reinforce the contribution of Mark 10:45 to our appreciation and understanding of the Second Gospel. Mark 10:45 is the first explication of the meaning of Jesus's passion and provides the foundation for the only other such expression in the narrative in 14:24. Although the various components listed above imply something about Mark's understanding of Jesus's death as atonement, the explicit statement in 10:45 makes those implications discernable and tangible. Without 10:45 (and 14:24, which is built on and confirms 10:45), it would be much harder for Mark's audience, then or now, to grasp the author's atonement theology. In this sense, the contribution of 10:45 to Mark's theology of atonement is undeniable, as is its contribution to how Mark wants his audience to understand the meaning of Jesus's death and to appreciate this narrative in which the passion of Jesus holds a vital position.

---

32. In Mark 8:29, Peter confesses Jesus as the Messiah, but his confession lacks explicit language of divine sonship. Although it is possible that divine sonship is implied in Peter's confession, it must be noted that his confession is portrayed as something deficient in view of (a) his subsequent rejection of the necessity of Jesus's suffering (8:32) and (b) Jesus's blunt rebuke of him as "Satan" and as one "not setting [his] mind on the things of God, but the things of people" (8:33).

THE PROMINENCE OF SERVANT-MINDED DISCIPLESHIP

Mark 10:45 further contributes to our reading of the Second Gospel in that it underscores the necessity of servanthood for those who would follow Jesus. As Tannehill notes on Mark 10:45, "Jesus' death as a ransom is used to explain the nature of Jesus' self-giving service."[33] Mark uses this first of only two explicit comments on the soteriological character of Jesus's death not just to stress its vicarious nature per se but to teach the sort of servanthood that such a death exemplifies. Within Mark's theological and ethical framework, embracing Jesus's atoning death directly and inescapably implies the necessity of self-giving service. As crucial as Christ's atoning death is in Mark's story, servanthood in the footsteps of the Son of Man is just as necessary. One may even say that, according to Mark's understanding, self-giving discipleship *authenticates* our genuine acceptance of Christ's atonement as a ransom for many.[34] Those who eschew self-giving discipleship are spurning Christ's atoning death. At the beginning of the Journey section, Mark clarifies that whoever wants to be a disciple of Jesus must deny themselves and follow the master in his cross-bearing footsteps (Mark 8:34; cf. vv. 35–38)—in that sense, there is no room in Mark's theology of atonement for what Dietrich Bonhoeffer called "cheap grace."[35] Whoever wants to follow the crucified Messiah must also follow his model of profound servanthood.

Servant-Minded Discipleship in the
Third Passion Prediction Cycle (10:32–45)

While Mark 10:45 does imply the vicarious nature of Christ's death, the overall thrust of the context (10:35–44) indicates the primary emphasis is on the example of servanthood that Jesus sets for his followers.

---

33. Tannehill, "The Gospel of Mark as Narrative Christology," 91n15.

34. See the section "To Give His Life as a Ransom for Many" in the previous chapter (see pp. 106–113).

35. Dietrich Bonhoeffer, *The Cost of Discipleship* (New York: Touchstone, 1995), 43–56.

Immediately following the third and final passion prediction (vv. 33–34), the most vivid and detailed among the three (8:31; 9:31; 10:33–34), Mark promotes servanthood by confronting the conceit and selfish ambition exemplified by the pagan rulers (v. 42) and even by Jesus's own disciples (vv. 35–41). These counterexamples seek honor for their own benefit, but Jesus contrasts such selfish pursuits with the upside-down lifestyle of servanthood that he expects from his followers (vv. 43–44) and that he himself embodies (v. 45). He is sharply critical of the worldly pursuit of power, and the criticism here is directed to the Twelve, whose minds are still set on not the things of God but the things of men (10:42; cf. 8:33). The Twelve, who were supposed to symbolize the restoration of the twelve tribes of Israel (cf. 3:13–16), instead exemplify the same worldly mindset that eventually led Israel to sacrifice to pagan deities and false gods, just like the gentile nations (cf. 10:42). In his correction, Jesus bluntly distinguishes between the ways of the pagan kingdoms and the kingdom of God (v. 43: "But it is not like this among you!"). These two operate on incompatible sets of principles. Worldly rulers coerce, threaten, and dominate their subjects (v. 42), ironically exposing their lack of true authority. By contrast, in the kingdom of God, the king himself serves and dies for his people, exercising his supreme authority through radical sacrifice, even at the cost of his own life (v. 45; cf. Phil 2:8). Though Jesus's words, "It is not like this among you" (Mark 10:43), are given in the indicative mood, they carry a hearty imperatival force. Disciples of Jesus must not conduct themselves like the pagan tyrants who are thirsty for power, dominion, and a distorted sense of influence. Instead, Jesus's followers should embody servanthood (vv. 43–44) and even be willing to emulate Jesus's ultimate example of self-sacrifice (v. 45). The servanthood that Jesus embodies in Mark's Gospel is a product of his utter devotion to God. In the same way, when disciples of Jesus give up everything they have and everything they are in order to follow him (cf. 10:28–31), when they deny themselves and take up their crosses—even at the cost of their own lives—they confirm their own devotion to Jesus and to the God he served. Embracing servanthood and self-sacrifice for the sake of Jesus and the gospel is one way that disciples of Jesus actualize and validate their loyalty and faithfulness to Jesus.

Another sign of Mark's focus on servanthood in 10:32–45 is the use of "cup"[36] and "baptism" in verses 38–39. In these verses, Mark repeatedly employs the vivid metaphors for suffering: "Are you able to drink the cup that I drink, or to be baptized with the baptism that I am baptized with? ... You will drink the cup that I drink, and you will be baptized with the baptism that I am baptized with" (10:38, 39). These verses link the suffering of Jesus to that of the disciples, further illustrating that the primary thrust of Mark 10:45 (and 10:32–45) is the promotion of profound servanthood and self-sacrifice as exemplified by Jesus's atoning death and not merely the vicarious nature of Jesus's atonement. This is not to deny the vicarious nature of Jesus's atoning death expressed in Mark 10:45 as "a ransom for many" (cf. 14:24). Jesus's death, in this sense, carries a unique significance that even the glorious martyrdom of his followers (e.g., Acts 12:2) never would nor could. Our point, instead, is that the emphasis on radical servanthood in the immediate context should not be overshadowed. In the third cycle (10:32–45), the main topic is the sacrificial servanthood that Jesus's disciples must live out, following his example. Though the saving significance of Jesus's death is clearly present in this passage (esp. v. 45) and important within Mark's narrative, atonement is not the predominant emphasis of the third cycle (vv. 32–45) itself. Instead, the Evangelist's primary focus is on following Jesus's example of cross-bearing and sacrificial servanthood—with the soteriological significance of his death as a ground for such an emphasis. Jesus has indeed paid the price (λύτρον) to redeem his people, but this means that they no longer belong to themselves. They belong to him. And they cannot follow him if they refuse to go where he went.

---

36. See also Mark 14:36.

Servant-Minded Discipleship
in the Journey Section (8:22–10:52)

Throughout the third cycle (10:32–45), Mark has been preparing his audience for this climactic statement on servanthood and self-sacrifice that presents Jesus's atoning death as the ultimate model (v. 45). The same can be said for the entire Journey section (8:22–10:52). The picture Mark paints of the disciples following Jesus on his journey toward the cross, coupled with the consistent emphasis on discipleship (see, e.g., 8:34–38; 9:7, 28–29, 31; 10:17–31, 32–45, 52), suggests that imitating Jesus's example of service through suffering is a major thrust of Mark's central section. Therefore, our point on servanthood as the primary emphasis of Mark 10:45 is supported not only by the thrust of the third cycle of passion prediction (10:32–45) but also by the impetus of the entire Journey section (8:22–10:52).

The prominence of the servanthood motif in Mark's narrative should be appreciated in connection to the suffering motif; the link between these two motifs amplifies the significance of each. Christ's suffering and his example of servanthood are unambiguously interwoven in the third cycle (Mark 10:32–45). The motif of suffering surfaces in 10:32–34, 38–39, 40, whereas servanthood (or its opposite, the desire to dominate others) is foregrounded in 10:35–37, 41, and 42–44. The ransom saying of verse 45 ("to serve, and to give his life as a ransom") then integrates these two motifs in its presentation of Jesus's self-giving death as the ultimate model to be emulated. For the Son of Man, giving his life as a ransom for many necessitates his suffering—in a radical, extreme, and ultimate way. But this is not suffering just for the sake of suffering; it is suffering endured for the sake of serving the many.

This inseparable bond between the suffering and servanthood motifs also appears in the earlier portions of Mark's Journey section, especially the second passion prediction cycle (9:30–10:31). Following Jesus's prediction of his suffering and death (9:31), this cycle presents a series of passages in which the emphasis on servanthood surfaces in one way or another (see 9:33-37, 38-41, 42; 10:13-16).[37] In this manner, the second cycle (9:30-10:31), too, intertwines the motifs of suffering and servanthood.

Although the first passion prediction cycle (8:27-9:29) does not highlight the servanthood motif as explicitly as the second and the third cycles, a careful examination of Mark's structuring of the three-fold passion prediction reveals the integration of the suffering and servanthood motifs across the middle Journey section (8:22-10:52). As mentioned earlier, each of the three passion prediction cycles presents a prophecy of Jesus's passion and resurrection, some misunderstanding by the disciples, and then Jesus's corrective teaching on discipleship. In the first cycle, the disciples' error and Jesus's corrective teaching concern the issue of suffering (8:32-38); in the second cycle, the topic of servanthood (9:33-37); and in the third, both suffering and servanthood (10:35-45). The third cycle's integration of the suffering motif (highlighted in the first cycle) and the servanthood motif (featured in the second cycle) implies the linkage between these two motifs within the author's deliberate structuring of the threefold passion prediction. Moreover, each motif—suffering, servanthood, and the integration of the two—occurs at the same location within the respective cycles, that is, immediately after the passion prediction proper (8:31; 9:31; 10:33-34). The common placement of each of these two motifs and their integration within their respective cycles further suggests the intentionality and care with which the central section of the Second Gospel was composed as well as the linkage between the motifs of suffering and servanthood. And this linkage magnifies the significance of each motif.

---

37. It is particularly noteworthy that the passage of 9:33-37, which depicts the disciples' power-driven competition (vv. 33-34) and Jesus's corrective teaching in response (vv. 35-37), prepares the arrival of the third and final cycle of passion prediction (10:32-45), in which a similar yet more intensified competition among the Twelve surfaces (vv. 35-41) and is followed by an equally intensified response from Jesus (vv. 42-45).

More could be said about Mark's emphasis on servanthood.[38] However, the discussion above has established the vital significance of servanthood within Mark's narrative. In light of the essential function of Mark 10:45 within the Second Gospel, its emphasis on servant-hood and suffering, and the prevalence of these two motifs (and their integration) in the central section of the narrative, it would be prudent to read the events in Jerusalem, especially the suffering and death of Jesus (Mark 14–15), not only as a portrayal and affirmation of his vicarious suffering on the cross but also as the Evangelist's pastoral plea that his audience follow Christ's example of radical servanthood and faithfulness to God.[39] Furthermore, given the linkage and integration of the motifs of suffering and service in Mark's portrayal of Jesus's ministry, the Second Gospel appears to express genuine consistency and connectivity between Jesus's life and death. He lived as a servant and died as a servant (10:43–45). His life and death are inseparably bound together in and through his radical service.

The importance of servanthood in Mark's Gospel is implied by various factors across the Gospel as just shown above, but it is Mark 10:45 that provides the climactic moment in the Evangelist's teaching on servanthood by (1) binding the passion theme—a major theme in Mark—with the notion of radical servanthood; (2) presenting the Son of Man's death as the ultimate example of that radical servanthood; and

---

38. There are several places beyond the Journey section in which discipleship is presented in terms of servanthood or self-denial (e.g., 3:13–14, 35; 6:12–13, 37, 41–43; 8:6–8; 13:9–14). It would also be helpful to elaborate further on the interrelation between servanthood and authority/power in Mark's narrative. For such discussions, see, e.g., Santos, *Slave of All*, 61–266; Kaminouchi, *'But It Is Not So Among You,'* 157–204.

39. If one reads the Great Command passage of Mark 12:28–34 in connection to the preceding threefold passion prediction cycles (8:27–10:45) and the subsequent passion narrative (chaps. 14–15), Christ's death can be seen as the ultimate expression of loving neighbor as oneself (12:31, v. 33; cf. Lev 19:18) and loving God without reservations (Mark 12:29–30, 32; cf. Deut 6:4–5); see George Keerankeri, *The Love Commandment in Mark: An Exegetico-Theological Study of Mark 12,28–34*, Analecta Biblica 150 (Rome: Pontifical Biblical Institute, 2003).

(3) showing that embracing the atoning significance of Jesus's death as a ransom for many carries the unavoidable implication of serving God and serving others with everything we have as we follow in his footsteps. These features appear or are suggested at various moments within Mark's narrative, not least the Journey section. But no other statement across Mark's Gospel integrates these features in as concentrated and climactic a manner as Mark 10:45. In that sense, Mark's theology of servanthood is uniquely distilled in this one verse.

So far, we have elaborated on two main implications of the case for Mark 10:45 as a key to the Second Gospel, namely, the prominence of Christ's atonement and of servanthood. However, these two are inseparably linked in that the former provides the foundation and model for the latter, while the latter expresses the ethical ramification of the former for Christ's followers. Thus, these two implications correspond with each other and are inextricably bound together.

OTHER CONTRIBUTIONS
TO OUR READING OF MARK'S GOSPEL

Mark 10:45 also contributes to our reading of Mark's Gospel in other ways that we should consider. Specifically, this verse contributes to our appreciation of (1) Mark's *narrative integrity*, (2) his pervasive use of *irony*, and (3) the *nature* of God's kingdom in the Second Gospel. We now turn to reflect briefly on those implications.

THE NARRATIVE INTEGRITY OF MARK'S GOSPEL

The first additional implication relates to the *narrative integrity* of Mark's Gospel. The placement of the climactic explanation of Jesus's death in Mark 10:45, rather than within the passion predictions, demonstrates the need to read and appreciate the Journey section as a whole. Likewise, by locating his explication of the meaning of Jesus's death in 10:45 (cf. 14:24), as opposed to the passion narrative proper (i.e., the crucifixion account in 15:16–41), Mark shows his intention that the entire narrative should be read holistically rather than fragmentarily. He has not crafted his narrative in the hope that his audience would abstract just a few passages or even sections from the larger whole. In this sense, even 10:45 in isolation from its context is no answer key, so to speak, for understanding Mark. Instead, we must read all of Mark's narrative carefully to appreciate how 10:45 contributes to its message since, as we have seen, many episodes early in the narrative point to later material, and this later material fulfills and makes sense of what precedes it. We must appreciate the Second Gospel in Mark's way—holistically.

MARK'S PERVASIVE USE OF IRONY

The second additional implication concerns the use of *irony*, that is, a situation in which expectation and reality are incongruous or in contrast. Acknowledging the function and contribution of 10:45 within Mark's narrative arrangement naturally draws our attention to his use of irony—something easily noted within 10:45 itself. The authoritative Son of Man (cf. Dan 7:13-14) came, but it was not so that he would be served by others, even though such service would be a natural expectation based on Daniel 7:14: "to [one like a son of man] was given dominion and glory and kingship that all the peoples, the nations, and languages would serve him."[40] Instead, this glorious Son of Man came to serve and to give his life. Thus, Mark 10:45 itself, a climactic statement in the Second Gospel, exhibits irony. This implies that irony exists at the core of Mark's narrative.

We do not have space to discuss the pervasive use of irony across Mark's Gospel, but Jerry Camery-Hoggatt's study offers valuable insights for those interested in the topic.[41] We simply note that the passage to which Mark 10:45 belongs (10:32-45, that is, the third cycle of passion prediction) exemplifies the pervasiveness of irony in the Second Gospel. Immediately following Jesus's final and most vivid passion prediction (10:33-34), two members of his inner circle, James and

---

40. For our case that Dan 7 is an appropriate background to Mark 10:45, see the section "The Son of Man" in chapter 4 (pp. 89-102).

41. Camery-Hoggatt, *Irony in Mark's Gospel.*

John, present a shocking and abrupt response to their teacher, "We want you to do for us whatever we ask you" (10:35). Their *response* to Jesus's prediction of his death seems completely oblivious to the gravity of what he has just announced (vv. 33-34; cf. 8:31; 9:12-13, 31). There is no real concern for their rabbi. Ironically, James and John, and even the other ten, are focused on themselves, acting in a manner directly opposed to Jesus's teaching (10:35-41). These are the men who have followed Jesus most closely and have been taught by him most directly (cf. v. 28). The *request* by James and John itself is also ironic. When they make their brazen petition to Jesus, "Grant to us that we may sit one at your right hand and one at your left in your glory" (v. 37), their desire for honor and power is obvious. Yet, the only other place where Mark mentions the positions right and left of Jesus is during his crucifixion, where the two criminals are executed alongside him: "with him they crucified two robbers, one on his right and one on his left" (15:27). Mark seems to imply through this irony that the most honorable position to which the disciples should aspire is, in fact, on a cross next to their Lord; they must deny themselves, take up their crosses, and follow the crucified Messiah (8:34). Irony also colors Jesus's *correction* of his power-driven disciples (10:42-45), especially his description of the pagan (Roman) leaders as "those who are considered to rule" (οἱ δοκοῦντες ἄρχειν; v. 42). In this phraseology, we discover the irony in the sense that although those pagan rulers *appear to be* in charge, they, in fact, are not.[42] It is Israel's God and the Lord Jesus, enthroned on his right (12:36; 14:62; cf. Ps 110:1), who exercise actual authority and sovereignty.[43]

---

42. See the discussion of this phrase in chapter 4, footnote 14.

43. See also Mark 6:14-29 and 15:1-15. Though holding a powerful position, Herod Antipas is controlled by Herodias (and by his own oath before the guests at his birthday party) in 6:14-29. Likewise, Pilate is manipulated by the chief priests and the crowd whom they stir up (15:1-15). These two figures, Herod and Pilate, illustrate "those who are considered to rule" (10:42) within Mark's overall narrative scheme. In spite of their powerful sociopolitical status, they ironically prove to be powerless. See Kaminouchi, *'But It Is Not So Among You,'* 163-97, for further discussion. In addition, it is notable that, in Mark's passion

Additionally, the episode of Mark 10:32-45 is surrounded by other instances of irony. The concluding verse of the preceding passage, which closes the second passion prediction cycle (9:30-10:31), provides a notably ironic statement: "many who are first will be last, and the last first" (10:31). On the other hand, the blind beggar in the pericope immediately following 10:32-45 seems to represent "the last" (cf. 9:35; 10:31) in Jericho. Mark initially describes Bartimaeus as "a blind beggar" who "was sitting beside the road" (10:46; cf. the unfavorable mentions of the roadside location in 4:4, 15). But later within the same episode, Bartimaeus is commended by Jesus for his faith (10:52) and becomes "first," a model disciple who is clear-sighted and eager to follow Jesus on his way to the cross (10:52). Mark's implicit contrast between the disciples (10:35-45) and Bartimaeus (vv. 46-52) is intriguing in at least two respects. First, Bartimaeus responds much more appropriately than James and John to Jesus's question, "What do you want me to do for you?" (compare vv. 37 and 51). Bartimaeus perceives his need for the Messiah's mercy even though he was still blind.[44] Second, at the very end of the episode, Bartimaeus follows Jesus on the way toward Jerusalem, which seems to imply, at least for Mark's audience, cross-focused discipleship (cf. 8:34-38). This favorable depiction of Bartimaeus contrasts with the portrayal of the power-hungry disciples (10:35-41). Bartimaeus's better example of faith and discipleship than that of the Twelve (vv. 35-41) is indeed quite ironic.

---

narrative, where Jesus is portrayed as betrayed, abandoned, captured, tried, abused, beaten, and crucified (chaps. 14-15), he is still seen to have control over the situations surrounding him (see, e.g., Jesus's instructions to his disciples on how to prepare the Passover meal in 14:12-16; cf. a report regarding the preparation of his entry to Jerusalem, i.e., the place of his death, in 11:1-6). It is ironic that in embracing his suffering and death, Jesus is still seen to be in charge of these circumstances, whereas those regarded as highly powerful, i.e., Herod Antipas (6:14-29) and Pilate (15:1-15), do not have control over their situations.

44. This contrast between Bartimaeus and the sons of Zebedee exposes the latter's spiritual blindness—they were more blind than he was!

Mark's repeated use of irony in and around 10:32–45 and the pervasiveness of irony throughout his narrative[45] are in line with Jesus's
frequent reversing of expectations in the story of the Second Gospel.
The kingdom of God Jesus proclaims (e.g., 1:14–15) requires that the
value system not just of his opponents but even of his own followers
be turned upside down (e.g., 10:14–16, 23–27, 31, 42–45).

THE UPSIDE-DOWN NATURE OF GOD'S KINGDOM

The third additional implication of Mark 10:45 for our reading of the
Second Gospel relates to *the upside-down nature* of God's kingdom,
a major theme in the Second Gospel. "The kingdom of God" (which
means the reign of God or his kingship) is, in fact, the central teaching of Jesus in Mark's Gospel (see 1:14–15; 3:24; 4:1–34, esp. vv. 11, 26, 30;
9:1, 47; 10:14–15; 10:17–31, esp. vv. 23–25; 12:34; 14:25; 15:43). If 10:45 is key
to understanding Mark's Gospel, then it would naturally have some
bearing on, or relation to, this fundamental theme of Jesus's teaching
presented by the Evangelist. To be clear, Mark 10:45 does not contain
the word "kingdom" (βασιλεία), nor does the third cycle of passion
prediction to which it belongs. Nevertheless, Mark's first report on
Jesus's public ministry describes nothing but his proclamation of the
kingdom of God (1:14–15), and the Evangelist consistently refers to this
kingdom across his narrative. In so doing, Mark interweaves other
critical motifs in his narrative with the theme of God's kingdom.[46]

---

45. Again, see Camery-Hoggatt, *Irony in Mark's Gospel*, as well as our discussion of dramatic irony in the section, "Mark's Competence as an Author,"
in chapter 3 above.

46. Mark's interweaving of Jesus's passion and God's kingdom, for instance,
is seen clearly in 14:24–25, which links the second of Mark's only two explicit
comments on soteriological nature of Jesus' death (v. 24) with the mention
of "the kingdom of God" (v. 25). For a succinct discussion of the connection
between these themes, see Peter Bolt, *The Cross from a Distance: Atonement
in Mark's Gospel*, New Studies in Biblical Theology 18 (Downers Grove, IL:
InterVarsity Press, 2004), 106. Mark's interweaving of the passion theme with
the notion of the kingdom of God is found from the outset of the narrative.
At the opening of his narrative, Mark names "Isaiah the Prophet" (1:2) and

While not mentioning the term "kingdom" explicitly, Mark 10:45 and the third cycle to which it belongs (10:32–45) do contain kingdom-sensitive language. There is enthronement imagery in 10:37 and 40 (namely, sitting on the right and the left of a royal figure [see 1 Kings 2:19; cf. Ps 110:1]) coupled with the expression of "glory" (Mark 10:37; cf. Isa 22:23; Jer 14:21; 17:12).[47] We also find the reference to "those considered to rule" in Mark 10:42. The repeated uses of "kingdom" and "kingship" language in Daniel 7 (from which the title "the Son of Man" was most likely drawn) in conjunction with the portrayal of the glorious

---

subsequently provides the composite citation of OT scriptures (1:2–3 [Mal 3:1; Isa 40:3]). This composite citation includes the mention of "the way of the Lord," a phrase taken directly from Isaiah 40:3 and appropriated christologically for Jesus the Messiah (Mark 1:3). In Mark's narrative, however, the Messiah's glorious way proves to be the way to his crucifixion—his soteriological death and self-giving service on the cross (10:45; 14:24). On the other hand, we are reminded that Isa 40:3 (quoted in Mark 1:3) is taken from an opening portion of Isa 40–55 (the so-called "Second Isaiah") which, in LXX, not only contains recurrent uses of the middle verb εὐαγγελίζομαι (i.e., the verb that means "to bring good news" [Isa 40:9; 52:7] and is a cognate to the Evangelist's key term "gospel" [εὐαγγέλιον; Mark 1:1, 14–15; 10:29; 13:10; 14:9]) but also links that verb with the notion of Yahweh's kingship: "How delightful on the mountains are the feet of him who brings good news, who announces peace, who brings good news, who announces salvation, who says to Zion, 'Your God reigns as a king'" (Isa 52:7). According to Isaiah, the content of the "good news" is Yahweh's kingship, namely, "the kingdom of God" (cf. Mark 1:15). The Markan author, who names and cites "Isaiah" in his opening (Mark 1:2, 3), is seen to adopt the Isaianic understanding of the "good news" as he binds the term "gospel" with God's kingship in his description of Jesus's inaugural proclamation: "The time is fulfilled and the kingdom of God has come near. Repent and believe in the gospel" (Mark 1:15). The Evangelist draws both "the way of the Lord" (1:3), i.e., Jesus's way to his soteriological death on the cross, and "the kingdom of God" (1:15), i.e., God's kingly reign, from Isaiah 40–55 and mentions each of them explicitly in the opening portion of his narrative, thus interweaving them with one other from very early on in his Gospel. For the connection between kingship and atonement in Mark's Gospel, refer also to Jensen, "Atonement Theology in the Gospel of Mark," 102–3.

47. Pitre, "The 'Ransom for Many,' the New Exodus, and the End of the Exile," 43–47.

man-like figure with universal authority in the same Danielic chapter
(esp. 7:13-14; cf. Mark 2:10, 28; 8:38; 13:26; 14:62) imply the fundamental
relevance of the kingdom/kingship idea for understanding Mark 10:45.
Finally, at numerous points across the Journey section (8:33; 9:35-37,
39-41; 10:13-16; 10:23-31), Jesus distinguishes how things work in the
kingdom of God from the way the kingdoms of this world operate.
And in 10:42-45 in particular, Jesus exemplifies honor and authority
in the divine kingdom by pointing to himself as the ultimate example
of power working for the benefit of and in service of others.

Looking at the passages surrounding Mark 10:32-45 only strength-
ens the relevance of the kingdom concept for 10:45. Among the most
notable references to God's kingdom in the Second Gospel are its
repeated mentions in 10:23-25, part of the episode found in 10:17-31
that immediately precedes the third cycle of passion prediction (10:32-
45). In 10:17-31, to inherit eternal life (vv. 17, 30) and to enter God's
Kingdom (vv. 23, 24, 25) are used synonymously,[48] with the notion
of "being saved" employed as another tantamount expression (v. 26).
Given that "eternal life" (vv. 17, 30) provides an inclusio to the episode
of 10:17-31 and that the ideas of salvation, entering the kingdom, and
inheriting eternal life overlap with one other across this episode, it is
reasonable to conclude that the whole pericope of 10:17-31 concerns
the kingdom of God.[49] Similarly, the Bartimaeus passage immediately
following Mark 10:32-45 repeatedly applies the kingdom-allusive title
"Son of David" (vv. 47, 48) to Jesus and thus anticipates the shout of the
crowd at Jesus's entry to Jerusalem: "Hosanna! Blessed is the one who
comes in the name of the Lord! Blessed is *the coming kingdom of our
father David!*" (11:9-10).[50]

---

48. For a similar interchange between entering into life and entering into
God's kingdom, see Mark 9:42-50, especially vv. 43, 45, 47.

49. The concluding verse of the passage (10:31) reveals the reversal of expectation that God's kingdom mandates: "But many who are first will be last, and
the last first."

50. The David's Son passage (Mark 12:35-37) does not refute Jesus's Davidic
sonship (something Bartimaeus confesses persistently in 10:47-48); instead,

Considering these several elements, Mark 10:32–45 appears to be a richly kingdom-oriented passage based on not only its own content but also that of the immediate narrative context—both preceding and following. Consequently, it is reasonable to expect that a crucial and culminating text such as Mark 10:45 and the third cycle to which this verse belongs (10:32–45), in turn, shed some light on the nature of the divine kingdom that the Evangelist presents. We specifically suggest that Mark 10:45 vividly displays that the kingdom of God operates according to different standards from those of worldly empires. God's kingdom frustrates Jesus's opponents and even his most passionate disciples because it requires not just a reordering but a total *transformation* of values. It is not enough to simply rearrange one's priorities; instead, they must be replaced altogether (see, e.g., 2:21–22; 10:14–16, 23–25). The kingdom of God is a reality that requires repentance (1:15), one in which "whoever wants to become great … must be [a] servant, and whoever wants to be most prominent … must be the slave of all" (10:43–44). God's kingdom is one in which the king does not threaten and domineer his subjects but instead serves them sacrificially and even lays down his own life for them. Jesus's atoning death as a ransom for many is the climatic and ultimate expression of this upside-down nature of divine kingship (10:45).[51]

---

this pericope of 12:35–37 intends to show that the nature of Jesus's messiahship is not bound by his contemporaries' expectation. This understanding of the David's Son passage seems also in line with Jesus's favorable response to Bartimaeus in 10:49–52, who professed him as Son of David, i.e., Davidic Messiah (10:47, 48), and Jesus's use of David as a precedent that justifies the exception he takes (2:25–26). Moreover, Mark does not seem to negatively portray the crowds' enthusiastic response containing expressly Davidic language ("Blessed is the coming kingdom of our father David!" [11:10]) at Jesus's entry to Jerusalem (11:1–11).

51. At the same time, Mark seems to hint that Christ's atoning death is a decisive means by which the divine kingdom is materialized on earth (see, e.g., Mark 2:5, 7, and esp. v. 10: "the Son of Man has authority *on earth* to forgive sins" [emphasis added]). See the section "The Authority to Forgive Sins" earlier in this chapter for our discussion of Mark 2:1–12 with attention to the

This chapter began by explaining the critical function of Mark 10:45 within the structure of the Second Gospel, a key text for understanding the Markan message. We have given special attention to this verse's content and its strategic placement within the narrative sequence. We have then reflected, in turn, on several implications of the case for 10:45 as key for understanding and appreciating the narrative and message of the Second Gospel. In that context, we have explored the vital significance of Jesus's atoning death and its unavoidable bearing on servant-minded discipleship and have also elaborated briefly on how this verse guides our reading of Mark's Gospel in terms of its narrative integrity, use of irony, and presentation of the upside-down nature of God's kingship. The final chapter of this book will offer, along with a brief summary, some practical considerations for those who seek to follow Jesus today, to which we now turn.

---

significance of Jesus's atoning death. It is also notable that the very last mention of the divine kingdom in Mark's narrative appears in the episode about Jesus' burial (15:42–47 [esp. v. 43]), which is located immediately after his death (15:33–41)—and right before his resurrection (16:1–8).

VI

LEARNING TO LIVE
THE MESSAGE OF MARK 10:45

OUR AIM IN THIS BOOK has been to explain precisely *why* and *how* Mark 10:45 is key to understanding Mark's message. To do this, we began by navigating the issues related to Mark's occasion and purpose. For the occasion of Mark's Gospel, we concluded that the middle to late 60s CE, especially the Neronian persecution of Roman Christians, would be a more plausible background for the composition of this Gospel than earlier or later periods and that Mark's original audience was facing suffering and trials because of their faith in Jesus of Nazareth. In examining Mark's purpose, we explored his competence as an author, indicated by various details in the story. The care and intricacy with which the Evangelist arranged his material contributes to the significance of Mark 10:45 within the Second Gospel and confirm that he wrote with a distinct purpose. Regarding this purpose, we examined his narrative for various clues to his intentions. We showed that Mark's narrative is focused on the person of Jesus from its beginning to its end. The identity of Jesus (who he is) and the mission of Jesus (what he has done and why) are the core content of the Second Gospel. However, we also noted that Mark has written his story not merely to provide or confirm historical data about Jesus but, more importantly, *to encourage his audience to remain faithful to Jesus and his teachings even in the face of shame and suffering.* We then surveyed the entirety of Mark's Gospel with an eye toward this purpose. In doing

so, we considered the various ways that each passage contributes to
Mark's purpose.

We then began a detailed analysis of Mark 10:45 preceded by some
observations about its narrative context. In the correction of James
and John's nearsighted request to share in his "glory," Jesus points his
disciples to the highest expression of honor and splendor, that of the
"one like a son of man" from Daniel 7:13-14. Even this glorious Son of
Man was not too exalted to become a servant to captives of sickness
and disease (1:34), of unclean spirits and demons (1:21-28, 34), and
of sin and unrighteousness (2:5, 17). He is not too exalted even to lay
down his life, being betrayed by a friend into the hands of men (9:32)
and delivered over to the Gentiles (10:33) to suffer shame, abuse, and
death. Most importantly, this glorious Son of Man is not too exalted
to give his life as a ransom for many (10:45).

Next, we outlined the function of Mark 10:45 within the narrative
of the Second Gospel and how it contributes to our appreciation of
Mark's message. We first examined the verse's strategic location as
the thematic pivot between the elaborately constructed passion prediction cycles (8:27-10:45) and the subsequent Jerusalem section (Mark
11:1-16:8), in which Mark narrates the very passion and resurrection
that Jesus had predicted (Mark 14-16). We also considered the details
of Mark 10:45 in relation to the purpose of Jesus's ministry and the
meaning of his death. We then presented several implications of this
verse's crucial importance for appreciating Mark's Gospel, with specific
attention to the significance of Jesus's atoning death, the organic and
inseparable connection between Jesus's atonement and Mark's emphasis on servanthood, and other ramifications including the importance
of Mark's literary features for interpreting the Second Gospel.

The relationship between suffering and servanthood, both in
10:45 specifically and in the passion prediction cycles more generally,
reminds us that following in the footsteps of Jesus means serving
others even when it hurts. In Mark's Gospel, "servanthood" that costs
us nothing will gain us nothing. Just as Jesus did not allow fear to divert
him from the path of suffering and shame, those who follow him must

also say, "Not what I will, but what you will" (14:36). This commitment to follow Jesus even if it means giving up all we have (8:34-36; 10:21, 28-30) indicates the authenticity of our commitment to the one who gave his life as a ransom for many.

The kingdom of God operates according to different principles from those of the empires of this world. Thriving in God's kingdom means serving others sacrificially. God's people achieve genuine success not by clinging to honor or wealth or connections or even their own lives but by using these things for the benefit of others (8:35-37; 9:35-37; 10:28-30, 42-45). Those who are truly great in God's kingdom follow the example of the Son of Man, who "did not come to be served but to serve" (10:45).

Exegetical and theological insights are essential for our understanding of Mark's message, but it is only as we continue to follow Christ's example of radical self-giving service that we can hope to have grasped the meaning and significance of Mark 10:45. As we close this book, we want to share a few additional thoughts on applying the message of Mark 10:45 today.

TRUE SERVANTHOOD
IN THE FOOTSTEPS OF JESUS

We believe that the term "service," as applied to the mission of Jesus, must be understood in a nuanced and refined manner. Its overuse in our era has cheapened the concept. When we think of "service" today, we imagine the service industry or maybe having a car "serviced." But in Jesus's case, "service" meant embracing the most shameful and despised fate of his time—death on a Roman cross. It meant being condemned by his fellow Jews as one accursed by Israel's God (cf. Gal 3:13; Deut 21:23). It meant being mocked by the Romans as a failed insurrectionist (cf. Mark 15:16-20). And the final phrase of Mark 10:45 ("to give his life as a ransom for many") points to the ultimate expression of the Son of Man's radical servanthood, his atoning death. Jesus did not allow his unique identity and authority to exempt him from the kingdom principle of sacrificial servanthood (cf. Phil 2:6-8). Instead,

he lived it out fully (Mark 10:45) and thus provided the foundation
and prototype for his followers' radical servanthood in his footsteps
(10:43-44; cf. 9:35-37).

This emphasis on sacrificial servanthood is not limited to Mark's
Gospel alone. It is found across the New Testament,[1] as the following
verses illustrate:

> Live in love, just as also Christ loved us, and gave himself for us
> an offering and sacrifice to God for a fragrant smell. (Eph 5:2)

> This is my commandment: that you love one another just as I
> have loved you. No one has greater love than this: that someone
> lay down his life for his friends. (John 15:12-13)

> We have come to know love by this: that he laid down his life
> on behalf of us, and we ought to lay down our lives on behalf
> of the brothers. (1 John 3:16)

Church history is replete with examples of radical servanthood in the
footsteps of Jesus. Just beyond the apostolic era, 1 Clement 55:2 reports,
"We know that many among ourselves have delivered themselves to
bondage, that they might ransom others. Many have sold themselves
to slavery, and receiving the price paid for themselves have fed others"
(trans. J. B. Lightfoot and J. R. Harmer). This reported practice among
early Christians reflects a *literal* application of Mark 10:45.[2] Other
examples of Christian servanthood across the centuries are not hard
to find. One of the most notable examples is Francis of Assisi. Before
his conversion, Francis felt a strong aversion to the sight of lepers.
But after his conversion, he went to live in a leprosarium to care for

---

1. For the reception of ransom saying (Mark 10:45//Matthew 20:28) in the
New Testament, see J. Christopher Edwards, *The Ransom Logion in Mark and
Matthew*, WUNT 2.327 (Tübingen: Mohr Siebeck, 2012), 30-53.

2. Garland, *A Theology of Mark's Gospel*, 459n62.

those with the disease.[3] Even at the end of his life, himself suffering
from many physical ailments and unable to walk,[4] Francis continually
demonstrated radical, sacrificial service toward others. On one occasion, during the winter, Francis heard about a woman in need, so he
sent the woman his own mantle to provide her with warmth—such
sacrificial generosity left Francis colder and weaker.[5]

Mark 10:45 does not describe service in general and abstract terms.
Instead, the portrayal is quite specific and personal. The service in
Mark 10:45 is a service that a particular person, Jesus, has offered in
a specific manner at a specific time and place, namely, giving his life
sacrificially for the sake of others by being crucified on a Roman cross.
And he did this despite the defeat that such a death signified in the eyes
of his contemporaries. If we want to follow in Jesus's footsteps, we
must also do so in a personal way in our own specific time and space.
The readers of this book will likely have one or two people they can
quickly identify as their models of sacrificial service. For some, time
would fail them to tell about their heroes of Christ-like servanthood
(cf. Heb 11:32).

However, following Jesus's example of servanthood may also take
less conspicuous forms and may have a more manageable and mun-
dane expression. For instance, welcoming neighbors over for dinner,
staying late after church to vacuum the building, serving in a food line
that feeds the hungry, or offering to babysit for a single parent can all
be meaningful ways of serving others sacrificially. The core thread
common to each of these acts is *a willingness to subordinate our liber-
ties, comforts, rights, and sometimes even our necessities to those of others*,
and, in so doing, we embody Jesus's own habit of sacrificial service in
a small yet meaningful way.

---

3. Augustine Thompson, *Francis of Assisi: The Life* (Ithaca: Cornell University
Press, 2013), 18–19.

4. Thompson, *Francis of Assisi*, 162–63.

5. Thompson, *Francis of Assisi*, 166.

To be clear, Mark's message is *not* that we must suffer or serve in order to get into heaven. Suffering and service do not earn our redemption and reconciliation with God. And not everyone who follows Jesus will face the same obstacles. Interestingly, Acts 12:2 mentions the death of James, which likely occurred only a decade or so after the request of Mark 10:37, yet church tradition indicates that his brother John lived to an old age. Likewise, in John 21:18-24, the resurrected Messiah foretells two very different paths for Peter and "the disciple whom Jesus loved." Mark does not claim that we will all experience the same afflictions and persecutions or identify the same needs among our neighbors.

Instead, the message of Mark is that those who follow Jesus must be *willing* to complete the journey. It is not enough simply to *hear* the message of the kingdom (Mark 4:4, 15). It is not even enough to receive that message with joy and start following Jesus if we are not committed to remaining with him to the end (4:5-7, 16-19). It is only those who receive the message of the kingdom *and* bear the fruit of loyal perseverance—committed to following Jesus wherever he leads and whatever it costs—who can say that they have truly followed him (4:8, 20). If you consider yourself a disciple of Jesus, it is worthwhile to ask yourself periodically, "What obstacles might deter me from staying on the path?" This world offers many distractions to lure us off the path of discipleship. For the rich man, it was his earthly treasure (10:17-22). For James and John, it was the pursuit of honor (10:35-37). For Peter, it was an aversion to shame and suffering (8:32; 14:66-72). What tempts you to sidestep the shame and suffering that may come with following Jesus? What are you unwilling to give in service to Jesus and others?

The spirit of competition and worldly success that once possessed James and John (10:35-40) is still rampant in our generation. Even churches, Christian institutions, and missions organizations are not immune. Too often, we view one another as competitors, not recognizing that Jesus sharply opposed this sort of perspective. Frequently, pastors look at larger, more successful churches and feel envious or even discouraged, carrying a weighty sense of failure and feeling pressure to outperform the church down the street. They may say they are just trying to thrive, but James and John, too, were trying to thrive—in their own way, according to the pattern of pagan rulers (10:42). We must again listen to Jesus, who sharply contrasted his way (Mark 1:3; cf. Isa 40:3) with that of the world: "it shall not be so among you" (10:43, ESV)! We who would follow Jesus on the way to the cross must deny ourselves and take up our own crosses (8:34), and we must learn to embrace the way of God rather than the ways of the world (8:33).

MARK'S MESSAGE TO THOSE
WHO FALL AWAY

By this point, we hope it is clear what we believe Mark wanted to accomplish with his story about who Jesus is and what he has done. And we hope we have made clear our view of how Mark 10:45 contributes to that purpose. In his effort to inspire followers of Jesus to remain loyal to Jesus even when it means giving up everything, the Evangelist provides both the positive example of Jesus's faithfulness to the will of God (e.g., 14:36) and the negative example of the disciples, who are continually stumbling, erring, and—honestly—failing to live up to the call of discipleship. Lest his audience, in the tradition of the Twelve, fail to grasp the imperative that comes with following Jesus, the author makes it explicit at the beginning of the Journey section:

> If anyone wants to come after me, let him deny himself and take up his cross and follow me. For whoever wants to save his life will lose it, but whoever loses his life on account of me and of the gospel will save it. ... For whoever is ashamed of me and my words in this adulterous and sinful generation, the Son of Man will also be ashamed of him when he comes in the glory of his Father with the holy angels. (Mark 8:34-35, 38)

When Jesus describes faithful discipleship, the expectations are extreme ("take up his cross"), and the consequences are severe ("save his life" or "lose his life"; "the Son of Man will be ashamed of him"). But the rationale for this extraordinary demand is found in the conclusion of the Journey section. Jesus demands so much from those who follow him because of the extraordinary price that he himself has paid for them: even the Son of Man did not come to be served but to serve and *give his life as a ransom for many.*

It certainly is motivating. There is clearly a lot riding on our faithfulness to Jesus. And yet, many of us read the words "whoever is ashamed of me" with a sense of timidity, even guilt. We know there are times when, to one degree or another, we have been ashamed. We know that we have not always denied ourselves. Self-denial is more than just giving up a vice or bad habit. Even good things, if we hold onto them more tightly than to Christ, are snares that can lure us off the path of discipleship (cf. Jas 1:14–15). So what would Mark say to those of us who are still clinging to these things, to those who have stumbled on the path? What would he say to those who have left the path altogether?

While Mark does not lighten the demands of discipleship in any way, he does know that many do stumble and even abandon the way of the Lord. Mark narrates the disciples' desertion of Jesus (14:50; cf. vv. 27–31). And Peter, never to be outdone (cf. 14:29, 31), not only deserts Jesus but blatantly denies even knowing him (14:71). Though Mark does not mention a restoration of Peter as we find in John's Gospel (John 21:15–22), he does anticipate it. When Jesus predicts the scattering of the disciples (Mark 14:27), he adds, "But after I am raised, I will go ahead of you into Galilee" (v. 28). This statement seems to imply that Jesus will not give up on the disciples. In Luke's Gospel, which is probably one of the earliest interpretations of Mark's narrative, Jesus includes the following exhortation when he predicts Peter's denial: "Once you have *turned back*, strengthen your brothers" (Luke 22:32, emphasis added). Jesus is not going to Galilee to scold the disciples for deserting him. Rather, the conjunction "but" (ἀλλά) that begins Mark 14:28 implies a *contrast* between the disciples' abandonment of Jesus and Jesus's gracious and hope-filled reunion with them in Galilee after his resurrection.

But, again, the warning "the Son of Man will also be ashamed of him" (8:38) is not an empty threat. So why does Jesus *not* reject those who have deserted him? What is the difference between someone like Peter—who was clearly ashamed to be associated with Jesus but goes down in history as one of the pillars of Christ's church (Gal 2:9; cf. Matt 16:17-19; Luke 22:32; Acts 1:15-22; 2:14-36; 15:6-11)—and someone like Judas, about whom Jesus warns, "It would be better for him if that man had not been born" (Mark 14:21)? What is the difference between a failure that leads to restoration and a failure that leads to condemnation?

One crucial difference is repentance. Repentance was, after all, the first message that Jesus proclaimed (1:15). John's baptism, which prepared Jesus's public ministry, was characterized as a baptism of repentance (1:4). And repentance was the message Jesus sent his disciples out to proclaim (6:12). Repentance is not just how we *start* following Jesus; it is how we *continue* to follow Jesus after we wander from the path of discipleship. Repentance and faith are not just how we *accept* the mindset focused on the things of God; it is how we *maintain* that mindset. Repentance is how we get back in our place, *behind Jesus* (8:33).

REPENT (AGAIN) AND BELIEVE

When Mark uses the verb "repent" (μετανοέω), it only appears in the present tense form. This may indicate that he views repentance as a process (1:15; 6:12).

"The time is fulfilled and the kingdom of God has come near. Repent [μετανοεῖτε] and believe in the gospel!" (Mark 1:15)

"And they went out and proclaimed that people should repent [μετανοῶσιν]." (Mark 6:12)

Mark also connects repentance to forgiveness at various points in his Gospel. The baptism that John proclaimed was a "baptism of repentance for the forgiveness of sins" (1:4). When Jesus explains his teachings about the kingdom to the disciples, he tells them that "those who are outside" receive only parables, specifically "so that they ... [would] not perceive ... and [would] not understand, *lest they turn* [ἐπιστρέψωσιν] and it be *forgiven* them" (4:12, emphasis added). Mark never explicitly mentions Peter's "turning," but he hints at it when he describes Peter's sorrowful reaction at the second crowing of the rooster (14:72). It would seem, then, that we may, in fact, have Mark's answer, subtle as it may be, to the difference between a disciple who stumbles but is restored and one for whom it would be better not to have been born. That difference seems to be *turning and being forgiven*.

Mark's response to those who have stumbled, fallen, and even abandoned the way of the Lord is really the same as Jesus's initial proclamation: "Repent and believe in the gospel!" (Mark 1:15). Just as we must continue in our faith in Christ, so also we must continue in our repentance. Has shame diverted you from the path of discipleship? Then turn back and be forgiven. Has a mind set on the things of this world lured you away from following after Jesus? Then get back to your proper place—*behind him* (8:33). Have you put your ultimate confidence, security, and even delight in something other than who Jesus is and what he has done for you (10:22)? Repent and believe in the gospel. He will not turn you away. He will not scold you, condemn you, or rub your nose in your failure. Those who see and perceive, those who hear and understand, those who turn back to the Messiah, they will be forgiven (4:12). He will have mercy on them (10:48) and heal them (10:52) because even the Son of Man did not come to be served but to serve and to give his life as a ransom for many.

APPENDIX I

ANNOTATED RECOMMENDATIONS
FOR FURTHER READING

I N RECENT DECADES, THERE HAVE been several studies on various aspects of Mark 10:45 or the passage to which it belongs (10:32–45). The literature is somewhat overwhelming. Here, we recommend a few books and articles with which to begin as the reader explores this verse and its context. To aid readers more efficiently, we provide annotations and full documentation for each entry below.

Jensen, Morten Hørning. "Atonement Theology in the Gospel of Mark." *Biblica* **100.1 (2019): 84–104.**

In his recent article, "Atonement Theology in the Gospel of Mark," M. H. Jensen asks whether Mark indeed presents Jesus's death as an atonement. In forming an answer to this question, Jensen engages two primary objections to the "vertical/cultic atonement theology in Mark."[1] The first objection denies the connection of Mark's view of the atonement to Isaiah's suffering servant. In responding to this objection, Jensen argues that an "Isaianic framework" underlies Mark's Gospel.[2] He points to six elements within the prologue, which place Mark's "narrative in the trajectory of Second Isaiah," and persuasively argues for "an over-arching Exodus motif."[3] The second objection challenges

---

1. Jensen, "Atonement Theology in the Gospel of Mark," 87.
2. Jensen, "Atonement Theology in the Gospel of Mark," 88–95.
3. Jensen, "Atonement Theology in the Gospel of Mark," 91–94 (quote on 91).

a cultic reading of the Gospel, denying Jesus's death as related or relevant to the temple. In response, Jensen points to several factors that indicate the importance of a Temple theme in Mark. For example, he shows that in Mark's Jerusalem section, especially chapters 11–12 of the Gospel, Mark not only "contrasts Jesus' program with that of the temple of Jerusalem, but he also ties the destiny of Jesus to Jesus's attack on the temple."[4] Thus Jesus's death is connected to the temple on various levels. In the final portion of his article, Jensen proposes that Mark 15:38 must be understood as central to Mark's theology of atonement: "In light of Mark's Isaianic framework and considering the solid connection between the temple and the death of Jesus, the rending of the temple veil becomes the perfect pivotal symbol of how Mark understands the effect that Jesus' death has on the vertical, God-human relationship, i.e., atonement."[5]

Kaminouchi, Alberto de Mingo. *'But It Is Not So Among You':* *Echoes of Power in Mark 10.32–45.* JSNTSS 249. London: T & T Clark International, 2003.

In his monograph, *'But It Is Not So Among You,'* Kaminouchi addresses the subject of power as presented in Mark's Gospel, particularly as it relates to the passage of 10:32–45. In so doing, he explores two main issues: first, the centrality of Mark 10:32–45's exposition on power "both to the plot and to the theology" of Mark's Gospel, and second, the Markan Jesus's "understanding of power radically opposed to the understanding of power prevalent in his society."[6] He approaches the text from a combination of "literary and social sensitivities," by following "the *echoes* of certain motifs."[7] According to Kaminouchi, an "echo" is the repetition of "a *formula* or *theme*" in a text that helps an

---

4. Jensen, "Atonement Theology in the Gospel of Mark," 97.

5. Jensen, "Atonement Theology in the Gospel of Mark," 99.

6. Kaminouchi, *'But It Is Not So Among You,'* 5.

7. Kaminouchi, *'But It Is Not So Among You,'* 43 (italics original).

oral audience follow the narrative.[8] Kaminouchi examines echoes within the three-part pattern of repetition in Mark's middle section (8:27–10:45), which reveals Mark 10:32–45 to be located in the climatic position of his Gospel.[9] As these echoes are repeated, the slight differences among them "create a crescendo" and accentuate Jesus's teaching on power and service.[10] Kaminouchi's study, he claims, shows that "Jesus' teachings in the section of the journey to Jerusalem" culminate in Mark 10:42–45.[11]

Santos, Narry F. *Slave of All: The Paradox of Authority and Servanthood in the Gospel of Mark*. JSNTSS 237.
London: Sheffield Academic, 2003.

In *Slave of All*, Santos explores the paradoxical relationship between authority and servanthood in the Gospel of Mark. Paradox, as Santos defines it, "is an unusual and apparently self-contradictory rhetorical statement or concept that departs dramatically from accepted opinion."[12] He argues that Mark uses paradox across his Gospel to challenge his audience's presuppositions that authority and servanthood are incompatible. Santos divides his study into three major sections according to the narrative sequence: Mark 1:1–8:21; 8:22–10:52; and 11:1–16:8. In the middle section of Mark's Gospel, the Evangelist intensifies the paradox in each subsequent passion prediction (8:31–35; 9:31–35; 10:32–45). In the first prediction discourse, the paradox is general: "'saving' and 'losing' one's life" (8:35). The second becomes more specific: "being 'first' and 'last' " (9:35). Mark's third discourse, however, contains the most vivid description: "becoming 'great' and becoming

---

8. Kaminouchi, *'But It Is Not So Among You,'* 55. Kaminouchi defines a *formula* as "a group of words repeated regularly to express the same idea" and a *theme* as "a group of ideas or images present in different moments of the text"; Kaminouchi, *'But It Is Not So Among You,'* 55.

9. Kaminouchi, *'But It Is Not So Among You,'* 43.

10. Kaminouchi, *'But It Is Not So Among You,'* 57.

11. Kaminouchi, *'But It Is Not So Among You,'* 209.

12. Santos, *Slave of All*, 3.

a 'servant', wishing to be 'first' and being a 'slave of all' " (10:43-44).[13] Santos argues that these intensifications reveal that "the authority-servanthood paradox" is essential for understanding all of Mark's discourses on discipleship.[14] In his analysis of 10:45, Santos argues that only by appreciating the paradox of this verse can readers understand that the supreme demonstration of greatness is found in Jesus's own serving and ransoming. In turn, by reflecting on Jesus's death, readers can then understand Mark's presentation of the threefold passion prediction—that Mark 10:45b explains why Jesus says he "must (δεῖ)" suffer and be rejected in 8:31. Only after this explanation of Jesus's death will readers see that 10:45 possesses a climactic role in the central section of Mark's Gospel. In his concluding summary of Mark's middle section, Santos offers a reminder that the stories placed between the first and second predictions (i.e., the transfiguration [9:2:13] and the healing of the demon-possessed boy [9:14-29]) demonstrate Jesus's authority, and the stories between the second and third predictions (i.e., the opposition of religious leaders [10:1-9], the misunderstanding of the disciples [10:10-16, 23-31], and a person's lack of faith [10:17-22]) work to "prompt the readers not to oppose Jesus in the way that the religious authorities do, nor to display lack of insight in the way the disciples do, but to appreciate Jesus's authority in light of his servanthood."[15]

---

13. Santos, *Slave of All*, 146.
14. Santos, *Slave of All*, 146-47 (quote on 146).
15. Santos, *Slave of All*, 212.

Watts, Rikki E. "Jesus' Death, Isaiah 53, and Mark 10:45:
A Crux Revisited." In *Jesus and the Suffering Servant:
Isaiah 53 and Christian Origins*. Edited by William H.
Bellinger, Jr., and William R. Farmer. Harrisburg, PA:
Trinity Press International, 1998.

In his essay "Jesus' Death, Isaiah 53, and Mark 10:45," which provides a
critical response to M. D. Hooker and C. K. Barrett's respective suggestions that Mark 10:45 does not allude to the suffering servant of Isaiah,[16]
Watts connects the broader horizon of Mark's Gospel to the Isaianic
New Exodus paradigm and devotes attention to Jesus's expressed purpose in Mark 9:12, arguing the verse's background is indeed Isaiah 53.
Watts also examines Mark's passion predictions in 8:31, 9:31, and 10:33–
34, concluding that "while there are various single linguistic connections" with plural OT texts in those predictions, Isaiah 53 is "by far the
dominant text overall."[17] Watts ultimately explores Mark 10:45, noting
linguistic usage and linking Mark 10:45 to the Isaianic New Exodus
paradigm. Specifically, he comments on three main issues: the concept
of "being given over to death, the meaning of λύτρον ἀντὶ ... , and the
significance of πολλῶν."[18] Taken individually, these concepts might
not evoke Isaiah 53. However, Watts believes their cumulative effect,
together with the broader New Exodus paradigm in Mark's Gospel,
makes Isaiah 53 a likely influence.

Pitre, Brant. "'The Ransom for Many,' the New Exodus,
and the End of the Exile: Redemption as the Restoration of
All Israel (Mark 10:35-45)." *Letter & Spirit* 1 (2005): 41-68.

In his article "The 'Ransom for Many,' the New Exodus, and the End
of the Exile," Pitre argues for an understanding of Mark 10:45 that
incorporates a Danielic background in combination with its Isaianic

---

16. Cf. Hooker, *Jesus and the Servant*; Barrett, "The Background of Mark
10:45."

17. Watts, "Jesus' Death, Isaiah 53, and Mark 10:45," 136.

18. Watts, "Jesus' Death, Isaiah 53, and Mark 10:45," 139.

background.[19] Pitre puts forward four lines of reasoning. First, the request by James and John (10:37) "presupposes the vision of the eschatological kingdom described in Daniel 7," which helps establish "an initial link to the eschatological restoration of Israel."[20] Second, Jesus's prediction of suffering before his exaltation "also presupposes the Danielic vision of the kingdom."[21] Third, Jesus combines the royal "Son of Man" figure in Daniel 7 with the dying Messiah in Daniel 9, which serves as "the origin of his claim that the Son of Man must 'give his life.'"[22] Fourth, Jesus's words "ransom" and "many" draw "on the widespread Old Testament hope for the restoration of all Israel: that is, the ingathering of the scattered tribes ... in a new exodus."[23] Pitre concludes that Jesus's words about a ransom "appear to be a *combination* of figures from Daniel and Isaiah that draws on their common hope for a new exodus and the restoration of Israel. In both, the exile is only brought to an end by a climactic period of tribulation or affliction in which a key figure, the Messiah/Son of Man, or the servant, dies, and thereby atones for the sins of Israel that have led her into exile in the first place."[24]

Howerzyl, Timothy. "Imaging Salvation: An Inquiry into the Function of Metaphor in Christian Soteriology, with Application to Mark 10:45 and the Metaphor of Ransom." PhD diss., Fuller Theological Seminary, 2014.

In his 2014 Fuller dissertation titled "Imaging Salvation," Timothy Howerzyl analyzes the role of metaphors as they relate to soteriology and the Christian portrayal of atonement. Howerzyl examines "the historical and cultural character of the biblical metaphors" and their

---

19. Pitre, "The 'Ransom for Many,'" 42–43.
20. Pitre, "The 'Ransom for Many,'" 42.
21. Pitre, "The 'Ransom for Many,'" 42
22. Pitre, "The 'Ransom for Many,'" 42.
23. Pitre, "The 'Ransom for Many,'" 43.
24. Pitre, "The 'Ransom for Many,'" 65.

continuing relevance "to communities which are removed from the time and place in which they were originally written."[25] First, however, Howerzyl expounds the methodology of Wolfhart Pannenberg, which proposes that Christology and soteriology should move "from below to above," that is, "begin from the perspective of Jesus as a human historical figure" rather than presupposing his divinity.[26] After discussing Pannenberg's methodology, Howerzyl examines Mark 10:45 (1) by exploring the "ransom" saying's linguistic background and (2) by considering the saying in the context of Mark's Gospel. Regarding the cultural and historical background of λύτρον, Howerzyl concludes that the phrase "ransom for many" (Mark 10:45) contains "quite clearly the notion of the payment of a price, though with emphasis on the deliverance which would result from the ransoming act."[27] The question of who receives the payment (e.g., Satan) would extend beyond the purpose of the metaphor. As a result of his investigation, Howerzyl finds three significant elements in the ransom language. First is the notion of deliverance that comes through the Son of Man. The metaphor leads readers to see their need for a ransoming. Second is the high price of the ransom. It is a cost that people themselves cannot afford to pay. The third element is that Jesus paid the price of the ransom willingly. Christ's willingness to serve as a ransom moves believers to cherish God's great mercy.

---

25. Howerzyl, "Imaging Salvation," 33.

26. Howerzyl, "Imaging Salvation," 45-46 (quote on p. 46); for a fuller description, see 41-94 (especially 45-47 and 91-94); cf. Wolfhart Pannenberg, *Jesus—God and Man*, 2nd ed., trans. Lewis L. Wilkins and Duane A. Priebe (Philadelphia: Westminster, 1977).

27. Howerzyl, "Imaging Salvation," 39; Howerzyl further states that in this context, λύτρον "would have been intended to conjure up ideas not only of the redemption of slaves or release of prisoners, but also to draw semantic currency from the cultic associations of the use of the term in the LXX translations of the Pentateuch" (39).

APPENDIX II

A SHORT HISTORY OF THE RANSOM VIEW OF THE ATONEMENT

T HE IMPORTANCE OF MARK 10:45 in early Christian interpretation revolves mainly around its use of ransom language. Christ's atonement as a ransom was a prominent view among the church fathers. J. Christopher Edwards, in *The Ransom Logion in Mark and Matthew*, provides a detailed study on the significance of the ransom view from the time of the New Testament until the year 300 CE.[1] During the Middle Ages, however, the prominent focus on Christ's death as a ransom diminished, and other atonement theories rose in popularity. This appendix primarily concerns the reception of the ransom saying (Mark 10:45/Matthew 20:28) and will briefly describe the shift from ransom language to other theories of atonement.[2]

Edwards notes that the early church father Clement of Alexandria utilized ransom language, placing it "alongside themes from John's

---

1. J. Christopher Edwards, *The Ransom Logion in Mark and Matthew: Its Reception and Its Significance for the Study of the Gospels*, WUNT 2.327 (Tübingen: Mohr Siebeck, 2012).

2. For the reception of the ransom view of the atonement, see also Gustaf Aulén, *Christus Victor: An Historical Study of the Three Main Types of the Idea of Atonement*, trans. A. G. Hebert (New York: Macmillan, 1951); Hastings Rashdall, *The Idea of Atonement in Christian Theology: Being the Bampton Lectures for 1915* (London: Macmillian, 1925).

Gospel, such as love and self-sacrifice."[3] Irenaeus (*Against Heresies* 5.1.1) employs ransom language when speaking of Jesus's blood.[4] Yet it is the church father Origen who is perhaps most responsible for the increased relevance of the ransom saying in discussions of the meaning of Jesus's death. In Origen's view, Jesus's death as a ransom serves in some way as a transaction or payment to the Devil.[5]

Augustine continued this notion that Jesus, in his death, paid a ransom to the Devil.[6] His sermon on John 6:9, for example, likens the ransom to that of a trap: "And what did our Redeemer to him who held us captive [i.e., the Devil]? For our ransom he held out His Cross as a trap; he placed in It as a bait His Blood."[7] Although Augustine acknowledges and describes Jesus's death as a ransom, he also understands his death in terms of its substitutionary benefit, with Jesus taking on the just punishment that sinful humanity had earned.[8] As Rashdall explains, "On the whole, in St. Augustine the idea of substituted or vicarious punishment is the central one."[9]

---

3. Edwards, *The Ransom Logion in Mark and Matthew*, 57. Edwards mentions *Paedagogus* 1.9.85.1–2 and *Quis Dives Salvetur* 37.4.

4. Edwards, *The Ransom Logion in Mark and Matthew*, 59–60.

5. Robert Guy Erwin, "The Passion and Death of Christ in the Piety and Theology of the Later Middle Ages and Martin Luther" (PhD diss., Yale University, 1999), 49–50, citing Origen, *Commentary in Matthew* 13.8–9; 16.8 (Griechischen Christlichen Schriftsteller 40:203–4; 498); Edwards, *The Ransom Logion in Mark and Matthew*, 78–79.

6. Rashdall, *The Idea of Atonement in Christian Theology*, 330-31; so also Paul Archbald, "A Comparative Study of John Calvin and Theodore Beza on the Doctrine of the Extent of the Atonement" (PhD diss., Westminster Theological Seminary, 1998). Archbald notes that Augustine believed "Christ's ransom price bound the devil to free us" (15).

7. Taken from Leon Morris, *The Cross of Jesus* (Grand Rapids: Eerdmans, 1988), 23n20.

8. Rashdall, *The Idea of Atonement in Christian Theology*, 331.

9. Rashdall, *The Idea of Atonement in Christian Theology*, 334.

The focus on Jesus's death as a "ransom" declined significantly during the time of Anselm and Abelard. Instead, theologians began debating whether the effect of Jesus's death was primarily objective or subjective. An objective atonement view sees Jesus's death as satisfying or quenching God's wrath. It is, therefore, a change *within God* that allows for reconciliation rather than any change within the person. The subjective view of the atonement sees Jesus's death as inspiring individuals toward repentance and faith. It is this change within the individual, then, that makes peace with God possible. Both Anselm and Abelard rejected the idea that Jesus's death was a ransom payment to the Devil.[10] For Anselm, Jesus's death satisfied God's justice[11] (an objective effect). On the other hand, Abelard denied both a payment to the Devil and satisfaction of God's justice.[12] Instead, Abelard believed that Jesus's death should be seen for its subjective effect—that is, in looking at Christ's death, sinners are stirred with gratitude toward repentance and devotion to God.[13]

Despite Abelard's preference for a subjective interpretation of the atonement, the objective understanding of Christ's atonement saw a revival with Thomas Aquinas. Like Anselm, Aquinas suggests that Jesus's death effectively satisfies God's sense of justice; rather than

---

10. Erwin, "The Passion and Death of Christ in the Piety and Theology of the Later Middle Ages and Martin Luther," 75; John R. W. Stott, *The Cross of Christ* (Downers Grove, IL: InterVarsity Press, 2006), 213.

11. Rashdall, *The Idea of Atonement in Christian Theology*, 351, citing *Cur Deus Homo* i.7, 13.

12. Stott, *The Cross of Christ*, 213.

13. Morris, *The Cross of Jesus*, 19. He writes, "On [Abelard's] view the death of Jesus has no objective effect: it does not pay a penalty or win a victory, other than symbolically. What it does is to show us the greatness of the love of God and move us to love in return." Rashdall, *The Idea of Atonement in Christian Theology*, 358, notes, "In Abelard not only the ransom theory but any kind of substitutionary or expiatory atonement is explicitly denied." See also Stott, *The Cross of Christ*, 213.

a payment to the Devil, the ransom is a payment to God.[14] As for the Reformers, Martin Luther and John Calvin emphasized Jesus's death as a "substitution" for believers—that Jesus was treated as guilty for humanity's sin.[15] Luther affirms in his sermon on John 3:16–21, "Christ teaches here that we are not lost, but have eternal life; that is, that God has so loved us that he allowed the ransom to cost him his only beloved child. Him he placed in our stead to suffer misery, hell and death, and let him drink our cup to the dregs."[16] Calvin similarly understood Jesus's death as a substitution,[17] but he also gave attention to the satisfaction of God's wrath. As Calvin writes, "It is not enough that Jesus Christ suffered in His person and was made a sacrifice for us; ... we must receive that testimony ... that He has made satisfaction for our sins."[18]

---

14. Thomas Aquinas, *Summa Theologica: A Concise Translation*, ed. Timothy McDermott (Westminster, MD: Christian Classics, 1989), 528. Refer also to Rashdall, *The Idea of Atonement in Christian Theology*, 376.

15. See, e.g., Martin Luther, *Through the Year with Martin Luther: A Selection of Sermons Celebrating the Feasts and Seasons of the Christian Year*, ed. Suzanne Tilton (Peabody, MA: Hendrickson, 2007), 346.

16. John Nicholas Lenker, *Luther's Church Postil Gospels: Pentecost or Missionary Sermons* (Minneapolis: Lutherans in All Lands, 1907), 343.

17. In his commentary on Romans 8:34, Calvin writes, "Now Christ is he, who, having once for all suffered the punishment due to us, thereby declared that he undertook our cause, in order to deliver us"; John Calvin, *Commentary on the Epistle of Paul the Apostle to the Romans*, ed. and trans. John Owen and Anthony Uyl (Ingersoll, Canada: Devoted Publishing, 2018), 325. Note also Calvin's claim that Jesus took on the form of a man in order to "present our flesh as the price of satisfaction to God's righteous judgement, and, in the same flesh, to pay the penalty that we had deserved"; Calvin, *Institutes of the Christian Religion*, ed. John T. McNeill, trans. Ford Lewis Battles (Louisville: Westminster Press, 1960), 466.

18. David Allen, *The Extent of the Atonement: A Historical and Critical Review* (Nashville: B&H Academic, 2016), 58, with reference to John Calvin, *Sermons on Isaiah's Prophecy of the Death and Passion of Christ*, Library of Ecclesiastical History, trans. T. H. L. Parker (Cambridge: James Clarke, 2010), 117.

In summary, when it comes to the idea of ransom, the church fathers often focused on the party to whom the payment was made (e.g., the Devil). This concern faded during the Middle Ages, and by the time of Reformation, theologians became more preoccupied with discerning whether the effect of Christ's death is subjective (inspiring Christians toward repentance and faith) or objective (satisfying God's wrath against sinners).

BIBLIOGRAPHY

Ådna, Jostein. "Jesus' Symbolic Act in the Temple (Mark 11:15-17): The Replacement of the Sacrificial Cult by His Atoning Death." In *Gemeinde ohne Tempel*, edited by Beate Ego, Armin Lange, and Peter Pilhofer, 461-75. WUNT 2.118. Tübingen: Mohr Siebeck, 1999.

Allen, David. *The Extent of the Atonement: A Historical and Critical Review.* Nashville: B&H Academic, 2016.

Anderson, Janice Capel, and Stephen D. Moore, eds. *Mark and Method: New Approaches in Biblical Studies.* 2nd ed. Minneapolis: Fortress, 2008.

Archbald, Paul. "A Comparative Study of John Calvin and Theodore Beza on the Doctrine of the Extent of the Atonement." PhD diss., Westminster Theological Seminary, 1998.

Arndt, William, Frederick W. Danker, and Walter Bauer. *A Greek-English Lexicon of the New Testament and Other Early Christian Literature.* Chicago: University of Chicago Press, 2000.

Aulén, Gustaf. *Christus Victor: An Historical Study of the Three Main Types of the Idea of Atonement.* Translated by A. G. Hebert. New York: Macmillan, 1951.

Aune, David Edward. "Genre Theory and the Genre-Function of Mark and Matthew." In *Matthew and Mark: Comparative Readings*, edited by Eve-Marie Becker and Anders Runesson, 2 vols, 145-75. WUNT 2.271. Tübingen: Mohr Siebeck, 2011.

Barrett, C. K. "The Background of Mark 10:45." In *New Testament Essays*, edited by A. J. B. Higgins, 1-18. Manchester: Manchester University Press, 1959.

Bauckham, Richard, ed. *The Gospels for All Christians: Rethinking the Gospel Audiences.* Grand Rapids: Eerdmans, 1998.

———. "For Whom Were Gospels Written?" *HTS Theological Studies* 55, no. 4 (1999): 865–82.

Becker, Eve-Marie, Troels Engberg-Pedersen, and Mogens Müller, eds. *Mark and Paul: Comparative Essays, Part 2.* Beihefte zur Zeitschrift für die neutestamentliche Wissenschaft und die Kunde der älteren Kirche 199. Berlin: De Gruyter, 2014.

Best, Ernest. *Following Jesus: Discipleship in the Gospel according to Mark.* JSNTSS 4. Sheffield: JSOT Press, 1981.

———. *Mark: The Gospel as Story.* Studies of the New Testament and Its World. Edinburgh: T&T Clark, 1985.

Bird, Michael. "Bauckham's *The Gospels for All Christians* Revisited." *European Journal of Theology* 15, no. 1 (2006): 5–13.

Blass, Friedrich, Albert Debrunner, and Robert Walter Funk. *A Greek Grammar of the New Testament and Other Early Christian Literature.* Chicago: University of Chicago Press, 1961.

Bolt, Peter. *The Cross from a Distance: Atonement in Mark's Gospel.* New Studies in Biblical Theology 18. Downers Grove, IL: InterVarsity Press, 2004.

Bond, Helen. *The First Biography of Jesus: Genre and Meaning in Mark's Gospel.* Grand Rapids: Eerdmans, 2020.

Bonhoeffer, Dietrich. *The Cost of Discipleship.* New York: Touchstone, 1995.

Boring, M. Eugene. *Mark: A Commentary.* New Testament Library. Louisville: Westminster John Knox, 2006.

Botner, Max. "The Role of Transcriptional Probability in the Text-Critical Debate on Mark 1:1." *Catholic Biblical Quarterly* 77, no. 3 (2015): 467–80.

———. "'Whoever Does the Will of God' (Mark 3:35): Mark's Christ as the Model Son." In *Son of God: Divine Sonship in Jewish and Christian Antiquity,* edited by Garrick V. Allen, Kai Akagi, Paul Sloan, and Madhavi Nevader, 106–17. Winona Lake, IN: Eisenbrauns, 2019.

Boyarin, Daniel. *The Jewish Gospels: The Story of the Jewish Christ.* New York: The New Press, 2012.

Bultmann, Rudolf K. *Theology of the New Testament.* 2 vols. London: SCM Press, 1952.

Burkett, Delbert. *The Son of Man Debate: A History and Evaluation.* New York: Cambridge University Press, 2000.

Burridge, Richard A. *What Are the Gospels? A Comparison with Graeco-Roman Biography*. Waco: Baylor University Press, 2018.

Calvin, John. *Commentary on the Epistle of Paul the Apostle to the Romans*. Edited and translated by John Owen and Anthony Uyl. Ingersoll, Canada: Devoted Publishing, 2018.

———. *Institutes of the Christian Religion*. Edited by John T. McNeill. Translated by Ford Lewis Battles. Louisville: Westminster Press, 1960.

Camery-Hoggatt, Jerry. *Irony in Mark's Gospel: Text and Subtext*. Society for New Testament Studies Monograph Series 72. Cambridge: Cambridge University Press, 1992.

Carey, Holly J. *Jesus' Cry from the Cross: Towards a First-Century Understanding of the Intertextual Relationship Between Psalm 22 and the Narrative of Mark's Gospel*. LNTS 398. New York: T&T Clark, 2009.

Casey, Maurice. *Aramaic Sources of Mark's Gospel*. Cambridge: Cambridge University Press, 1998.

———. *The Solution to the 'Son of Man' Problem*. New York: T&T Clark, 2009.

Choi, Jin Young. "Mark." Pages 297–314 in *The State of New Testament Studies*, edited by Scot McKnight and Nijay Gupta. Grand Rapids: Baker Academic, 2019.

Clement of Alexandria. "Fragments of Clemens Alexandrinus." *Fathers of the Second Century: Hermas, Tatian, Athenagoras, Theophilus, and Clement of Alexandria (Entire)*. Edited by Alexander Roberts, James Donaldson, and A. Cleveland Coxe. Translated by William Wilson. The Ante-Nicene Fathers, vol. 2. Buffalo: Christian Literature Company, 1885.

Collins, John C. *The Apocalyptic Imagination: An Introduction to Jewish Apocalyptic Literature*. 3rd ed. Grand Rapids: Eerdmans, 2016.

Comfort, Philip. *New Testament Text and Translation Commentary: Commentary on the Variant Readings of the Ancient New Testament Manuscripts and How They Relate to the Major English Translations*. Carol Stream, IL: Tyndale House, 2008.

Cranfield, Charles E. B. *The Gospel According to St. Mark*. The Cambridge Greek Testament Commentary. Cambridge: Cambridge University Press, 1959.

Crossley, James G. *The Date of Mark's Gospel: Insight from the Law in Earliest Christianity*. New York: T&T Clark, 2004.

———. *Mark 9-16: A Handbook on the Greek Text*. Baylor Handbook on the Greek New Testament. Waco, Texas: Baylor University Press, 2014.

Deppe, Dean B. *The Theological Intentions of Mark's Literary Devices: Markan Intercalations, Frames, Allusionary Repetitions, Narrative Surprises, and Three Types of Mirroring*. Eugene, OR: Wipf & Stock, 2015.

Dewey, Joanna. "Mark as Interwoven Tapestry: Forecasts and Echoes for a Listening Audience." *Catholic Biblical Quarterly* 53 (1991): 221–36.

Donahue, John R. *The Theology and Setting of Discipleship in the Gospel of Mark*. Milwaukee: Marquette University Press, 1998.

Dowd, Sharyn. *Reading Mark*. Macon, GA: Smyth & Helwys, 2000.

Edwards, J. Christopher. *The Ransom Logion in Mark and Matthew*. WUNT 2.327. Tübingen: Mohr Siebeck, 2012.

Edwards, James R. *The Gospel According to Mark*. Pillar New Testament Commentary. Grand Rapids: Eerdmans, 2002.

Ehrman, Bart. *The Orthodox Corruption of Scripture: The Effect of Early Christological Controversies on the Text of the New Testament*. New York: Oxford University Press, 1993.

Elliott, J. K. *The Language and Style of the Gospel of Mark: An Edition of C. H. Turner's "Notes on Marcan Usage" Together with Other Comparable Studies*. Supplements to Novum Testamentum 71. New York: Brill, 1993.

Ellis, Edward Earle. "The Date and Provenance of Mark's Gospel." In *The Four Gospels, 1992*, edited by Frans van Segbroeck, 3 vols, 801–15. Leuven: Peeters, 1992.

Erwin, Robert Guy. "The Passion and Death of Christ in the Piety and Theology of the Later Middle Ages and Martin Luther." PhD diss., Yale University, 1999.

Eusebius of Caesarea. *Eusebius: Church History, Life of Constantine the Great, and Oration in Praise of Constantine*. Edited by Philip Schaff and Henry Wace. A Select Library of the Nicene and Post-Nicene Fathers of the Christian Church, Second Series 1. New York: Christian Literature Company, 1890.

Evans, Craig A. *Mark 8:27–16:20*. Word Biblical Commentary, 34B. Nashville: Thomas Nelson, 2001.

Farrer, Austin. *A Study in St. Mark*. New York: Oxford University Press, 1952.

Fee, Gordon. *Pauline Christology: An Exegetical-Theological Study*. Peabody, MA: Hendrickson, 2007.

Fowler, Robert M. *Loaves and Fishes: The Function of the Feeding Stories in the Gospel of Mark*. Society of Biblical Literature Dissertation Series 54. Chico, CA: Scholars Press, 1981.

France, R. T. *The Gospel of Mark: A Commentary on the Greek Text*. New International Greek Testament Commentary. Grand Rapids: Eerdmans, 2002.

———. "The Servant of the Lord in the Teaching of Jesus." *Tyndale Bulletin* 19 (1968): 26–52.

Fuller, R. H. *The Foundations of New Testament Christology*. London: Collins, 1969.

———. *A Theology of Mark's Gospel: Good News about Jesus the Messiah, the Son of God*. Biblical Theology of the New Testament Series. Grand Rapids: Zondervan, 2015.

Garland, David E. *A Theology of Mark's Gospel: Good News about Jesus the Messiah, the Son of God*. Grand Rapids: Zondervan, 2015.

Gathercole, Simon. *The Preexistent Son: Recovering the Christologies of Matthew, Mark, and Luke*. Grand Rapids: Eerdmans, 2006.

Gatti, Pierluigi Leone. "Much Ado about Nothing: An Answer to B. D. Shaw's The Myth of the Neronian Persecution." *Augustinianum* 59 (2019): 201–15.

Goodrich, John K. "Rule of the Congregation in Mark 10:32–52: Glory and Greatness in Eschatological Israel." In *Reading Mark in Context: Jesus and Second Temple Judaism*, edited by Ben C. Blackwell, John K. Goodrich, and Jason Maston, 166–73. Grand Rapids: Zondervan, 2018.

Guelich, Robert. *Mark 1–8:26*. Word Biblical Commentary. Dallas: Word, 1989.

Gundry, Robert H. *Mark: A Commentary on His Apology for the Cross*. Grand Rapids: Eerdmans, 1993.

Harnack, Adolf. *The Date of Acts and the Synoptic Gospels*. New York: Putnam's Sons, 1911.

Harris, Murray J. *Prepositions and Theology in the Greek New Testament: An Essential Reference Resource for Exegesis*. Grand Rapids: Zondervan, 2012.

Hedrick, Charles W. "What Is a Gospel? Geography, Time and Narrative Structure." *Perspectives in Religious Studies* 10, no. 3 (1983): 255–68.

Henderson, Suzanne. *Christology and Discipleship in the Gospel of Mark*. Society of New Testament Studies Monograph Series 135. Cambridge: Cambridge University Press, 2005.

Hengel, Martin. *The Atonement*. Philadelphia: Fortress, 1981.

——. *Crucifixion*. Philadelphia: Fortress, 1977.

——. *Studies in the Gospel of Mark*. Minneapolis: Fortress, 1985.

Holtzmann, Heinrich J. *Die Synoptischen Evangelien*. Leipzig: Engelmann, 1863.

Homer. *The Odyssey with an English Translation by A.T. Murray, Ph.D. in Two Volumes*. Perseus Classics Collection. Cambridge, MA: Harvard University Press, 1919.

Hooker, Morna D. *The Gospel According to Saint Mark*. Black's New Testament Commentary. Peabody, MA: Hendrickson, 1991.

——. *Jesus and the Servant: The Influence of the Servant Concept of Deutero-Isaiah in the New Testament*. London: SPCK, 1959.

——. *The Son of Man in Mark: A Study of the Background of the Term and Its Use in St. Mark's Gospel*. London: SPCK, 1967.

Howerzyl, Timothy. "Imaging Salvation: An Inquiry into the Function of Metaphor in Christian Soteriology, with Application to Mark 10:45 and the Metaphor of Ransom." PhD diss., Fuller Theological Seminary, 2015.

Hurtado, Larry W. *Lord Jesus Christ: Devotion to Jesus in Earliest Christianity*. Grand Rapids: Eerdmans, 2003.

Irenaeus of Lyons. "Irenæus against Heresies." *The Apostolic Fathers with Justin Martyr and Irenaeus*. Edited by Alexander Roberts, James Donaldson, and A. Cleveland Coxe. The Ante-Nicene Fathers, vol. 1. Buffalo: Christian Literature Company, 1885.

Jensen, Irving L. *Jensen's Survey of the New Testament*. Chicago: Moody Press, 1977.

Jensen, Morten Hørning. "Atonement Theology in the Gospel of Mark."
   Biblica 100, no. 1 (2019): 84–104.

Jones, Christopher. "The Historicity of the Neronian Persecution: A
   Response to Brent Shaw." *NTS* 63 (2017): 146–52.

Josephus. *The Jewish War: Books 1–7: Greek Text*. Edited by Jeffrey Henderson,
   T. E. Page, E. Capps, and W. H. D. Rouse. Loeb Classical Library. New
   York: Harvard University Press, 1927–28.

Justin Martyr. "Dialogue of Justin with Trypho, a Jew." *The Apostolic Fathers
   with Justin Martyr and Irenaeus*. Edited by Alexander Roberts, James
   Donaldson, and A. Cleveland Coxe. The Ante-Nicene Fathers, vol. 1.
   Buffalo, NY: Christian Literature Company, 1885.

Kähler, Martin. *The So-Called Historical Jesus and the Historic Biblical Christ*.
   Translated by Carl E. Braaten. Philadelphia: Fortress, 1964.

Kaminouchi, Alberto de Mingo. *'But It Is Not So Among You': Echoes of Power in
   Mark 10.32–45*. JSNTSS 249. New York: T&T Clark, 2003.

Kealy, Sean P. *A History of the Interpretation of Mark's Gospel*. 2 vols. Lewiston,
   NY: Edward Mellen, 2007.

Keener, Craig S. *Christobiography: Memory, History, and the Reliability of the
   Gospels*. Grand Rapids: Eerdmans, 2019.

Keener, Craig S., and Edward Wright, eds. *Biographies and Jesus: What Does It
   Mean for the Gospels to Be Biographies?* Lexington: Emeth, 2016.

Keerankeri, George. *The Love Commandment in Mark: An Exegetico-Theological
   Study of Mark 12,28–34*. Analecta Biblica 150. Rome: Pontifical Biblical
   Institute, 2003.

Kelber, Werner H. *The Kingdom in Mark: A New Time and a New Place*.
   Philadelphia: Fortress, 1974.

Klink III, Edward W., ed. *The Audience of the Gospels: The Origin and Function of
   the Gospels in Early Christianity*. LNTS 353. London: T&T Clark, 2010.

Kloppenborg, John S. "Evocatio Deorum and the Date of Mark," *JBL* 124, no. 3
   (2005): 419–50.

Lane, William L. *The Gospel According to Mark*. New International
   Commentary on the New Testament. Grand Rapids: Eerdmans, 1974.

Lee, John J. R. *Christological Rereading of the Shema (Deut 6.4) in Mark's Gospel*.
   WUNT 2.533. Tübingen: Mohr Siebeck, 2020.

Lenker, John Nicholas. *Luther's Church Postil Gospels: Pentecost or Missionary Sermons*. Minneapolis: Lutherans in All Lands, 1907.

Lightfoot, J. B., and J. R. Harmer. *The Apostolic Fathers*. London: Macmillan, 1891.

Lucado, Max. *The Lucado Life Lessons Study Bible: NKJV*. Nashville: Thomas Nelson, 2010.

Luther, Martin. *Through the Year with Martin Luther: A Selection of Sermons Celebrating the Feasts and Seasons of the Christian Year*. Edited by Suzanne Tilton. Peabody, MA: Hendrickson, 2007.

Marcus, Joel. "The Jewish War and the *Sitz im Leben* of Mark." *JBL* 111, no. 3 (1992): 441–62.

———. *Mark 1–8: A New Translation with Introduction and Commentary*. The Anchor Yale Bible 27. New Haven: Yale University Press, 2008.

———. *Mark 8–16: A New Translation with Introduction and Commentary*. The Anchor Yale Bible 28. New Haven: Yale University Press, 2009.

———. "Mark—Interpreter of Paul." *NTS* 46, no. 4 (2000): 473–87.

———. *The Way of the Lord: Christological Exegesis of the Old Testament in the Gospel of Mark*. New York: T&T Clark, 2004.

Markusse, Gabi. *Salvation in the Gospel of Mark: The Death of Jesus and the Path of Discipleship*. Eugene, OR: Pickwick, 2018.

Marxsen, Willi. *Mark the Evangelist: Studies on the Redaction History of the Gospel*. Translated by James Boyce, Donald Juel, William Poehlmann, and Roy A. Harrisville. Nashville: Abingdon, 1969. Originally published in German as *Der Evangelist Markus: Studien zur Redaktionsgeschichte des Evangeliums*. Göttingen: Vandenhoeck & Ruprecht, 1956.

Moore, Mark E. *Kenotic Politics: The Reconfiguration of Power in Jesus' Political Praxis*. Library of Biblical Studies 482. New York: T&T Clark, 2013.

Morris, Leon. *The Cross of Jesus*. Grand Rapids: Eerdmans, 1988.

Moulder, W. J. "Old Testament Background and the Interpretation of Mark X.45." *NTS* 24, no. 1 (1977): 120–27.

Omanson, Roger L., and Bruce Manning Metzger. *A Textual Guide to the Greek New Testament: An Adaptation of Bruce M. Metzger's Textual Commentary for the Needs of Translators*. Stuttgart: Deutsche Bibelgesellschaft, 2006.

Ortlund, Dane. "What Does It Mean to Cast a Mountain into the Sea? Another Look at Mark 11:23." *BBR* 28, no. 2 (2018): 218–39.

Painter, John. *Mark's Gospel*. London: Routledge, 1997.

Pannenberg, Wolfhart. *Jesus—God and Man*. 2nd ed. Translated by Lewis L. Wilkins and Duane A. Priebe. Philadelphia: Westminster, 1977.

Peterson, Dwight. *The Origins of Mark: The Markan Community in Current Debate*. Boston: Brill, 2000.

Petersen, Norman R. "'Point of View' in Mark's Narrative." *Semeia* 12 (1978): 97–121.

Pitre, Brant. "The 'Ransom for Many,' the New Exodus, and the End of the Exile: Redemption as the Restoration of All Israel (Mark 10:35–45)." *Letter & Spirit* 1 (2005): 41–68.

Rahlfs, Alfred. *Septuaginta*. Stuttgart: Deutsche Bibelgesellschaft, 1996.

Rashdall, Hastings. *The Idea of Atonement in Christian Theology: Being the Bampton Lectures for 1915*. London: Macmillian, 1925.

Rhoads, David M., Joanna Dewey, and Donald Michie. *Mark as Story: An Introduction to the Narrative of a Gospel*. 2nd ed. Minneapolis: Fortress, 1999.

Roberts, Alexander, James Donaldson, and A. Cleveland Coxe, eds. *Fathers of the Second Century: Hermas, Tatian, Athenagoras, Theophilus, and Clement of Alexandria (Entire)*. The Ante-Nicene Fathers, vol. 2. Buffalo: Christian Literature Company, 1885.

Robinson, J. A. T. *Redating the New Testament*. London: SCM, 1976.

Roskam, Hendrika. *The Purpose of the Gospel of Mark in Its Historical and Social Context*. Leiden: Brill, 2004.

Santos, Narry F. *Slave of All: The Paradox of Authority and Servanthood in the Gospel of Mark*. JSNTSS 237. New York: Sheffield Academic, 2003.

Shaw, Brent D. "The Myth of the Neronian Persecution." *Journal of Roman Studies* 105 (2015): 73–100.

Sim, David. "The Gospel for All Christians? A Response to Richard Bauckham." *JSNT* 84, no. 1 (2001): 3–27.

Snow, Robert. *Daniel's Son of Man in Mark*. Eugene, OR: Pickwick, 2016.

Spurgeon, Charles Haddon. *The Metropolitan Tabernacle Pulpit Sermons* Vol. 39. London: Passmore & Alabaster, 1893.

Stein, Robert H. *Jesus, the Temple, and the Coming Son of Man: A Commentary on Mark 13*. Downers Grove, IL: IVP Academic, 2014.

———. *Mark*. Baker Exegetical Commentary on the New Testament. Grand Rapids: Baker Academic, 2008.

Stott, John R. W. *The Cross of Christ*. Downers Grove, IL: InterVarsity Press, 2006.

Strauss, Mark L. *Mark*. Zondervan Exegetical Commentary on the New Testament. Grand Rapids: Zondervan, 2014.

Suetonius Tranquillus. *Suetonius: The Lives of Caesars, The Lives of Illustrious Men*. Translated by J. C. Rolfe. The Loeb Classical Library vol. 1. Cambridge, MA: Harvard University Press, 1914.

Swindoll, Chuck. "Mark." *The Bible Teaching Ministry of Pastor Chuck Swindoll*. https://www.insight.org/resources/bible/the-gospels/mark.

Tannehill, Robert C. "The Disciples in Mark: The Function of a Narrative Role." *Journal of Religion* 57 (1977): 386–405.

———. "The Gospel of Mark as Narrative Christology." *Semeia* 16 (1979): 57–95.

Taylor, Vincent. *The Gospel According to St. Mark: The Greek Text with Introduction, Notes, and Indexes*. London: Macmillan, 1952.

Telford, William, ed. *The Interpretation of Mark*. 2nd ed. Edinburgh: T&T Clark, 1995.

Tertullian. "The Five Books against Marcion." *Latin Christianity: Its Founder, Tertullian*. Edited by Alexander Roberts, James Donaldson, and A. Cleveland Coxe. Translated by Peter Holmes. The Ante-Nicene Fathers, vol. 3. Buffalo: Christian Literature Company, 1885.

———. "The Prescription against Heretics." In *Latin Christianity: Its Founder, Tertullian*. Edited by Alexander Roberts, James Donaldson, and A. Cleveland Coxe. Translated by Peter Holmes. The Ante-Nicene Fathers, vol. 3. Buffalo: Christian Literature Company, 1885.

Theissen, Gerd. *The Gospels in Context: Social and Political History in the Synoptic Tradition*. Translated by Linda Maloney. Minneapolis: Fortress, 1991.

Thomas Aquinas. *Summa Theologica: A Concise Translation*. Edited by Timothy McDermott. Westminster, MD: Christian Classics, 1989.

Thompson, Augustine. *Francis of Assisi: The Life*. Ithaca, NY: Cornell

University Press, 2013.

Torrey, C. C. *The Four Gospels: A New Translation*. 2nd ed. New York: Harper, 1947.

Trakatellis, Demetrios. *Authority and Passion: Christological Aspects of the Gospel According to Mark*. Brookline: Holy Cross Orthodox Press, 1987.

Vermes, Geza. *The Authentic Gospel of Jesus*. London: Penguin, 2004.

———. *Jesus the Jew*. London: Collins, 1973.

———. "The Son of Man Debate Revisited (1960-2010)." *Journal of Jewish Studies* 61, no. 2 (2010): 193-206.

Vinzent, Markus. *Marcion and the Dating of the Synoptic Gospels*. Studia Patristica Supplement 2. Leuven: Peeters, 2014.

Voelz, James W. *Mark 1:1-8:26*. Concordia Commentary. St. Louis: Concordia, 2013.

Wallace, Daniel B. *Greek Grammar Beyond the Basics: An Exegetical Syntax of the New Testament*. Grand Rapids: Zondervan, 1996.

Wasserman, Tommy. "The 'Son of God' Was in the Beginning (Mark 1:1)." *Journal for Theological Studies* 62, no. 1 (2011): 20-50.

Watson, David. *Honor Among Christians: The Cultural Key to the Messianic Secret*. Minneapolis: Fortress, 2010.

Watts, Rikki E. *Isaiah's New Exodus and Mark*. Tübingen: Mohr Siebeck, 1997.

———. "Jesus' Death, Isaiah 53, and Mark 10:45: A Crux Revisited." In *Jesus and the Suffering Servant: Isaiah 53 and Christian Origins*, edited by William Bellinger and William R. Farmer, 125-51. Harrisburg, PA: Trinity, 1998.

———. "Mark." In *Commentary on the New Testament Use of the Old Testament*, edited by G. K. Beale and D. A. Carson, 111-237. Grand Rapids: Baker Academic, 2007.

Weeden, Theodore. "The Heresy that Necessitated Mark's Gospel." *Zeitschrift für die neutestamentliche Wissenschaft und die Kunde der älteren Kirche* 59 (1968): 145-58.

Wellhausen, Julius. *Das Evangelium Marci*. 2nd ed. Berlin: Reimer, 1909.

Wenham, David. *Paul: Follower of Jesus or Founder of Christianity?* Grand Rapids: Eerdmans, 1995.

Werner, Martin. *Der Einfluss paulinischer Theologie im Markusevangelium: Eine Studie zur neutestamentlichen Theologie*. Zeitschrift für die

neutestamentliche Wissenschaft und die Kunde der älteren Kirche
Beihefte 1. Berlin: de Gruyter, 1923.

Wiersbe, Warren W. *The Wiersbe Bible Commentary: Complete Set.* Colorado
Springs: David C. Cook, 2007.

Wilke, Christian G. *Der Urevangelist oder exegetisch kritische Untersuchung über
das Verwandtschafts-verhältniss der drei ersten Evangelien.* Dresden:
Fleischer, 1838.

Williams, Joel F. *Other Followers of Jesus: Minor Characters as Major Figures in
Mark's Gospel.* Sheffield: Sheffield Academic, 1994.

Winn, Adam. *The Purpose of Mark's Gospel: An Early Christian Response to Roman
Imperial Propaganda.* WUNT 2.245. Tübingen: Mohr Siebeck, 2008.

———. *Reading Mark's Christology under Caesar: Jesus the Messiah and Roman
Imperial Ideology.* Downers Grove, IL: IVP Academic, 2018.

———. "Resisting Honor: The Markan Secrecy Motif and Roman Imperial
Ideology." *JBL* 133, no. 3 (2014): 583–601.

———. "Tyrant or Servant? Roman Political Ideology and Mark 10.42–45."
JSNT 36, no. 4 (2014): 325–52.

Witherington III, Ben. *The Gospel of Mark: A Socio-Rhetorical Commentary.*
Grand Rapids: Eerdmans, 2001.

Wrede, William. *The Messianic Secret.* Cambridge: Clarke, 1971. Originally
published in German as *Das Messiasgeheimnis in den Evangelien.*
Göttingen: Vandenhoeck & Ruprecht, 1901.

Wright, N. T. *Jesus and the Victory of God.* Christian Origins and the Question
of God 2. London: SPCK, 1996.

Yarbro Collins, Adela. "Finding Meaning in the Death of Jesus." *Journal of
Religion* 78, no. 2 (1998): 175–96.

———. *Mark: A Commentary.* Hermeneia. Minneapolis: Fortress, 2007.

———. "Mark's Interpretation of the Death of Jesus." *JBL* 128, no. 3 (2009): 545–54.

———. "The Signification of Mark 10:45 among Gentile Christians." *Harvard
Theological Review* 90, no. 4 (1997): 371–82.

Yarbro Collins, Adela, and John J. Collins. *King and Messiah as Son of God:
Divine, Human, and Angelic Messianic Figures in Biblical and Related
Literature.* Grand Rapids: Eerdmans, 2008.

SUBJECT AND AUTHOR INDEX

D

Deppe, Dean B., 42, 43, 45
Dewey, Joanna, 40
discipleship, 37–38, 39, 41, 46, 56,
　59–60, 66, 79, 88, 114, 118–19,
　130, 138–44, 147, 152, 158, 159,
　160, 161, 162, 166
Donahue, John R., 38
Dowd, Sharyn, 74

E

Edwards, J. Christopher, 156, 171–72
Edwards, James R., 15, 43, 45, 73
Ehrman, Bart, 48
Elliott, J. K., 87
Ellis, Edward Earle, 12, 20
Engberg-Pedersen, Troels, 13
epitome, 5, 7
Erwin, Robert Guy, 172, 173
Eusebius, 6, 11
Evans, Craig A., 73, 132
evocatio deorum, 17–18, 19
ex eventu prophecy, 14–15

F

faithfulness, 31, 33, 36, 37, 38, 39, 46,
　51, 59–60, 66, 71, 84, 125, 140,
　143, 153, 159, 160
fall of Jerusalem, 14–15, 16–19,
　20, 27–28. See also Olivet
　Discourse.
Farrer, Austin, 15
Fee, Gordon, 13
forgiveness, 43, 52, 94–95, 133–35
Fowler, Robert M., 45
France, R. T., 73, 86, 112
Francis of Assisi, 156–57

G

Garland, David E., 38, 41, 42, 45, 73,
　74, 77, 112, 131, 132, 135, 156
Gathercole, Simon, 103

Gatti, Pierluigi Leone, 9
glory, 58, 65, 82, 84–85, 87, 99–100,
　102, 114–16, 146, 149, 154. See
　also authority; honor. See
　also under Jesus.
Goodrich, John K., 80
"gospel," 32–33
Grayson, A. K., 15
Guelich, Robert, 74
Gundry, Robert H., 20, 81, 87

H

Harnack, Adolf, 20
Harris, Murray J., 110, 112
Hedrick, Charles W., 76
Henderson, Suzanne, 38
Hengel, Martin, 10, 15, 22, 26, 46, 119,
　122, 124–25, 129, 132, 135
Holtzmann, Heinrich, 7
Homer, 32
honor, 3, 26, 58–59, 67, 78–80, 82, 87,
　99, 102, 104–6, 113, 114–16,
　139, 146, 154, 155, 158. See also
　authority; glory. See also
　under Jesus.
Hooker, Morna D., 73, 81, 89, 100–101,
　112, 123, 167
Howerzyl, Timothy, 109, 168–69
Hurtado, Larry W., 122

I

Irenaeus, 6, 10, 11, 12, 172

J

Jensen, Irving L., 2
Jensen, Morten Hørning, 127, 135, 135,
　148, 163–64
Jesus,
　authority, 26, 34, 35, 38, 39, 43–45,
　　51–55, 60–61, 66–68, 75, 80,
　　84, 88, 92, 94, 96, 101–2, 114,

SCRIPTURE INDEX

Old Testament

195

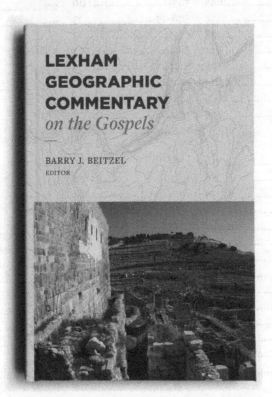